Sundays and Solemnities

YEAR

C

PSALMS

FOR THE

LITURGICAL YEAR

The PSALMS *from*
the LECTIONARY *for* CANADA

Sundays and Solemnities

YEAR

C

PSALMS

FOR THE LITURGICAL YEAR

The PSALMS *from
the* LECTIONARY *for* CANADA

Music by Gordon Johnston

NOVALIS

Table of Contents

Introduction   vii

Advent Season

Common Psalm for Advent	Psalm 25	2
Common Psalm for Advent	Psalm 85	4
Common Psalm for Advent	Psalm 146	6
First Sunday of Advent – C	Psalm 25	8
Second Sunday of Advent – C	Psalm 126	10
Third Sunday of Advent – C	Canticle – Isaiah 12	12
Fourth Sunday of Advent – C	Psalm 80	14

Christmas Season

Common Psalm for Christmas	Psalm 98	16
Common Psalm for Christmas	Psalm 34	18
Common Psalm for Christmas	Psalm 72	20
Christmas: Nativity of the Lord (Vigil) – ABC	Psalm 89	22
Christmas: Nativity of the Lord (Night) – ABC	Psalm 96	24
Christmas: Nativity of the Lord (Dawn) – ABC	Psalm 97	26
Christmas: Nativity of the Lord (Day) – ABC	Psalm 98	28
Holy Family of Jesus, Mary and Joseph – C	Psalm 84	30
Holy Family of Jesus, Mary and Joseph – ABC	Psalm 128	32
January 1 – Solemnity of Mary, the Holy Mother of God – ABC	Psalm 67	34
Second Sunday after Christmas – ABC	Psalm 147	36
Epiphany of the Lord – ABC	Psalm 72	38
Baptism of the Lord – C	Psalm 104	40
Baptism of the Lord – ABC	Psalm 29	42

Lenten Season

Common Psalm for Lent	Psalm 51	44
Common Psalm for Lent	Psalm 91	46
Common Psalm for Lent	Psalm 130	48
Common Psalm for Holy Week	Psalm 22	50
Ash Wednesday – ABC	Psalm 51	52
First Sunday of Lent – C	Psalm 91	54

Second Sunday of Lent – C | Psalm 27 | 56
Third Sunday of Lent – C | Psalm 103 | 58
Third Sunday of Lent (Christian Initiation) | Psalm 95 | 60
Fourth Sunday of Lent – C | Psalm 34 | 62
Fourth Sunday of Lent (Christian Initiation) | Psalm 23 | 64
Fifth Sunday of Lent – C | Psalm 126 | 66
Fifth Sunday of Lent (Christian Initiation) | Psalm 130 | 68
Passion Sunday – C | Psalm 22 | 70
Mass of Chrism – ABC | Psalm 89 | 72

Easter Triduum

Mass of the Lord's Supper – ABC | Psalm 116 | 74
Celebration of the Lord's Passion – ABC | Psalm 31 | 76
Resurrection of the Lord – Easter Vigil (1.1) – ABC | Psalm 104 | 78
Resurrection of the Lord – Easter Vigil (1.2) – ABC | Psalm 33 | 80
Resurrection of the Lord – Easter Vigil (2) – ABC | Psalm 16 | 82
Resurrection of the Lord – Easter Vigil (3) – ABC | Canticle – Exodus 15 | 84
Resurrection of the Lord – Easter Vigil (4) – ABC | Psalm 30 | 86
Resurrection of the Lord – Easter Vigil (5) – ABC | Canticle – Isaiah 12 | 88
Resurrection of the Lord – Easter Vigil (6) – ABC | Psalm 19 | 90
Resurrection of the Lord – Easter Vigil (7.1) – ABC | Psalm 42/43 | 92
Resurrection of the Lord – Easter Vigil (7.2) – ABC | Psalm 51 | 94
Resurrection of the Lord – Easter Vigil – Solemn Alleluia – ABC | Psalm 118 | 96
Resurrection of the Lord – Easter Sunday – ABC | Psalm 118 | 98

Easter Season

Common Psalm for Easter | Psalm 118 | 100
Common Psalm for Easter | Psalm 66 | 102
Common Psalm for after Ascension | Psalm 47 | 104
Common Psalm for Pentecost | Psalm 104 | 106
Second Sunday of Easter – C | Psalm 118 | 108
Third Sunday of Easter – C | Psalm 30 | 110
Fourth Sunday of Easter – C | Psalm 100 | 112
Fifth Sunday of Easter – C | Psalm 145 | 114
Sixth Sunday of Easter – C | Psalm 67 | 116
Ascension of the Lord – C | Psalm 47 | 118
Seventh Sunday of Easter – C | Psalm 97 | 120
Pentecost (Vigil) – ABC | Psalm 104 | 122
Extended Vigil of Pentecost (1) – ABC | Psalm 8 | 124

Extended Vigil of Pentecost (2) – ABC   Psalm 80   126
Extended Vigil of Pentecost (3) – ABC   Psalm 97   128
Extended Vigil of Pentecost (4) – ABC   Psalm 139   130
Extended Vigil of Pentecost (5) – ABC   Psalm 105   132
Extended Vigil of Pentecost (6) – ABC   Psalm 90   134
Extended Vigil of Pentecost (7) – ABC   Psalm 104   136
Pentecost Sunday – C   Psalm 104   138

Solemnities of the Lord during Ordinary Time

The Most Holy Trinity – C   Psalm 8   140
The Most Holy Body and Blood of Christ – C   Psalm 110   142
The Most Sacred Heart of Jesus – C   Psalm 23   144

Ordinary Time

Common Psalm for Ordinary Time   Psalm 19   146
Common Psalm for Ordinary Time   Psalm 27   148
Common Psalm for Ordinary Time   Psalm 34   150
Common Psalm for Ordinary Time   Psalm 63   152
Common Psalm for Ordinary Time   Psalm 95   154
Common Psalm for Ordinary Time   Psalm 100   156
Common Psalm for Ordinary Time   Psalm 103   158
Common Psalm for Ordinary Time   Psalm 145   160
Common Psalm for the Last Weeks of Ordinary Time   Psalm 122   162
Second Sunday in Ordinary Time – C   Psalm 96   164
Third Sunday in Ordinary Time – C   Psalm 19   166
Fourth Sunday in Ordinary Time – C   Psalm 71   168
Fifth Sunday in Ordinary Time – C   Psalm 138   170
Sixth Sunday in Ordinary Time – C   Psalm 1   172
Seventh Sunday in Ordinary Time – C   Psalm 103   174
Eighth Sunday in Ordinary Time – C   Psalm 92   176
Ninth Sunday in Ordinary Time – C   Psalm 117   178
Tenth Sunday in Ordinary Time – C   Psalm 30   180
Eleventh Sunday in Ordinary Time – C   Psalm 32   182
Twelfth Sunday in Ordinary Time – C   Psalm 63   184
Thirteenth Sunday in Ordinary Time – C   Psalm 16   186
Fourteenth Sunday in Ordinary Time – C   Psalm 66   188
Fifteenth Sunday in Ordinary Time (1) – C   Psalm 69   190
Fifteenth Sunday in Ordinary Time (2) – C   Psalm 19   192
Sixteenth Sunday in Ordinary Time – C   Psalm 15   194

Seventeenth Sunday in Ordinary Time – C | Psalm 138 | 196
Eighteenth Sunday in Ordinary Time – C | Psalm 90 | 198
Nineteenth Sunday in Ordinary Time – C | Psalm 33 | 200
Twentieth Sunday in Ordinary Time – C | Psalm 40 | 202
Twenty-first Sunday in Ordinary Time – C | Psalm 117 | 204
Twenty-second Sunday in Ordinary Time – C | Psalm 68 | 206
Twenty-third Sunday in Ordinary Time – C | Psalm 90 | 208
Twenty-fourth Sunday in Ordinary Time – C | Psalm 51 | 210
Twenty-fifth Sunday in Ordinary Time – C | Psalm 113 | 212
Twenty-sixth Sunday in Ordinary Time – C | Psalm 146 | 214
Twenty-seventh Sunday in Ordinary Time – C | Psalm 95 | 216
Twenty-eighth Sunday in Ordinary Time – C | Psalm 98 | 218
Twenty-ninth Sunday in Ordinary Time – C | Psalm 121 | 220
Thirtieth Sunday in Ordinary Time – C | Psalm 34 | 222
Thirty-first Sunday in Ordinary Time – C | Psalm 145 | 224
Thirty-second Sunday in Ordinary Time – C | Psalm 17 | 226
Thirty-third Sunday in Ordinary Time – C | Psalm 98 | 228
Thirty-fourth Sunday in Ordinary Time (Christ the King) – C | Psalm 122 | 230

Feasts and Solemnities Replacing Sundays

February 2 – Presentation of the Lord – ABC | Psalm 24 | 232
March 19 – St. Joseph, Husband of the Blessed Virgin Mary – ABC | Psalm 89 | 234
March 25 – Annunciation of the Lord – ABC | Psalm 40 | 236
June 24 – Nativity of St. John the Baptist (Vigil) – ABC | Psalm 71 | 238
June 24 – Nativity of St. John the Baptist (Day) – ABC | Psalm 139 | 240
June 29 – Sts. Peter and Paul, Apostles (Vigil) – ABC | Psalm 19 | 242
June 29 – Sts. Peter and Paul, Apostles (Day) – ABC | Psalm 34 | 244
August 6 – Transfiguration of the Lord – ABC | Psalm 97 | 246
August 15 – Assumption of the Blessed Virgin Mary (Vigil) – ABC | Psalm 132 | 248
August 15 – Assumption of the Blessed Virgin Mary (Day) – ABC | Psalm 45 | 250
September 14 – Exaltation of the Holy Cross – ABC | Psalm 78 | 252
November 1 – All Saints – ABC | Psalm 24 | 254
November 2 – Commemoration of All the Faithful Departed I – ABC | Psalm 103 | 256
November 2 – Commemoration of All the Faithful Departed II – ABC | Psalm 23 | 258
November 2 – Commemoration of All the Faithful Departed III – ABC | Psalm 116 | 260
November 9 – Dedication of the Lateran Basilica – ABC | Psalm 46 | 262
December 8 – Immaculate Conception of the Blessed Virgin Mary – ABC | Psalm 98 | 264

Table of Responsorial Psalms and Canticles

266

Table of Psalm Refrains

270

Introduction

These psalm settings are intended to be sung by a solo cantor, with the response sung by the choir and congregation. Accompaniment parts are given for keyboard, guitar, C instrument (flute, oboe, recorder, etc.) and B-flat instrument (trumpet, clarinet, etc.). The instrumental lines are meant to accompany the refrain. Instruments may also be used to double the melody line of the refrain.

A unique characteristic of this music is the "bridge" which connects the cantor's verse to the congregational refrain. The fermata ⌢ over the final note of the refrain is intended to show the end of the phrase, not to indicate that the music should slow down or hold on that note. The symbol D.C. (*da capo*) at the end of the second line of music indicates that the accompaniment returns to the beginning without stopping.

How the psalms are sung

These psalms should be performed in the following manner:

- As an introduction, play the refrain through, stopping at the fermata.

- The cantor sings the refrain. This time, the accompaniment doesn't stop at the fermata, but continues on, playing the bridge, and then repeats the refrain for the congregation to sing, this time stopping at the fermata.

- Now the cantor sings the first verse. On the last note of the psalm tone, the tempo is re-established; play the bridge in tempo, returning to the refrain for everyone to sing, stopping at the fermata.

- Subsequent verses continue this pattern, so there is a break between the congregational refrain and the new verse by the cantor, but a smooth transition from the cantor back to the congregation.

The purpose of the musical bridge which connects the cantor's verse to the congregation's refrain is to indicate the tempo and pitch of the refrain for the congregation so that they can sing their part with confidence. In order for them to do that, it's important that the accompanist ***not* slow down** just before they begin singing; the purpose is to lead the congregation into their part, so a steady, reliable tempo is essential.

How the psalms are pointed

The psalm tones in this collection have been written to match the lines of the psalm. Each line is pointed using a bullet and bold print to indicate when to move. You move **on** the bold word. For example, if the music has a reciting tone and one note following, the text would be pointed:

I will bless the Lord at all · **times.**

If two words are to be sung to one note, they are joined together with an underscore:

With my whole heart **I** · **seek_you.**

If a word of several syllables is to be divided over more than one note, the hyphen shows the division:

Let me not stray from your com·-**mandments.**

Most psalm texts are divided into groups of four lines each. The accompanying psalm tone will have four measures, one for each line. In a few rare instances, one verse will have fewer lines than the other verses. In that case, the number of the measure precedes the text. For example,

1 – Be glad in the Lord and rejoice, O · **righteous,**
4 – and shout for joy, all you upright in · **heart.**

In this case, you would sing the first line to the first measure of the psalm tone, then omit measures 2 and 3, and sing the second line to measure 4, continuing on to the bridge and the refrain.

The singing of the psalms should be like musical speech, free and natural, never measured or forced. The note values of the refrain are exact, but the verses are meant to be sung and played in free time, following the natural flow of the text.

A few general thoughts

It is always important to teach the people the psalm refrain before the celebration begins, unless it is a seasonal refrain that is well known. Play the refrain on the keyboard, if you're using one, then sing the refrain and invite the congregation to sing it back.

Music ministers and cantors should always learn the psalm well before the liturgy so they can lead the assembly in singing the refrain, and enable the assembly to meditate on the Word as the cantor sings the verses. Respect for Christ's presence in the Word and in the worshipping assembly should motivate us to prepare and give only our best.

If you would like to hear a recording of a particular psalm, play the mp3 file on the accompanying CD (located inside the back cover). As well, to hear the psalm for the coming Sunday, visit

www.livingwithchrist.ca

and click on "Music."

Sundays and Solemnities

YEAR

C

Common Psalm for Advent

Psalm 25

Make me to know your ways, O · **Lord,**
teach me your · **paths.**
Lead me in your truth and · **teach_me,**
for you are the God of my · **sal**-vation. R.

Good and upright is the · **Lord,**
therefore he instructs sinners in the · **way.**
He leads the humble in what is · **right,**
and teaches the humble · **his** way. R.

All the paths of the Lord are steadfast love and · **faithfulness,**
for those who keep his covenant and his de·-**crees.**
The friendship of the Lord is for those who · **fear_him,**
and he makes his covenant known · **to** them. R.

Common Psalm for Advent

Psalm 25

Guitar

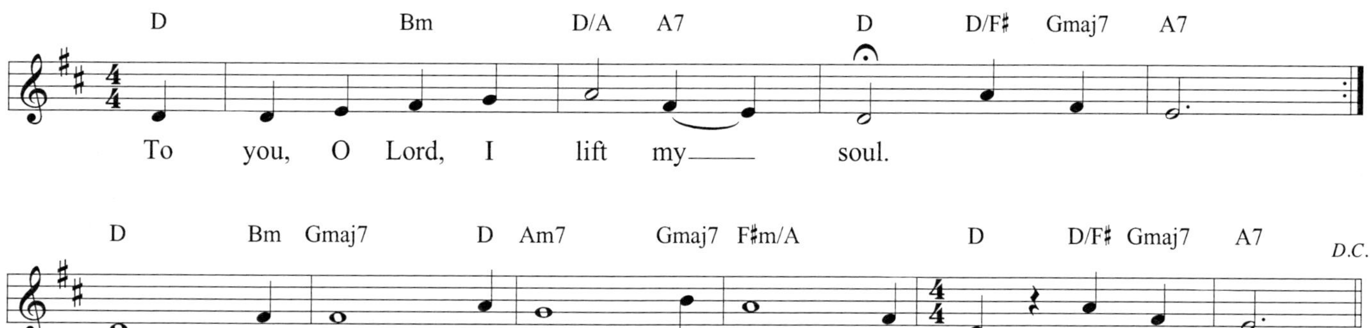

Make me to know your ways, O · **Lord,**
teach me your · **paths.**
Lead me in your truth and · **teach_me,**
for you are the God of my · **sal**-vation. R.

Good and upright is the · **Lord,**
therefore he instructs sinners in the · **way.**
He leads the humble in what is · **right,**
and teaches the humble · **his** way. R.

All the paths of the Lord are steadfast love and · **faithfulness,**
for those who keep his covenant and his de·-**crees.**
The friendship of the Lord is for those who · **fear_him,**
and he makes his covenant known · **to** them. R.

Common Psalm for Advent

Psalm 85

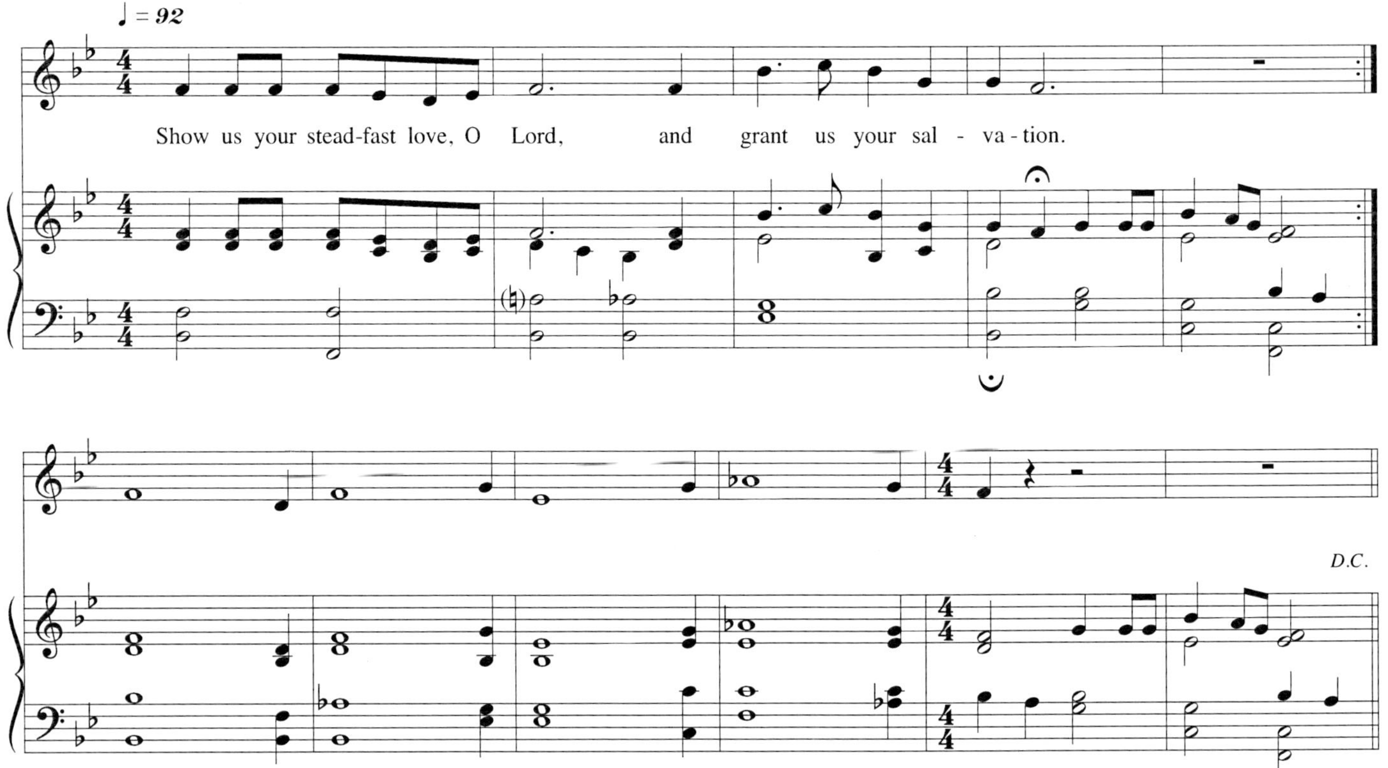

Let me hear what God the Lord will · **speak,**
for he will speak peace to his · **people.**
Surely his salvation is at hand for those who · **fear_him,**
that his glory may dwell · **in_our** land. R.

Steadfast love and faithfulness will · **meet;**
righteousness and peace will · **kiss_each_other.**
Faithfulness will spring up from the · **ground,**
and righteousness will look down · **from_the** sky. R.

The Lord will give what is · **good,**
and our land will yield its · **increase.**
Righteousness will go be·-**fore_him,**
and will make a path · **for_his** steps. R.

Common Psalm for Advent

Psalm 85

Guitar

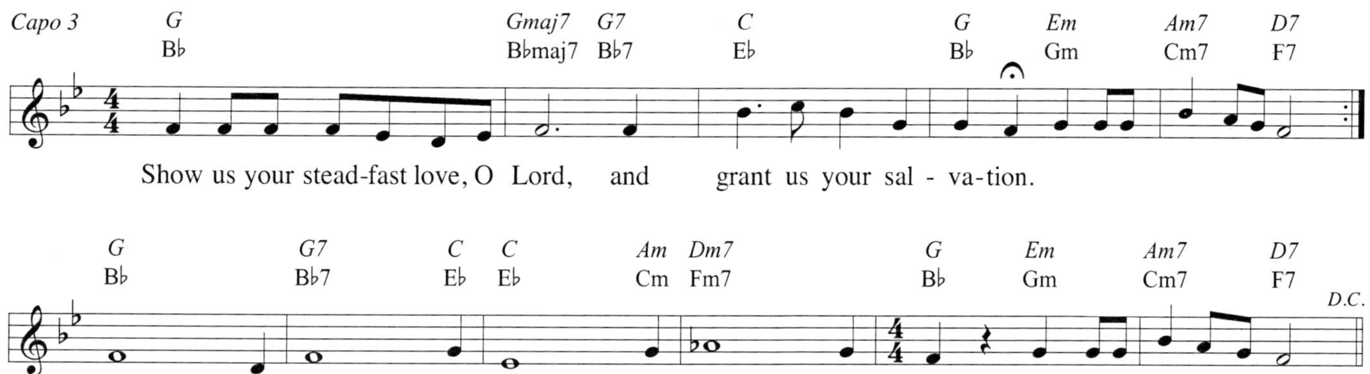

Let me hear what God the Lord will · **speak,**
for he will speak peace to his · **people.**
Surely his salvation is at hand for those who · **fear_him,**
that his glory may dwell · **in_our** land. R.

Steadfast love and faithfulness will · **meet;**
righteousness and peace will · **kiss_each_other.**
Faithfulness will spring up from the · **ground,**
and righteousness will look down · **from_the** sky. R.

The Lord will give what is · **good,**
and our land will yield its · **increase.**
Righteousness will go be·-**fore_him,**
and will make a path · **for_his** steps. R.

C Instrument

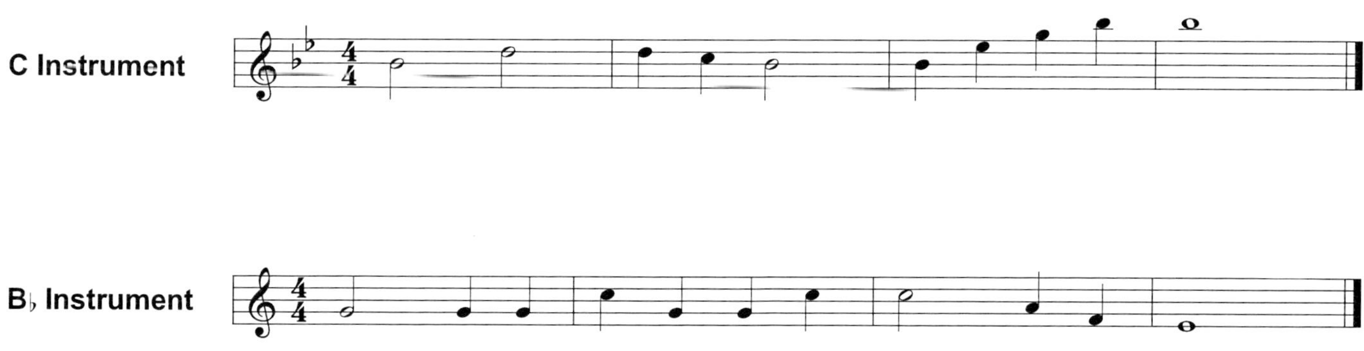

Bb Instrument

Common Psalm for Advent

Psalm 146

It is the Lord who keeps faith for·-**ever,**
who executes justice for the op·-**pressed;**
who gives food to the · **hungry.**
The Lord sets the · **prisoners** free. R.

The Lord opens the eyes of the · **blind**
and lifts up those who are bowed · **down;**
the Lord loves the · **righteous**
and watches over · **the** strangers. R.

The Lord upholds the orphan and the · **widow,**
but the way of the wicked he brings to · **ruin.**
The Lord will reign for·-**ever,**
your God, O Zion, for all · **gener**-ations. R.

Common Psalm for Advent

Psalm 146

Guitar

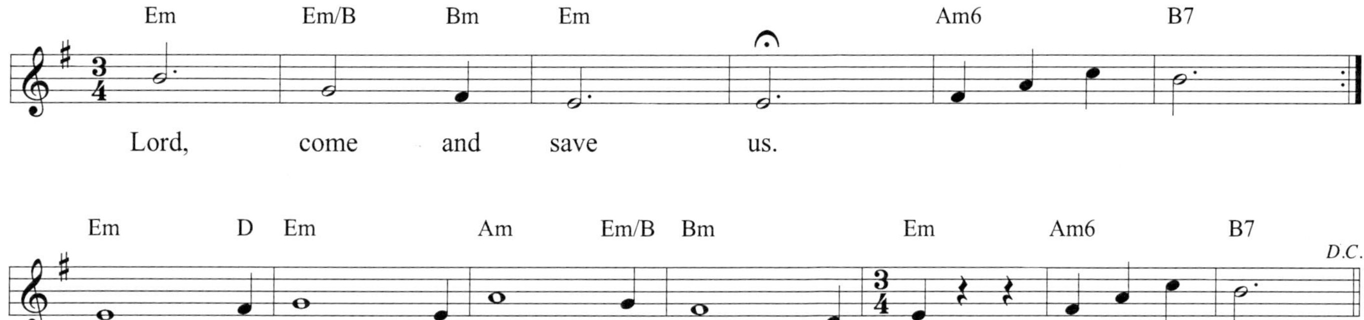

It is the Lord who keeps faith for·-**ever,**
who executes justice for the op·-**pressed;**
who gives food to the · **hungry.**
The Lord sets the · **prisoners** free. R.

The Lord opens the eyes of the · **blind**
and lifts up those who are bowed · **down;**
the Lord loves the · **righteous**
and watches over · **the** strangers. R.

The Lord upholds the orphan and the · **widow,**
but the way of the wicked he brings to · **ruin.**
The Lord will reign for·-**ever,**
your God, O Zion, for all · **gener**-ations. R.

C Instrument

B♭ Instrument

First Sunday of Advent – C

Psalm 25

Make me to know your ways, O · **Lord,**
teach me your · **paths.**
Lead me in your truth and · **teach_me,**
for you are the God of my · **sal**-vation. R.

Good and upright is the · **Lord;**
therefore he instructs sinners in the · **way.**
He leads the humble in what is · **right,**
and teaches the humble · **his** way. R.

All the paths of the Lord are steadfast love and · **faithfulness,**
for those who keep his covenant and his de·-**crees.**
The friendship of the Lord is for those who · **fear_him,**
and he makes his covenant known · **to** them. R.

First Sunday of Advent – C

Psalm 25

Guitar

Make me to know your ways, O · **Lord,**
teach me your · **paths.**
Lead me in your truth and · **teach_me,**
for you are the God of my · **sal**-vation. R.

Good and upright is the · **Lord;**
therefore he instructs sinners in the · **way.**
He leads the humble in what is · **right,**
and teaches the humble · **his** way. R.

All the paths of the Lord are steadfast love and · **faithfulness,**
for those who keep his covenant and his de·-**crees.**
The friendship of the Lord is for those who · **fear_him,**
and he makes his covenant known · **to** them. R.

C Instrument

B♭ Instrument

9

Second Sunday of Advent – C

Psalm 126

♩ = 112

When the Lord restored the fortunes of · **Zion,**
we were like those who · **dream.**
Then our mouth was filled with · **laughter,**
and our tongue with shouts · **of** joy. R.

Then it was said among the · **nations,**
"The Lord has done great things for · **them.**"
The Lord has done great things for · **us,**
and we · **re**-joiced. R.

Restore our fortunes, O · **Lord,**
like the watercourses in the desert of the · **Negev.**
May those who sow in · **tears**
reap with shouts · **of** joy. R.

Those who go out · **weeping,**
bearing the seed for · **sowing,**
shall come home with shouts of · **joy,**
carrying · **their** sheaves. R.

Second Sunday of Advent – C

Psalm 126

Guitar

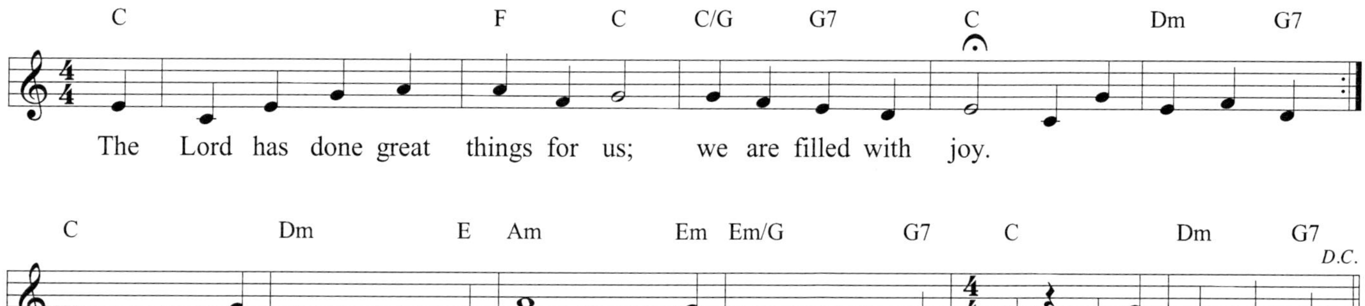

When the Lord restored the fortunes of · **Zion,**
we were like those who · **dream.**
Then our mouth was filled with · **laughter,**
and our tongue with shouts · **of** joy. R.

Then it was said among the · **nations,**
"The Lord has done great things for · **them.**"
The Lord has done great things for · **us,**
and we · **re**-joiced. R.

Restore our fortunes, O · **Lord,**
like the watercourses in the desert of the · **Negev.**
May those who sow in · **tears**
reap with shouts · **of** joy. R.

Those who go out · **weeping,**
bearing the seed for · **sowing,**
shall come home with shouts of · **joy,**
carrying · **their** sheaves. R.

C Instrument

B♭ Instrument

11

Third Sunday of Advent – C

Isaiah 12

Surely God is my salvation; I will trust, and will not · **be** a-fraid,
for the Lord God is my strength and my might; he has be·-**come_my** sal-vation.
With joy · **you_will** draw water
from the wells · **of** sal-vation. R.

Give thanks · **to** the Lord,
call · **on** his name;
make known his deeds a·-**mong** the nations;
proclaim that his · **name_is** ex-alted. R.

Sing praises to the Lord, for he · **has** done gloriously;
let this be known in · **all** the earth.
Shout aloud and sing for joy, O · **roy**-al Zion,
for great in your midst is the Holy · **One** of Israel. R.

Third Sunday of Advent – C

Isaiah 12

Guitar

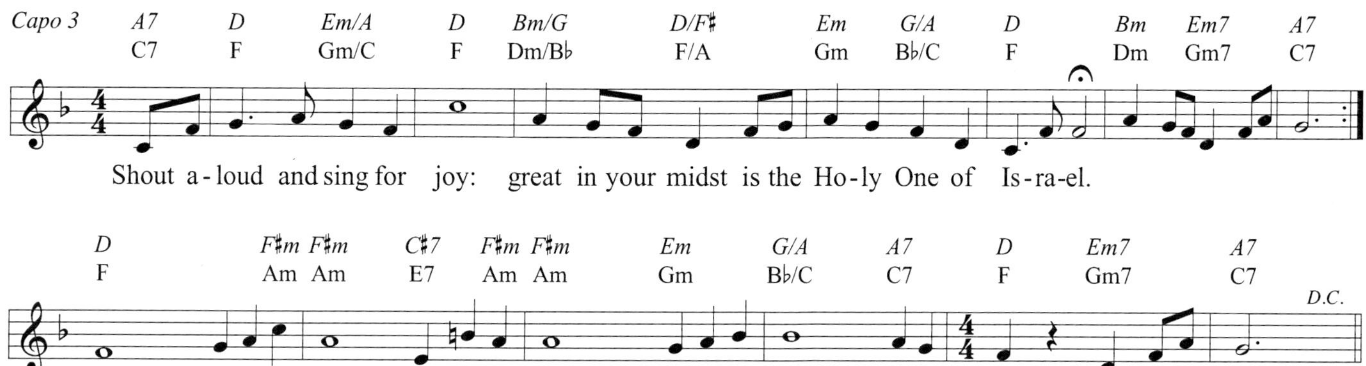

Surely God is my salvation; I will trust, and will not · **be** a-fraid,
for the Lord God is my strength and my might; he has be·-**come_my** sal-vation.
With joy · **you_will** draw water
from the wells · **of** sal-vation. R.

Give thanks · **to** the Lord,
call · **on** his name;
make known his deeds a·-**mong** the nations;
proclaim that his · **name_is** ex-alted. R.

Sing praises to the Lord, for he · **has** done gloriously;
let this be known in · **all** the earth.
Shout aloud and sing for joy, O · **roy**-al Zion,
for great in your midst is the Holy · **One** of Israel. R.

C Instrument

B♭ Instrument

13

Fourth Sunday of Advent – C

Psalm 80

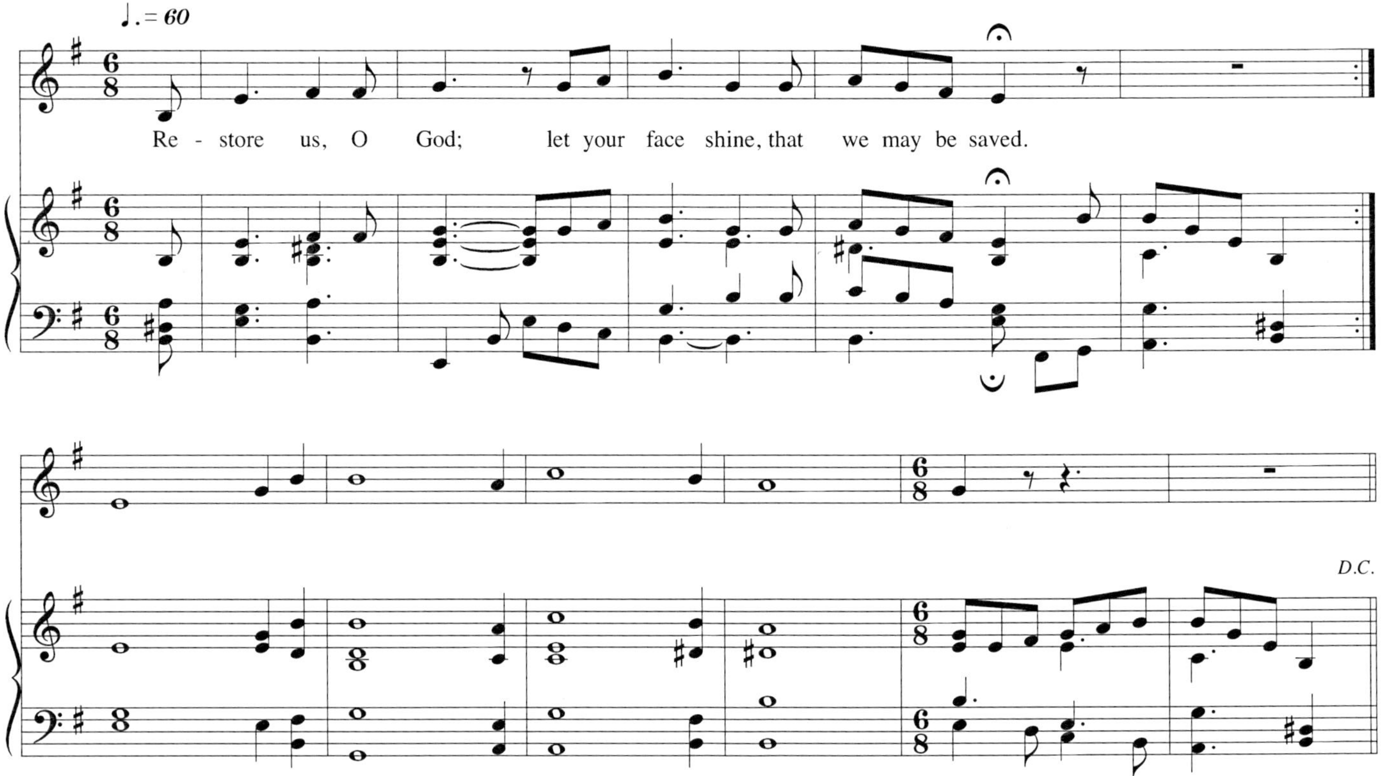

Give ear, O Shepherd · **of** Israel,
you who are enthroned upon the cherubim, shine · **forth.**
Stir up your · **might,**
and come to · **save_us.** R.

Turn again, O God · **of** hosts,
look down from heaven, and · **see;**
have regard for this · **vine,**
the stock that your right hand has · **planted.** R.

But let your hand be upon the man at · **your** right,
the son of man you have made strong for your·-**self.**
Then we will never turn · **back_from_you;**
give us life, and we will call on your · **name.** R.

Fourth Sunday of Advent – C

Psalm 80

Guitar

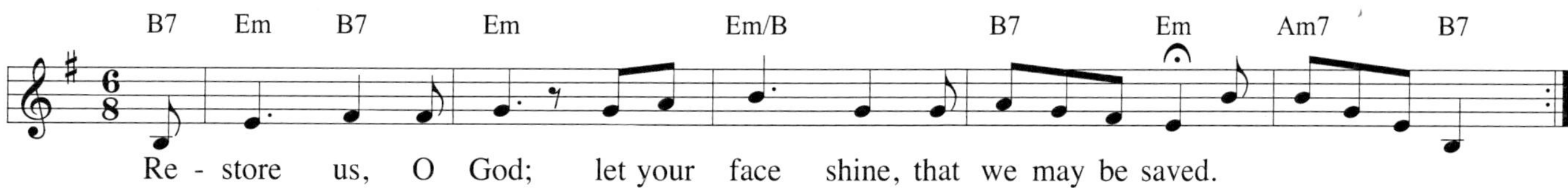

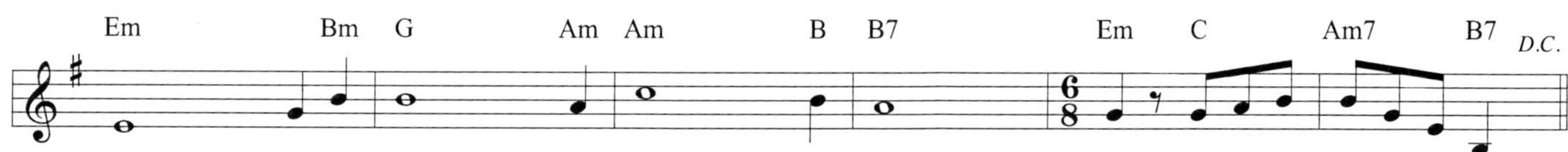

Give ear, O Shepherd · **of** Israel,
you who are enthroned upon the cherubim, shine · **forth.**
Stir up your · **might,**
and come to · **save_us.** R.

Turn again, O God · **of** hosts,
look down from heaven, and · **see;**
have regard for this · **vine,**
the stock that your right hand has · **planted.** R.

But let your hand be upon the man at · **your** right,
the son of man you have made strong for your·-**self.**
Then we will never turn · **back_from_you;**
give us life, and we will call on your · **name.** R.

C Instrument

B♭ Instrument

Common Psalm for Christmas

Psalm 98

O sing to the Lord a · **new** song,
for he has done · **marvellous** things.
His right hand and his holy · **arm**
have brought · **him** victory. R.

The Lord has made known · **his** victory;
he has revealed his vindication in the sight of · **the** nations.
He has remembered his steadfast love and · **faithfulness**
to the house · **of** Israel. R.

All the ends of the earth · **have** seen
the victory of · **our** God.
Make a joyful noise to the Lord, all the · **earth;**
break forth into joyous song and · **sing** praises. R.

Sing praises to the Lord with · **the** lyre,
with the lyre and the sound · **of** melody.
With trumpets and the sound of the · **horn**
make a joyful noise before the King, · **the** Lord. R.

Common Psalm for Christmas

Psalm 98

Guitar

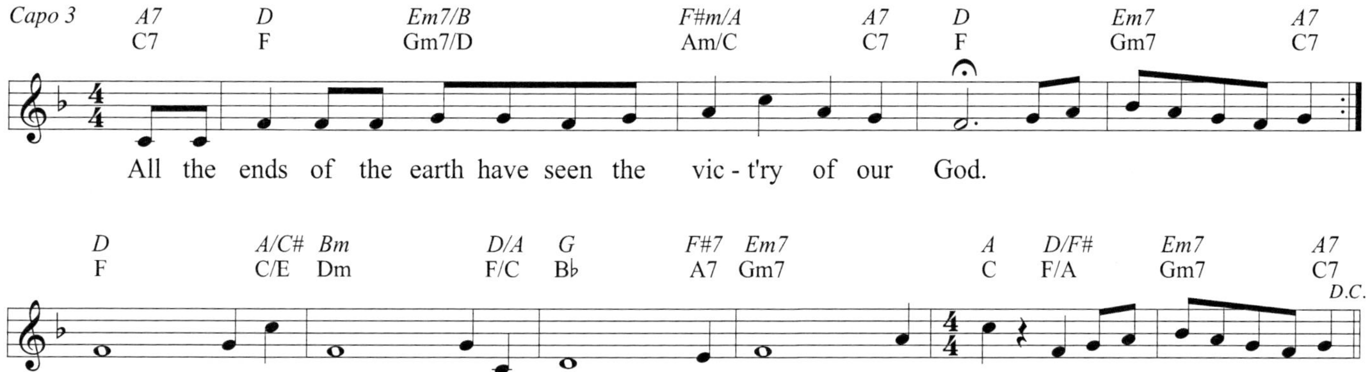

O sing to the Lord a · **new** song,
for he has done · **marvellous** things.
His right hand and his holy · **arm**
have brought · **him** victory. R.

The Lord has made known · **his** victory;
he has revealed his vindication in the sight of · **the** nations.
He has remembered his steadfast love and · **faithfulness**
to the house · **of** Israel. R.

All the ends of the earth · **have** seen
the victory of · **our** God.
Make a joyful noise to the Lord, all the · **earth;**
break forth into joyous song and · **sing** praises. R.

Sing praises to the Lord with · **the** lyre,
with the lyre and the sound · **of** melody.
With trumpets and the sound of the · **horn**
make a joyful noise before the King, · **the** Lord. R.

Common Psalm for Christmas

Psalm 34

I will bless the Lord at all · **times;**
his praise shall continually be in · **my** mouth.
My soul makes its boast in the · **Lord;**
let the humble hear and · **be** glad. R.

O fear the Lord, you his · **holy_ones,**
for those who fear him have · **no** want.
The young lions suffer want and · **hunger,**
but those who seek the Lord lack no · **good** thing. R.

Come, O children, · **listen_to_me;**
I will teach you the fear of · **the** Lord.
Which of you desires · **life,**
and covets many days to en·-**joy** good? R.

Keep your tongue from · **evil,**
and your lips from speaking · **de**-ceit.
Depart from evil, and do · **good;**
seek peace, and · **pur**-sue_it. R.

Common Psalm for Christmas

Psalm 34

Guitar

I will bless the Lord at all · **times;**
his praise shall continually be in · **my** mouth.
My soul makes its boast in the · **Lord;**
let the humble hear and · **be** glad. R.

O fear the Lord, you his · **holy_ones,**
for those who fear him have · **no** want.
The young lions suffer want and · **hunger,**
but those who seek the Lord lack no · **good** thing. R.

Come, O children, · **listen_to_me;**
I will teach you the fear of · **the** Lord.
Which of you desires · **life,**
and covets many days to en·-**joy** good? R.

Keep your tongue from · **evil,**
and your lips from speaking · **de**-ceit.
Depart from evil, and do · **good;**
seek peace, and · **pur**-sue_it. R.

C Instrument

B♭ Instrument

Common Psalm for Christmas

Psalm 72

Give the king your justice, O · **God,**
and your righteousness to a king's · **son.**
May he judge your · **people** with righteousness,
and your · **poor** with justice. R.

In his days may righteousness · **flourish**
and peace abound, until the moon is no · **more.**
May he have dominion from · **sea** to sea,
and from the River to the · **ends_of** the earth. R.

May the kings of Tarshish and of the isles render him · **tribute,**
may the kings of Sheba and Seba bring · **gifts.**
May all kings fall · **down** be-fore_him,
all nations · **give** him service. R.

For he delivers the needy one who · **calls,**
the poor and the one who has no · **helper.**
He has pity on the · **weak_and** the needy,
and saves the · **lives_of** the needy. R.

Common Psalm for Christmas

Psalm 72

Guitar

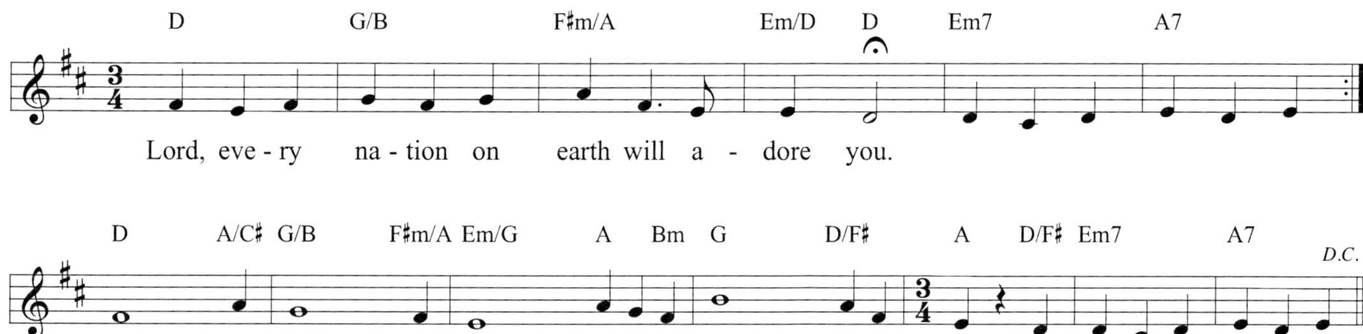

Give the king your justice, O · **God,**
and your righteousness to a king's · **son.**
May he judge your · **people** with righteousness,
and your · **poor** with justice. R.

In his days may righteousness · **flourish**
and peace abound, until the moon is no · **more.**
May he have dominion from · **sea** to sea,
and from the River to the · **ends_of** the earth. R.

May the kings of Tarshish and of the isles render him · **tribute,**
may the kings of Sheba and Seba bring · **gifts.**
May all kings fall · **down** be-fore_him,
all nations · **give** him service. R.

For he delivers the needy one who · **calls,**
the poor and the one who has no · **helper.**
He has pity on the · **weak_and** the needy,
and saves the · **lives_of** the needy. R.

C Instrument

B♭ Instrument

Christmas: Nativity of the Lord (Vigil) – ABC

Psalm 89

You said, "I have made a covenant with my · **chosen_one,**
I have sworn to my servant · **David:**
I will establish your descendants for·-**ever,**
and build your throne for all · **gener**-ations." R.

Blessed are the people who know the festal · **shout,**
who walk, O Lord, in the light of your · **countenance;**
they exult in your name all day · **long,**
and extol · **your** righteousness. R.

He shall cry to me, "You are my · **Father,**
my God, and the Rock of my sal·-**vation!**"
Forever I will keep my steadfast love for · **him,**
and my covenant with him will · **stand** firm. R.

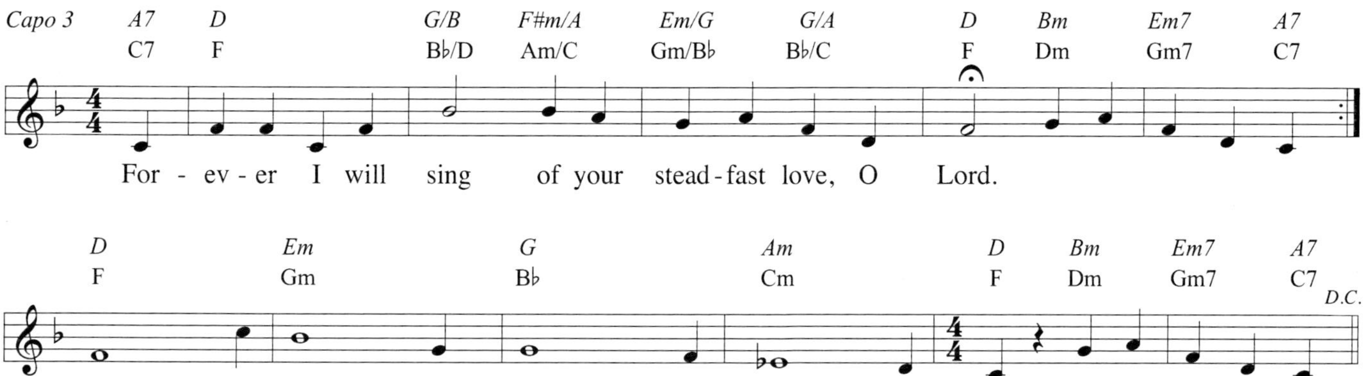

Christmas: Nativity of the Lord (Vigil) – ABC
Psalm 89

You said, "I have made a covenant with my · **chosen_one,**
I have sworn to my servant · **David:**
I will establish your descendants for·-**ever,**
and build your throne for all · **gener**-ations." R.

Blessed are the people who know the festal · **shout,**
who walk, O Lord, in the light of your · **countenance;**
they exult in your name all day · **long,**
and extol · **your** righteousness. R.

He shall cry to me, "You are my · **Father,**
my God, and the Rock of my sal·-**vation!**"
Forever I will keep my steadfast love for · **him,**
and my covenant with him will · **stand** firm. R.

Christmas: Nativity of the Lord (Night) – ABC

Psalm 96

O sing to the Lord a · **new** song;
sing to the Lord, · **all_the** earth.
Sing to the Lord, · **bless_his** name;
tell of his salvation from day · **to** day. R.

Declare his glory among · **the** nations,
his marvellous works among all · **the** peoples.
For great is the Lord, and greatly · **to_be** praised;
he is to be revered above · **all** gods. R.

Let the heavens be glad, and let the earth · **re**-joice;
let the sea roar, and all · **that** fills_it;
let the field exult, and every·-**thing** in_it.
Then shall all the trees of the forest sing · **for** joy. R.

Rejoice before the Lord; for · **he_is** coming,
for he is coming to judge · **the** earth.
He will judge the world · **with** righteousness,
and the peoples · **with_his** truth. R.

Christmas: Nativity of the Lord (Night) – ABC

Psalm 96

Guitar

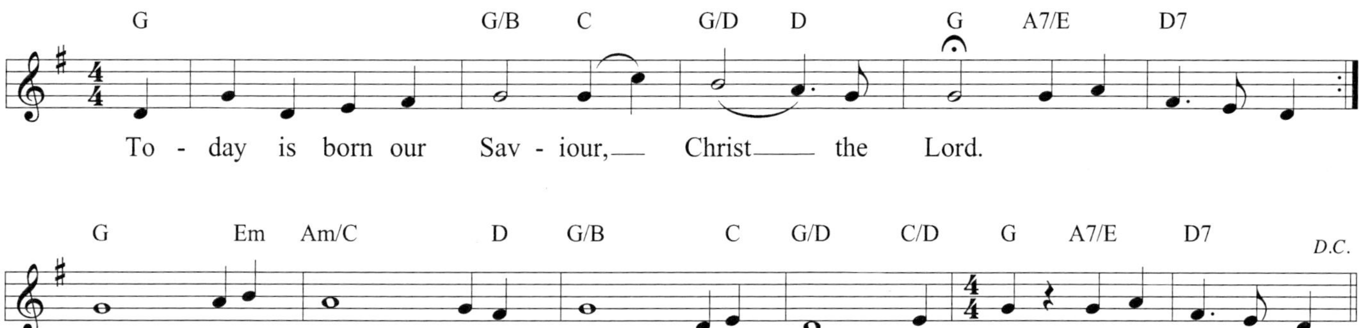

O sing to the Lord a · **new** song;
sing to the Lord, · **all_the** earth.
Sing to the Lord, · **bless_his** name;
tell of his salvation from day · **to** day. R.

Declare his glory among · **the** nations,
his marvellous works among all · **the** peoples.
For great is the Lord, and greatly · **to_be** praised;
he is to be revered above · **all** gods. R.

Let the heavens be glad, and let the earth · **re**-joice;
let the sea roar, and all · **that** fills_it;
let the field exult, and every·-**thing** in_it.
Then shall all the trees of the forest sing · **for** joy. R.

Rejoice before the Lord; for · **he_is** coming,
for he is coming to judge · **the** earth.
He will judge the world · **with** righteousness,
and the peoples · **with_his** truth. R.

C Instrument

B♭ Instrument

Christmas: Nativity of the Lord (Dawn) – ABC

Psalm 97

The Lord is king! Let the earth re·-**joice;**
let the many coastlands be · **glad!**
Clouds and thick darkness are all a·-**round_him;**
righteousness and justice are the foundation of his · **throne.** R.

The mountains melt like wax before the · **Lord,**
before the Lord of all the · **earth.**
The heavens proclaim his · **righteousness;**
and all the peoples behold his · **glory.** R.

Light dawns for the · **righteous,**
and joy for the upright in · **heart.**
Rejoice in the Lord, O you · **righteous,**
and give thanks to his holy · **name!** R.

Christmas: Nativity of the Lord (Dawn) – ABC

Psalm 97

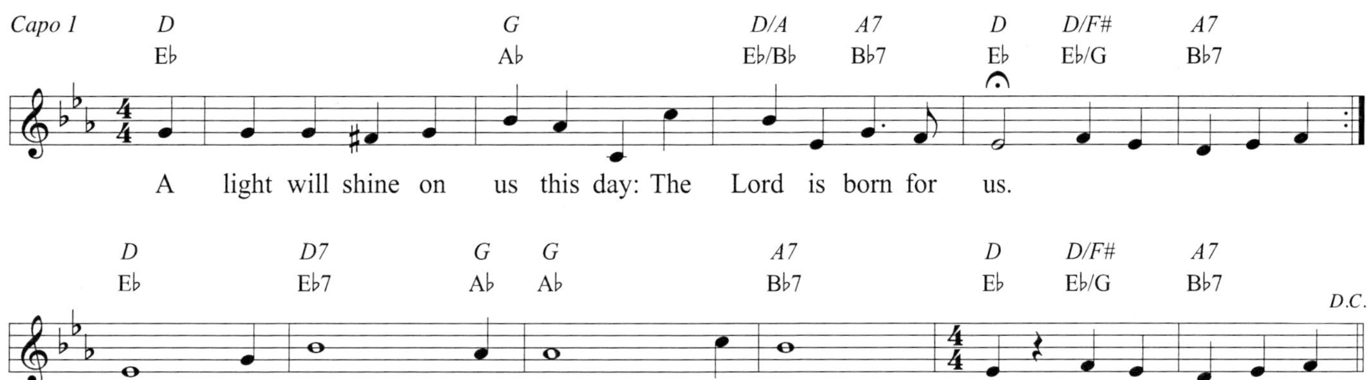

The Lord is king! Let the earth re·-**joice;**
let the many coastlands be · **glad!**
Clouds and thick darkness are all a·-**round_him;**
righteousness and justice are the foundation of his · **throne.** R.

The mountains melt like wax before the · **Lord,**
before the Lord of all the · **earth.**
The heavens proclaim his · **righteousness;**
and all the peoples behold his · **glory.** R.

Light dawns for the · **righteous,**
and joy for the upright in · **heart.**
Rejoice in the Lord, O you · **righteous,**
and give thanks to his holy · **name!** R.

27

Christmas: Nativity of the Lord (Day) – ABC

Psalm 98

O sing to the Lord a · **new** song,
for he has done · **marvellous** things.
His right hand and his holy · **arm**
have brought · **him** victory. R.

The Lord has made known · **his** victory;
he has revealed his vindication in the sight of · **the** nations.
He has remembered his steadfast love and · **faithfulness**
to the house · **of** Israel. R.

All the ends of the earth · **have** seen
the victory of · **our** God.
Make a joyful noise to the Lord, all the · **earth;**
break forth into joyous song and · **sing** praises. R.

Sing praises to the Lord with · **the** lyre,
with the lyre and the sound · **of** melody.
With trumpets and the sound of the · **horn**
make a joyful noise before the King, · **the** Lord. R.

Christmas: Nativity of the Lord (Day) – ABC

Psalm 98

Guitar

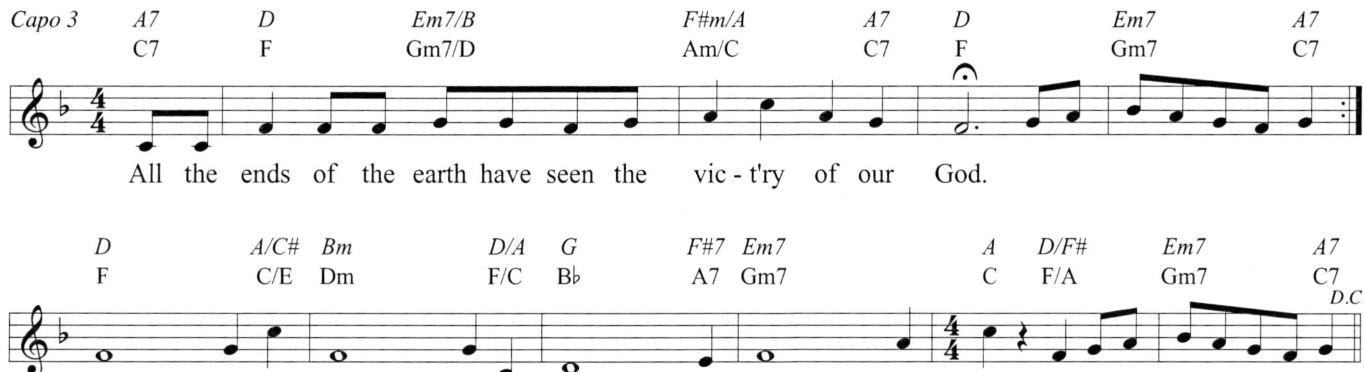

O sing to the Lord a · **new** song,
for he has done · **marvellous** things.
His right hand and his holy · **arm**
have brought · **him** victory. R.

The Lord has made known · **his** victory;
he has revealed his vindication in the sight of · **the** nations.
He has remembered his steadfast love and · **faithfulness**
to the house · **of** Israel. R.

All the ends of the earth · **have** seen
the victory of · **our** God.
Make a joyful noise to the Lord, all the · **earth;**
break forth into joyous song and · **sing** praises. R.

Sing praises to the Lord with · **the** lyre,
with the lyre and the sound · **of** melody.
With trumpets and the sound of the · **horn**
make a joyful noise before the King, · **the** Lord. R.

Holy Family of Jesus, Mary and Joseph – C

Psalm 84

How lovely is · **your** dwelling_place,
O Lord · **of** hosts!
My soul longs, indeed it faints for the courts of · **the** Lord;
my heart and my flesh sing for joy to the · **liv**-ing God. R.

Blessed are those who live in · **your** house,
ever singing · **your** praise.
Blessed are those whose strength is · **in** you,
in whose heart are the · **highways** to Zion. R.

O Lord God of hosts, hear · **my** prayer;
give ear, O God · **of** Jacob!
Behold our shield, · **O** God;
look on the face of · **your** a-nointed. R.

For a day in your courts · **is** better
than a thou·-**sand** elsewhere.
I would rather be a doorkeeper in the house of · **my** God
than live in the · **tents** of wickedness. R.

Holy Family of Jesus, Mary and Joseph – C
Psalm 84

How lovely is · **your** dwelling_place,
O Lord · **of** hosts!
My soul longs, indeed it faints for the courts of · **the** Lord;
my heart and my flesh sing for joy to the · **liv**-ing God. R.

Blessed are those who live in · **your** house,
ever singing · **your** praise.
Blessed are those whose strength is · **in** you,
in whose heart are the · **highways** to Zion. R.

O Lord God of hosts, hear · **my** prayer;
give ear, O God · **of** Jacob!
Behold our shield, · **O** God;
look on the face of · **your** a-nointed. R.

For a day in your courts · **is** better
than a thou·-**sand** elsewhere.
I would rather be a doorkeeper in the house of · **my** God
than live in the · **tents** of wickedness. R.

Holy Family of Jesus, Mary and Joseph – ABC

Psalm 128

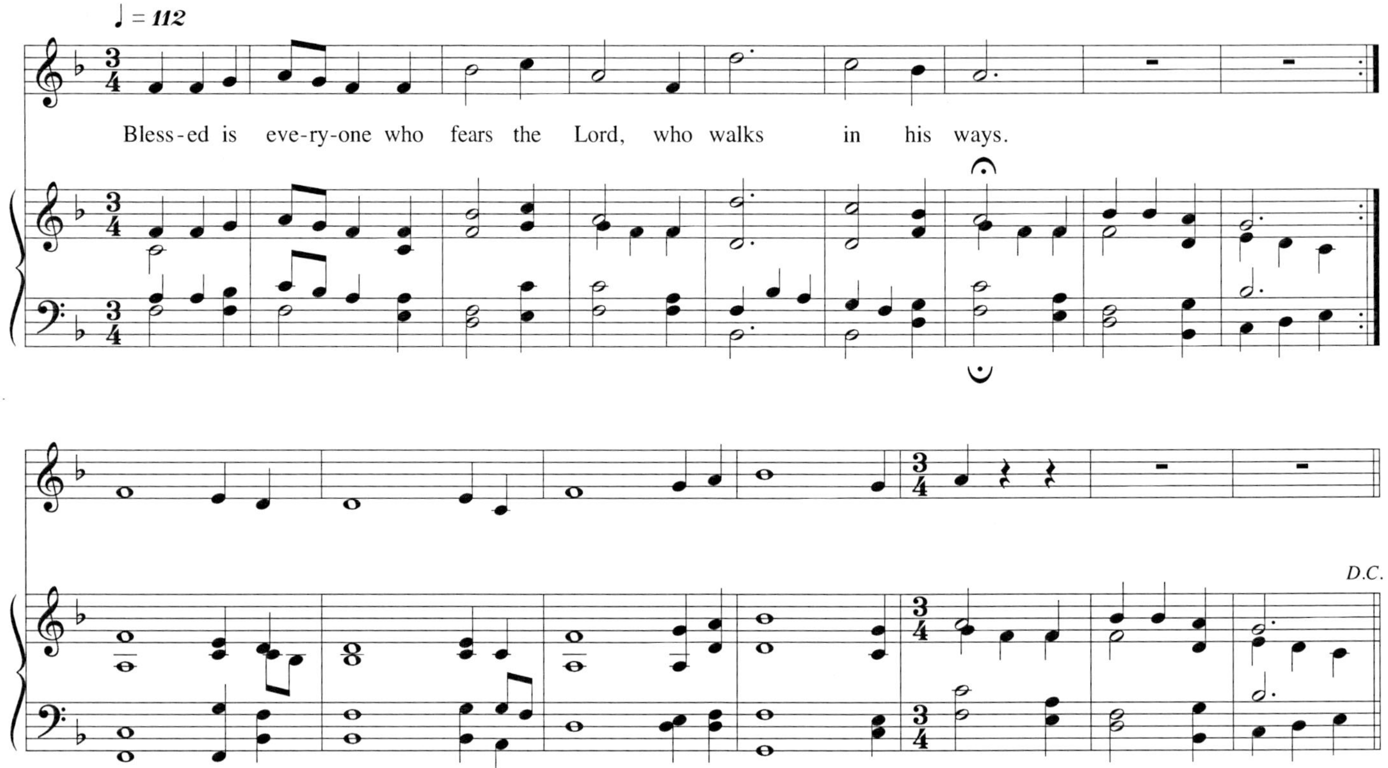

Blessed is everyone who fears · **the** Lord,
who walks in · **his** ways.
You shall eat the fruit of the labour of · **your** hands;
you shall be happy, and it shall go well · **with** you. R.

Your wife will be like a fruit·-**ful** vine
within · **your** house;
your children will be · **like** olive_shoots
around · **your** table. R.

Thus shall the man be blessed who fears · **the** Lord.
The Lord bless you · **from** Zion.
May you see the prosperity of · **Je**-rusalem
all the days of · **your** life. R.

Holy Family of Jesus, Mary and Joseph – ABC

Psalm 128

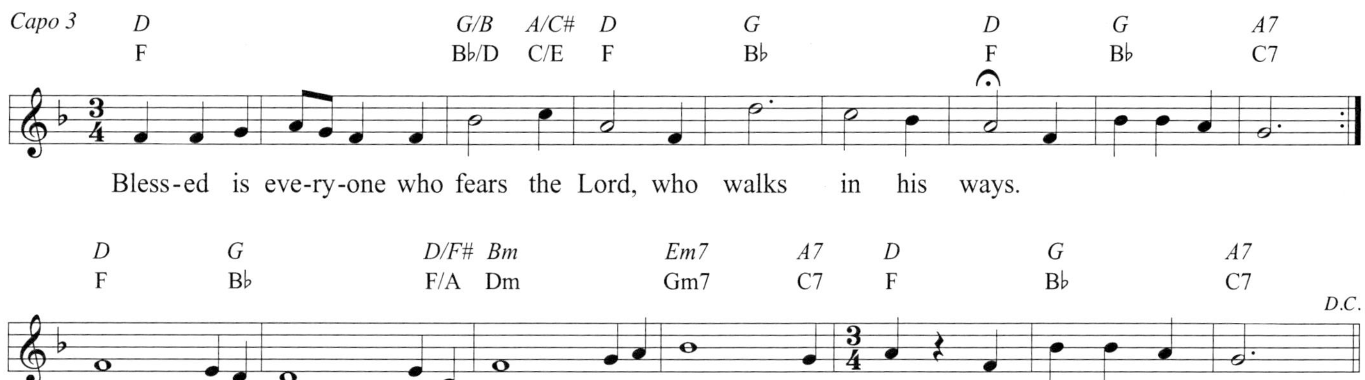

Blessed is everyone who fears · **the** Lord,
who walks in · **his** ways.
You shall eat the fruit of the labour of · **your** hands;
you shall be happy, and it shall go well · **with** you. R.

Your wife will be like a fruit·-**ful** vine
within · **your** house;
your children will be · **like** olive_shoots
around · **your** table. R.

Thus shall the man be blessed who fears · **the** Lord.
The Lord bless you · **from** Zion.
May you see the prosperity of · **Je**-rusalem
all the days of · **your** life. R.

33

January 1 – Solemnity of Mary, the Holy Mother of God – ABC

Psalm 67

May God be gracious to us · **and** bless_us
and make his face to shine · **up**-on_us,
that your way may be known up·-**on** earth,
your saving power a·-**mong** all nations. R.

Let the nations be glad and sing · **for** joy,
for you judge the peoples with equity and guide the nations up·-**on** earth.
Let the peoples praise you, · **O** God;
let all the · **peo**-ples praise_you. R.

The earth has yielded · **its** increase;
God, our God, · **has** blessed_us.
May God continue · **to** bless_us;
let all the ends of the · **earth** re-vere_him. R.

January 1 – Solemnity of Mary, the Holy Mother of God – ABC

Psalm 67

Guitar

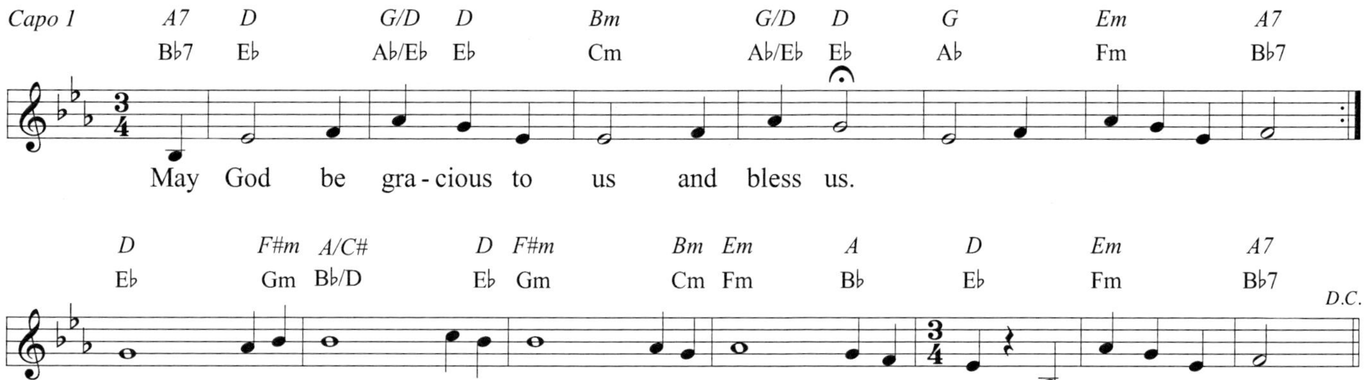

May God be gracious to us · **and** bless_us
and make his face to shine · **up**-on_us,
that your way may be known up·-**on** earth,
your saving power a·-**mong** all nations. R.

Let the nations be glad and sing · **for** joy,
for you judge the peoples with equity and guide the nations up·-**on** earth.
Let the peoples praise you, · **O** God;
let all the · **peo**-ples praise_you. R.

The earth has yielded · **its** increase;
God, our God, · **has** blessed_us.
May God continue · **to** bless_us;
let all the ends of the · **earth** re-vere_him. R.

C Instrument

B♭ Instrument

35

Second Sunday after Christmas – ABC

Psalm 147

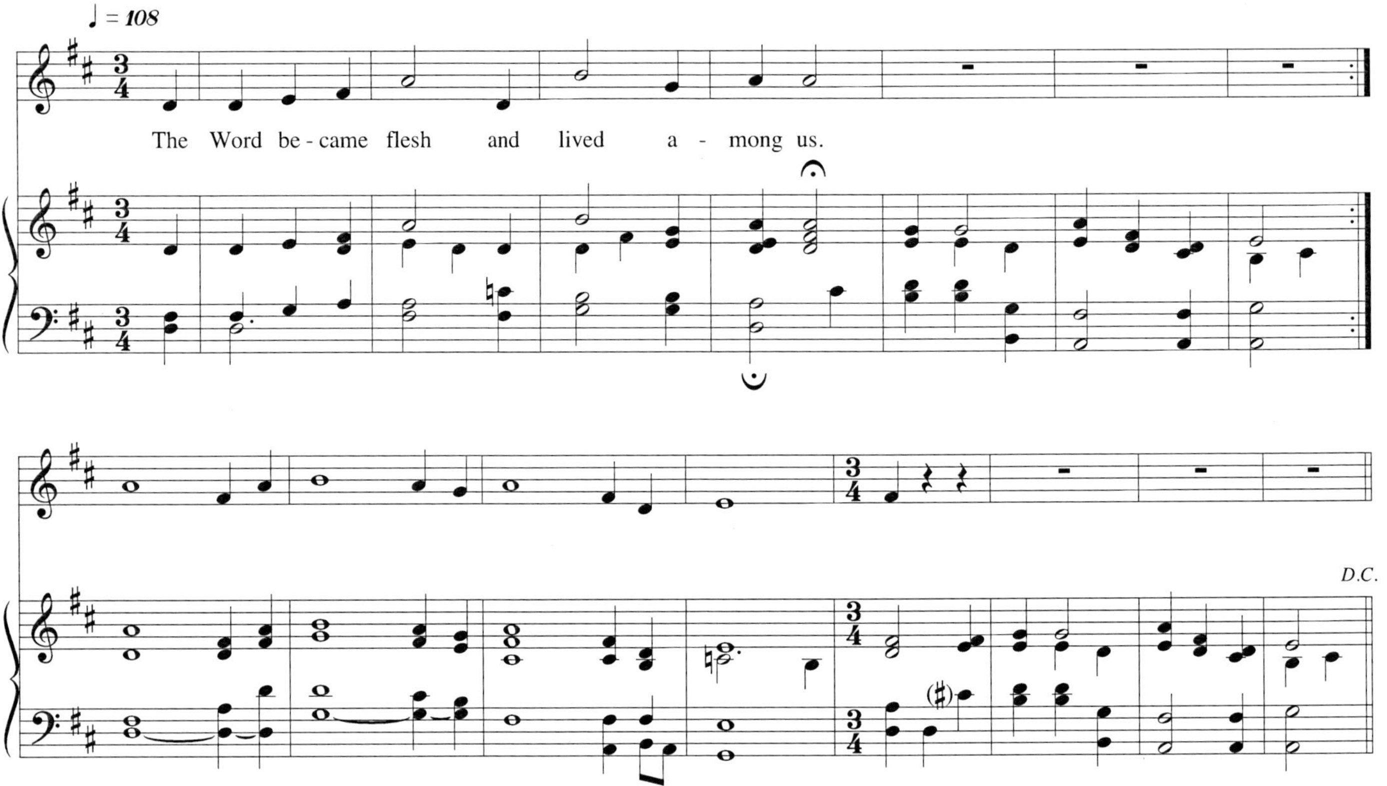

Praise the Lord, O · **Je**-rusalem!
Praise your God, · **O** Zion!
For he strengthens the bars of · **your** gates;
he blesses your children with·-**in_you.** R.

He grants peace within · **your** borders;
he fills you with the finest · **of** wheat.
He sends out his command · **to_the** earth;
his word runs · **swiftly.** R.

He declares his word · **to** Jacob,
his statutes and ordinances · **to** Israel.
He has not dealt thus with any · **other** nation;
they do not know his · **ordinances.** R.

Second Sunday after Christmas – ABC

Psalm 147

Guitar

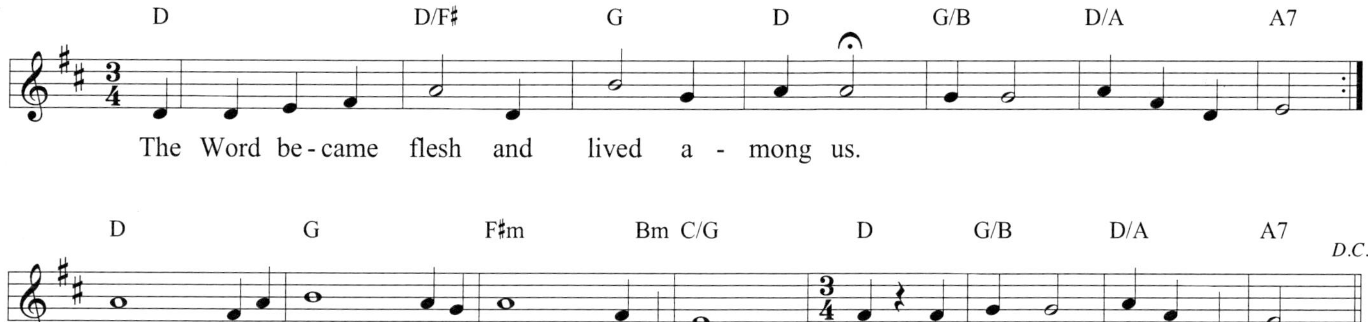

Praise the Lord, O · **Je**-rusalem!
Praise your God, · **O** Zion!
For he strengthens the bars of · **your** gates;
he blesses your children with·-**in_you.** R.

He grants peace within · **your** borders;
he fills you with the finest · **of** wheat.
He sends out his command · **to_the** earth;
his word runs · **swiftly.** R.

He declares his word · **to** Jacob,
his statutes and ordinances · **to** Israel.
He has not dealt thus with any · **other** nation;
they do not know his · **ordinances.** R.

C Instrument

B♭ Instrument

Epiphany of the Lord – ABC

Psalm 72

Give the king your justice, O · **God,**
and your righteousness to a king's · **son.**
May he judge your · **people** with righteousness,
and your · **poor** with justice. R.

In his days may righteousness · **flourish**
and peace abound, until the moon is no · **more.**
May he have dominion from · **sea** to sea,
and from the River to the · **ends_of** the earth. R.

May the kings of Tarshish and of the isles render him · **tribute,**
may the kings of Sheba and Seba bring · **gifts.**
May all kings fall · **down** be-fore_him,
all nations · **give** him service. R.

For he delivers the needy one who · **calls,**
the poor and the one who has no · **helper.**
He has pity on the · **weak_and** the needy,
and saves the · **lives_of** the needy. R.

Epiphany of the Lord – ABC

Psalm 72

Guitar

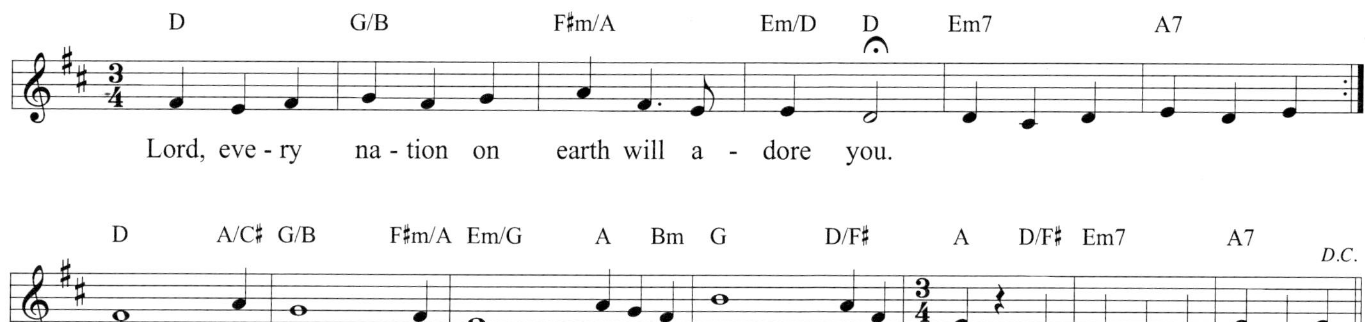

Give the king your justice, O · **God,**
and your righteousness to a king's · **son.**
May he judge your · **people** with righteousness,
and your · **poor** with justice. R.

In his days may righteousness · **flourish**
and peace abound, until the moon is no · **more.**
May he have dominion from · **sea** to sea,
and from the River to the · **ends_of** the earth. R.

May the kings of Tarshish and of the isles render him · **tribute,**
may the kings of Sheba and Seba bring · **gifts.**
May all kings fall · **down** be-fore_him,
all nations · **give** him service. R.

For he delivers the needy one who · **calls,**
the poor and the one who has no · **helper.**
He has pity on the · **weak_and** the needy,
and saves the · **lives_of** the needy. R.

C Instrument

B♭ Instrument

Baptism of the Lord – C

Psalm 104

O Lord my God, you are · **very** great.
You are clothed with honour and · **majesty,**
wrapped in light as · **with** a garment.
You stretch out the heavens · **like_a** tent. R.

You set the beams of your dwelling place on · **the** waters,
you make the clouds your chariot, you ride on the wings of the · **wind,**
you make the · **winds** your messengers,
fire and flame · **your** ministers. R.

O Lord, how manifold are · **your** works!
In wisdom you have made them all; the earth is full of your · **creatures.**
Yonder is the sea, · **great** and wide,
creeping things innumerable are there, living things both small · **and** great. R.

Living things all look · **to** you
to give them their food in due · **season;**
when you give to them, they · **gather** it up;
when you open your hand, they are filled with · **good** things. R.

When you take away · **their** breath,
they die and return to their · **dust.**
When you send forth your spirit, they · **are** cre-ated;
and you renew the face of · **the** earth. R.

Psalm 104

Guitar

O Lord my God, you are · **very** great.
You are clothed with honour and · **majesty,**
wrapped in light as · **with** a garment.
You stretch out the heavens · **like_a** tent. R.

You set the beams of your dwelling place on · **the** waters,
you make the clouds your chariot, you ride on the wings of the · **wind,**
you make the · **winds** your messengers,
fire and flame · **your** ministers. R.

O Lord, how manifold are · **your** works!
In wisdom you have made them all; the earth is full of your · **creatures.**
Yonder is the sea, · **great** and wide,
creeping things innumerable are there, living things both small · **and** great. R.

Living things all look · **to** you
to give them their food in due · **season;**
when you give to them, they · **gather** it up;
when you open your hand, they are filled with · **good** things. R.

When you take away · **their** breath,
they die and return to their · **dust.**
When you send forth your spirit, they · **are** cre-ated;
and you renew the face of · **the** earth. R.

Baptism of the Lord – ABC

Psalm 29

Ascribe to the Lord, O heavenly · **beings,**
ascribe to the Lord glory · **and** strength.
Ascribe to the Lord the glory of his · **name;**
worship the Lord in · **holy** splendour. R.

The voice of the Lord is over the · **waters;**
the Lord, over · **mighty** waters.
The voice of the Lord is · **powerful;**
the voice of the Lord is · **full_of** majesty. R.

The God of glory · **thunders,**
and in his temple all · **say,** "Glory!"
The Lord sits enthroned over the · **flood;**
the Lord sits enthroned as king · **for-**ever. R.

Baptism of the Lord – ABC

Psalm 29

Guitar

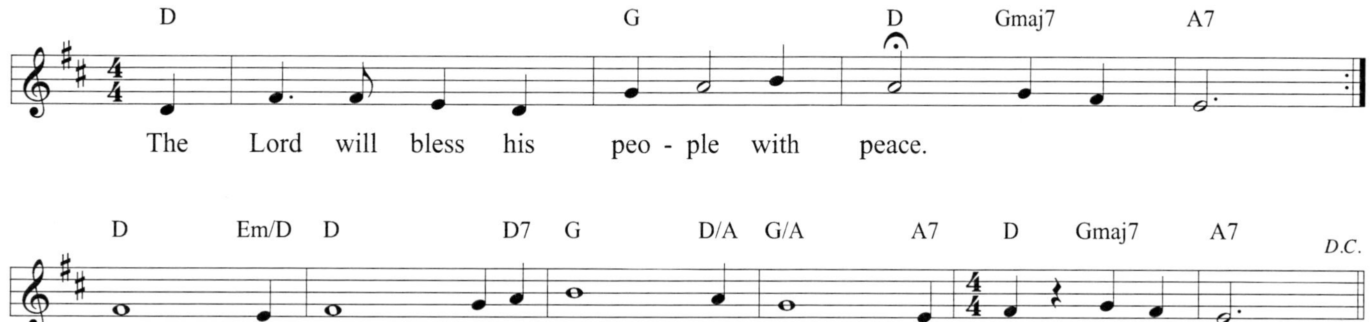

Ascribe to the Lord, O heavenly · **beings,**
ascribe to the Lord glory · **and** strength.
Ascribe to the Lord the glory of his · **name;**
worship the Lord in · **holy** splendour. R.

The voice of the Lord is over the · **waters;**
the Lord, over · **mighty** waters.
The voice of the Lord is · **powerful;**
the voice of the Lord is · **full_of** majesty. R.

The God of glory · **thunders,**
and in his temple all · **say,** "Glory!"
The Lord sits enthroned over the · **flood;**
the Lord sits enthroned as king · **for**-ever. R.

C Instrument

B♭ Instrument

43

Common Psalm for Lent

Psalm 51

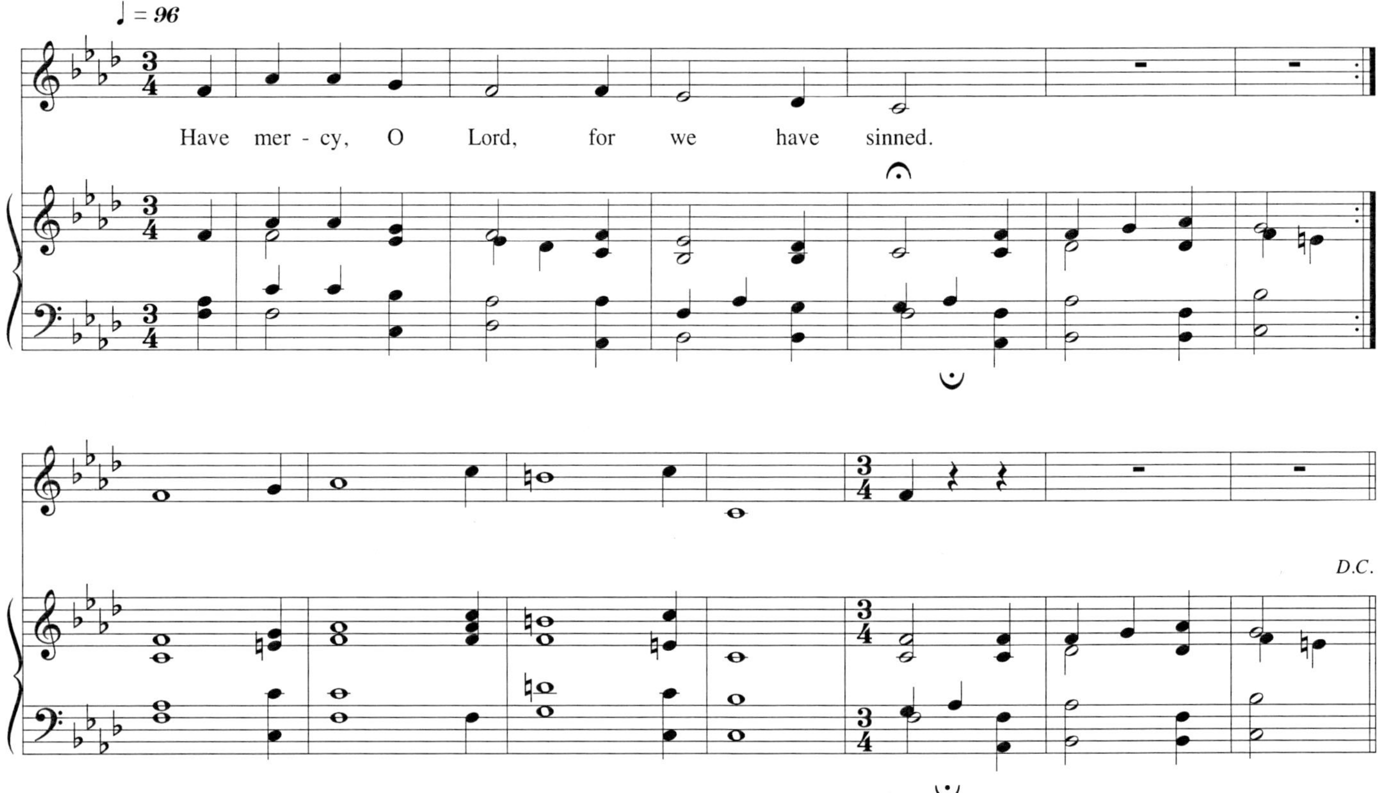

Have mercy on me, O God, according to your steadfast · **love;**
according to your abundant mercy blot out my trans·-**gressions.**
Wash me thoroughly from my in·-**iquity,**
and cleanse me from my · **sin.** R.

For I know my trans·-**gressions,**
and my sin is ever be·-**fore_me.**
Against you, you alone, have I · **sinned,**
and done what is evil in your · **sight.** R.

Create in me a clean heart, O · **God,**
and put a new and right spirit with·-**in_me.**
Do not cast me away from your · **presence,**
and do not take your holy spirit from · **me.** R.

Restore to me the joy of your sal·-**vation,**
and sustain in me a willing · **spirit.**
O Lord, open my · **lips,**
and my mouth will declare your · **praise.** R.

Common Psalm for Lent

Psalm 51

Guitar

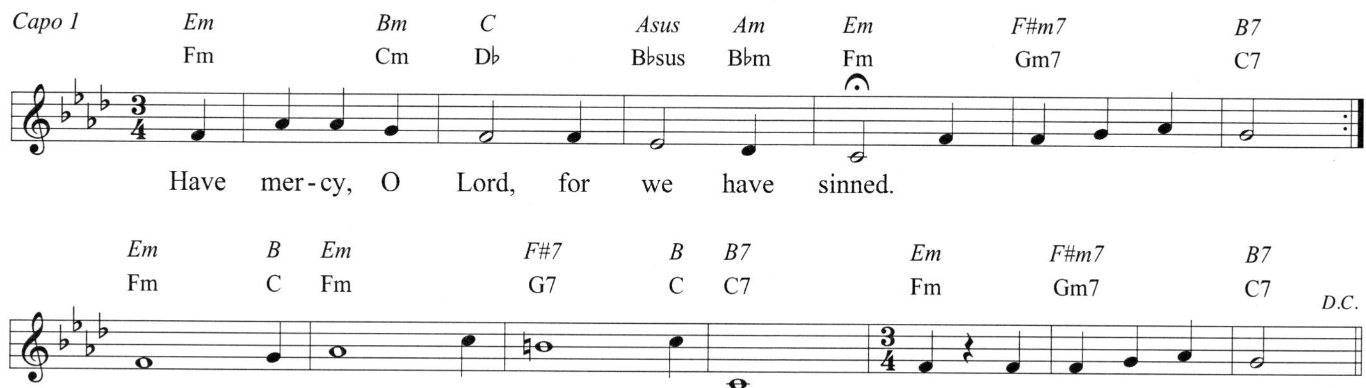

Have mercy on me, O God, according to your steadfast · **love;**
according to your abundant mercy blot out my trans·-**gressions.**
Wash me thoroughly from my in·-**iquity,**
and cleanse me from my · **sin.** R.

For I know my trans·-**gressions,**
and my sin is ever be·-**fore_me.**
Against you, you alone, have I · **sinned,**
and done what is evil in your · **sight.** R.

Create in me a clean heart, O · **God,**
and put a new and right spirit with·-**in_me.**
Do not cast me away from your · **presence,**
and do not take your holy spirit from · **me.** R.

Restore to me the joy of your sal·-**vation,**
and sustain in me a willing · **spirit.**
O Lord, open my · **lips,**
and my mouth will declare your · **praise.** R.

C Instrument

B♭ Instrument

45

Common Psalm for Lent

Psalm 91

You who live in the shelter of the Most · **High,**
who abide in the shadow of the · **Al**-mighty,
will say to the Lord, "My refuge and my · **fortress;**
my God, in whom · **I** trust." R.

No evil shall be·-**fall_you,**
no scourge come near · **your** tent.
For he will command his Angels con·-**cerning_you**
to guard you in all · **your** ways. R.

On their hands they will bear you · **up,**
so that you will not dash your foot against · **a** stone.
You will tread on the lion and the · **adder,**
the young lion and the serpent you will trample · **under** foot. R.

The one who loves me, I will de·-**liver;**
I will protect the one who knows · **my** name.
When he calls to me, I will · **answer_him;**
I will be with him in trouble, I will rescue him · **and** honour_him. R.

Common Psalm for Lent

Psalm 91

Guitar

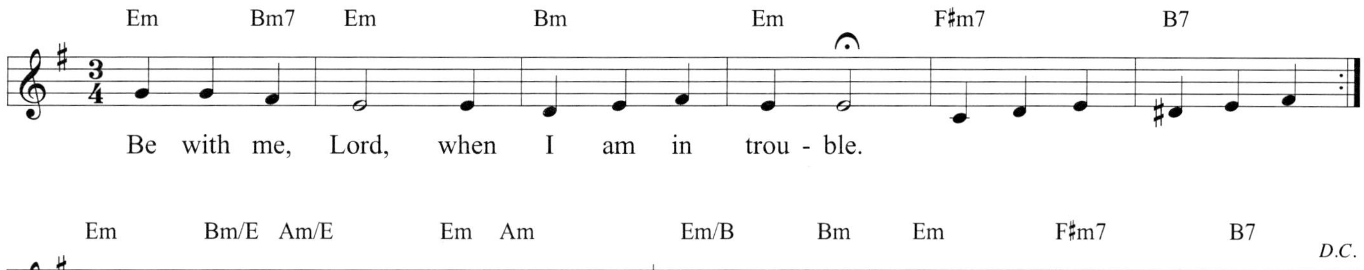

You who live in the shelter of the Most · **High,**
who abide in the shadow of the · **Al**-mighty,
will say to the Lord, "My refuge and my · **fortress;**
my God, in whom · **I** trust." R.

No evil shall be·-**fall_you,**
no scourge come near · **your** tent.
For he will command his Angels con·-**cerning_you**
to guard you in all · **your** ways. R.

On their hands they will bear you · **up,**
so that you will not dash your foot against · **a** stone.
You will tread on the lion and the · **adder,**
the young lion and the serpent you will trample · **under** foot. R.

The one who loves me, I will de·-**liver;**
I will protect the one who knows · **my** name.
When he calls to me, I will · **answer_him;**
I will be with him in trouble, I will rescue him · **and** honour_him. R.

C Instrument

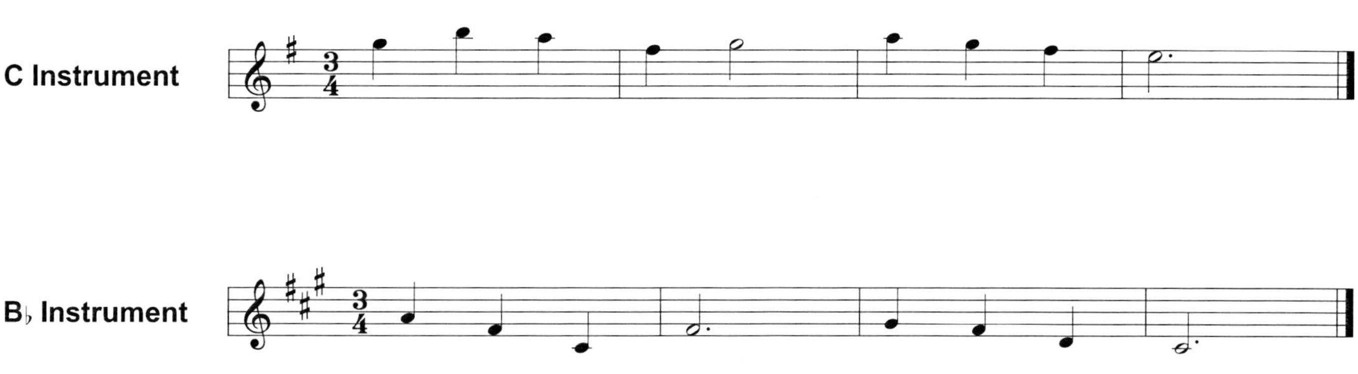

B♭ Instrument

47

Common Psalm for Lent

Psalm 130

Out of the depths I cry to you, O · **Lord.**
Lord, hear · **my** voice!
Let your ears be at·-**tentive**
to the voice of my sup·-**pli**-cations! R.

If you, O Lord, should mark in·-**iquities,**
Lord, who · **could** stand?
But there is forgiveness with · **you,**
so that you may be · **re**-vered. R.

I wait for the · **Lord,**
my soul waits, and in his word · **I** hope;
my soul waits for the · **Lord**
more than watchmen for · **the** morning. R.

For with the Lord there is steadfast · **love,**
and with him is great power to · **re**-deem.
It is he who will redeem · **Israel**
from all its · **in**-iquities. R.

Common Psalm for Lent

Psalm 130

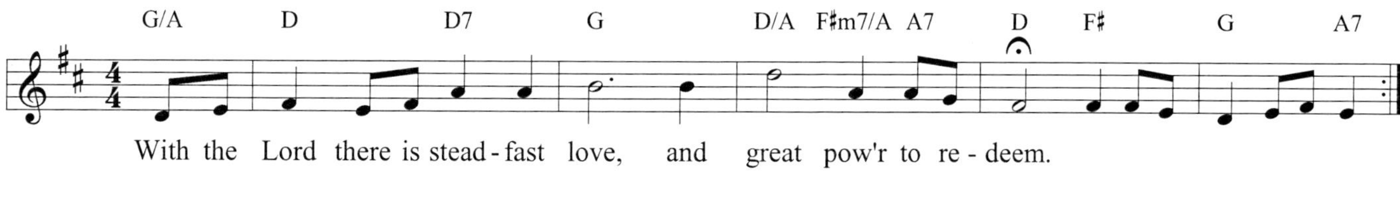

Out of the depths I cry to you, O · **Lord.**
Lord, hear · **my** voice!
Let your ears be at·-**tentive**
to the voice of my sup·-**pli**-cations! R.

If you, O Lord, should mark in·-**iquities,**
Lord, who · **could** stand?
But there is forgiveness with · **you,**
so that you may be · **re**-vered. R.

I wait for the · **Lord,**
my soul waits, and in his word · **I** hope;
my soul waits for the · **Lord**
more than watchmen for · **the** morning. R.

For with the Lord there is steadfast · **love,**
and with him is great power to · **re**-deem.
It is he who will redeem · **Israel**
from all its · **in**-iquities. R.

Common Psalm for Holy Week

Psalm 22

All who see me · **mock_at_me;**
they make mouths at me, they shake · **their** heads;
"Commit your cause to the Lord; let him de·-**liver;**
let him rescue the one in whom he · **de**-lights!" R.

For dogs are all a·-**round_me;**
a company of evildoers · **en**-circles_me.
My hands and feet have · **shrivelled;**
I can count all · **my** bones. R.

They divide my clothes a·-**mong_themselves,**
and for my clothing they · **cast** lots.
But you, O Lord, do not be far a·-**way!**
O my help, come quickly · **to_my** aid! R.

I will tell of your name to my brothers and sisters;
    in the midst of the congregation I will · **praise_you:**
You who fear the · **Lord,** praise_him!
All you offspring of Jacob, · **glorify_him;**
stand in awe of him, all you offspring · **of** Israel! R.

Common Psalm for Holy Week

Psalm 22

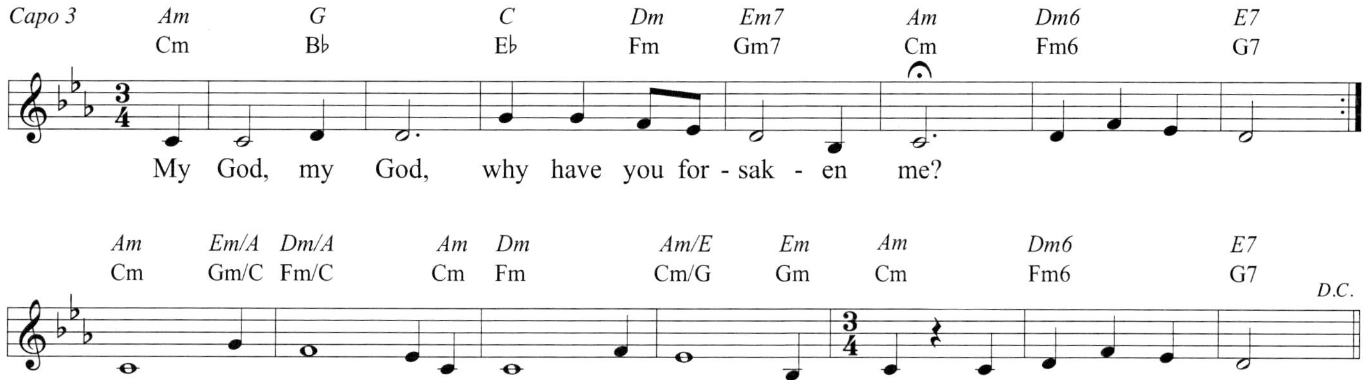

All who see me · **mock_at_me;**
they make mouths at me, they shake · **their** heads;
"Commit your cause to the Lord; let him de·-**liver;**
let him rescue the one in whom he · **de**-lights!" R.

For dogs are all a·-**round_me;**
a company of evildoers · **en**-circles_me.
My hands and feet have · **shrivelled;**
I can count all · **my** bones. R.

They divide my clothes a·-**mong_themselves,**
and for my clothing they · **cast** lots.
But you, O Lord, do not be far a·-**way!**
O my help, come quickly · **to_my** aid! R.

I will tell of your name to my brothers and sisters;
    in the midst of the congregation I will · **praise_you:**
You who fear the · **Lord,** praise_him!
All you offspring of Jacob, · **glorify_him;**
stand in awe of him, all you offspring · **of** Israel! R.

Ash Wednesday – ABC

Psalm 51

Have mercy on me, O God, according to your steadfast · **love;**
according to your abundant mercy blot out my trans·-**gressions.**
Wash me thoroughly from my in·-**iquity,**
and cleanse me from my · **sin.** R.

For I know my trans·-**gressions,**
and my sin is ever be·-**fore_me.**
Against you, you alone, have I · **sinned,**
and done what is evil in your · **sight.** R.

Create in me a clean heart, O · **God,**
and put a new and right spirit with·-**in_me.**
Do not cast me away from your · **presence,**
and do not take your holy spirit from · **me.** R.

Restore to me the joy of your sal·-**vation,**
and sustain in me a willing · **spirit.**
O Lord, open my · **lips,**
and my mouth will declare your · **praise.** R.

Ash Wednesday – ABC

Psalm 51

Guitar

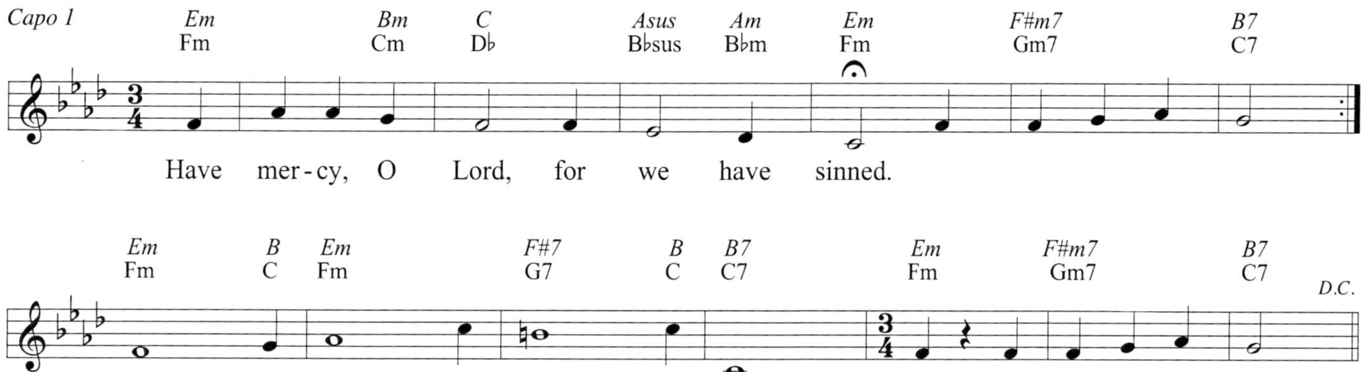

Have mercy on me, O God, according to your steadfast · **love;**
according to your abundant mercy blot out my trans·-**gressions.**
Wash me thoroughly from my in·-**iquity,**
and cleanse me from my · **sin.** R.

For I know my trans·-**gressions,**
and my sin is ever be·-**fore_me.**
Against you, you alone, have I · **sinned,**
and done what is evil in your · **sight.** R.

Create in me a clean heart, O · **God,**
and put a new and right spirit with·-**in_me.**
Do not cast me away from your · **presence,**
and do not take your holy spirit from · **me.** R.

Restore to me the joy of your sal·-**vation,**
and sustain in me a willing · **spirit.**
O Lord, open my · **lips,**
and my mouth will declare your · **praise.** R.

C Instrument

B♭ Instrument

First Sunday of Lent – C

Psalm 91

You who live in the shelter of the Most · **High,**
who abide in the shadow of the · **Al**-mighty,
will say to the Lord, "My refuge and my · **fortress;**
my God, in whom · **I** trust." R.

No evil shall be·-**fall_you,**
no scourge come near · **your** tent.
For he will command his Angels con·-**cerning_you**
to guard you in all · **your** ways. R.

On their hands they will bear you · **up,**
so that you will not dash your foot against · **a** stone.
You will tread on the lion and the · **adder,**
the young lion and the serpent you will trample · **under** foot. R.

The one who loves me, I will de·-**liver;**
I will protect the one who knows · **my** name.
When he calls to me, I will · **answer_him;**
I will be with him in trouble, I will rescue him · **and** honour_him. R.

First Sunday of Lent – C

Psalm 91

Guitar

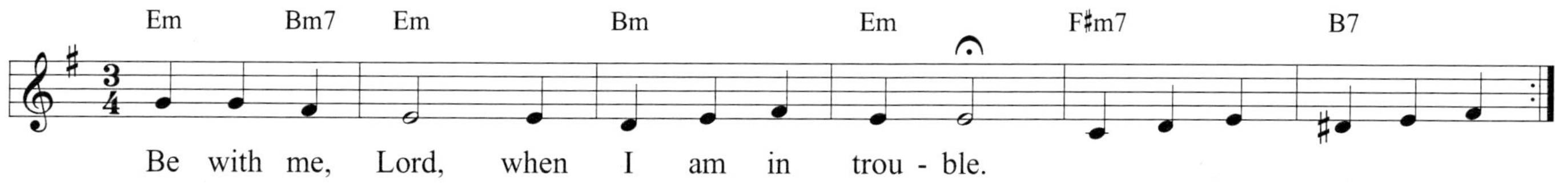

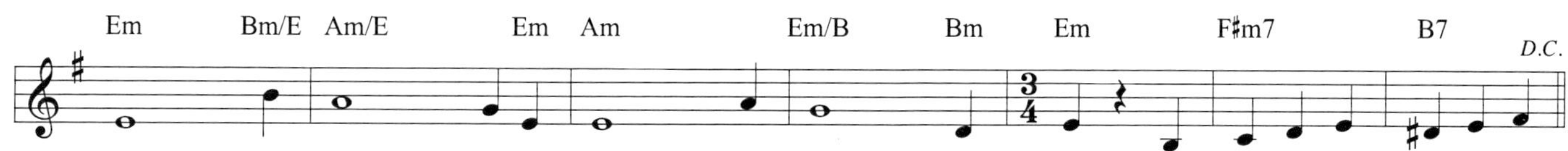

You who live in the shelter of the Most · **High,**
who abide in the shadow of the · **Al**-mighty,
will say to the Lord, "My refuge and my · **fortress;**
my God, in whom · **I** trust." R.

No evil shall be·-**fall_you,**
no scourge come near · **your** tent.
For he will command his Angels con·-**cerning_you**
to guard you in all · **your** ways. R.

On their hands they will bear you · **up,**
so that you will not dash your foot against · **a** stone.
You will tread on the lion and the · **adder,**
the young lion and the serpent you will trample · **under** foot. R.

The one who loves me, I will de·-**liver;**
I will protect the one who knows · **my** name.
When he calls to me, I will · **answer_him;**
I will be with him in trouble, I will rescue him · **and** honour_him. R.

C Instrument

B♭ Instrument

55

Second Sunday of Lent – C

Psalm 27

The Lord is my light and my sal·-**vation;**
whom shall · **I** fear?
The Lord is the stronghold of my · **lif**e**;**
of whom shall I be · **a**-fraid?

Hear, O Lord, when I cry a·-**loud,**
be gracious to me · **and** answer_me!
"Come," my heart says, "seek his · **face!"**
Your face, Lord, do · **I** seek. R.

Do not hide your face from · **me.**
Do not turn your servant away · **in** anger,
you who have been my · **help.**
Do not cast me off, do not forsake me, O God of my · **sal**-vation! R.

I believe that I shall see the goodness of the · **Lord**
in the land of · **the** living.
Wait for the Lord; be · **strong,**
and let your heart take courage; wait · **for_the** Lord!

Second Sunday of Lent – C

Psalm 27

Guitar

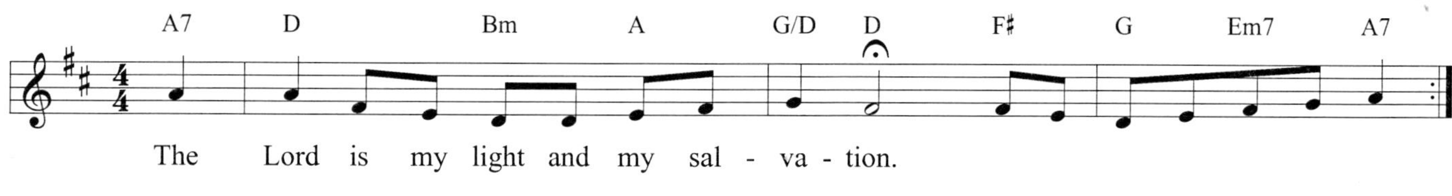

The Lord is my light and my sal·-**vation;**
whom shall · **I** fear?
The Lord is the stronghold of my · **lif**e**;**
of whom shall I be · **a**-fraid?

Hear, O Lord, when I cry a·-**loud,**
be gracious to me · **and** answer_me!
"Come," my heart says, "seek his · **face!"**
Your face, Lord, do · **I** seek. R.

Do not hide your face from · **me.**
Do not turn your servant away · **in** anger,
you who have been my · **help.**
Do not cast me off, do not forsake me, O God of my · **sal**-vation! R.

I believe that I shall see the goodness of the · **Lord**
in the land of · **the** living.
Wait for the Lord; be · **strong,**
and let your heart take courage; wait · **for_the** Lord!

C Instrument

B♭ Instrument

Third Sunday of Lent – C

Psalm 103

Bless the Lord, O my · **soul,**
and all that is within me, bless his · **holy** name.
Bless the Lord, O my · **soul,**
and do not forget all · **his** benefits. R.

It is the Lord who forgives all your in·-**iquity,**
who heals all your · **dis**-eases,
who redeems your life from the · **Pit,**
who crowns you with steadfast love · **and** mercy. R.

The Lord works vindi·-**cation**
and justice for all who are · **op**-pressed.
He made known his ways to · **Moses,**
his acts to the people · **of** Israel. R.

The Lord is merciful and · **gracious,**
slow to anger and abounding in stead·-**fast** love.
For as the heavens are high above the · **earth,**
so great is his steadfast love toward those · **who** fear_him. R.

Third Sunday of Lent – C
Psalm 103

Guitar

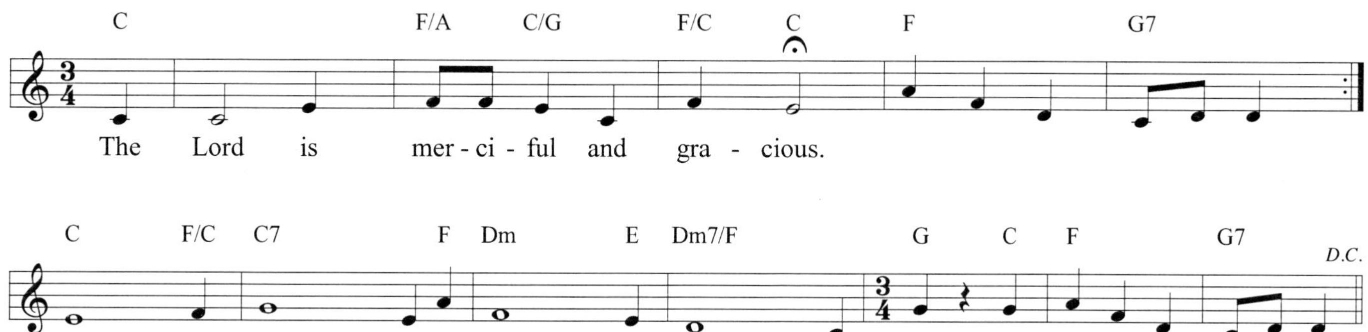

Bless the Lord, O my · **soul,**
and all that is within me, bless his · **holy** name.
Bless the Lord, O my · **soul,**
and do not forget all · **his** benefits. R.

It is the Lord who forgives all your in·-**iquity,**
who heals all your · **dis**-eases,
who redeems your life from the · **Pit,**
who crowns you with steadfast love · **and** mercy. R.

The Lord works vindi·-**cation**
and justice for all who are · **op**-pressed.
He made known his ways to · **Moses,**
his acts to the people · **of** Israel. R.

The Lord is merciful and · **gracious,**
slow to anger and abounding in stead·-**fast** love.
For as the heavens are high above the · **earth,**
so great is his steadfast love toward those · **who** fear_him. R.

C Instrument

B♭ Instrument

Third Sunday of Lent (Christian Initiation)

Psalm 95

O come, let us sing to · **the** Lord;
let us make a joyful noise to the rock of our · **sal**-vation!
Let us come into his presence with · **thanks**-giving;
let us make a joyful noise to him with songs · **of** praise! R.

O come, let us worship and · **bow** down,
let us kneel before the Lord, · **our** Maker!
For he is our God, and we are the people of · **his** pasture,
and the sheep of · **his** hand. R.

O that today you would listen to · **his** voice!
Do not harden your hearts, as at Meribah, as on the day at Massah in · **the** wilderness,
when your ancestors tested me, and put me to · **the** proof,
though they had seen · **my** work. R.

60

Third Sunday of Lent (Christian Initiation)

Psalm 95

Guitar

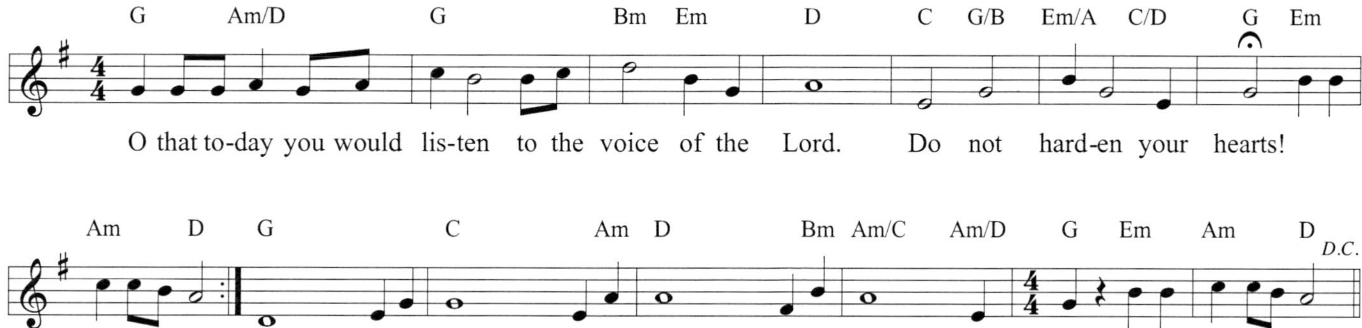

O come, let us sing to · **the** Lord;
let us make a joyful noise to the rock of our · **sal**-vation!
Let us come into his presence with · **thanks**-giving;
let us make a joyful noise to him with songs · **of** praise! R.

O come, let us worship and · **bow** down,
let us kneel before the Lord, · **our** Maker!
For he is our God, and we are the people of · **his** pasture,
and the sheep of · **his** hand. R.

O that today you would listen to · **his** voice!
Do not harden your hearts, as at Meribah, as on the day at Massah in · **the** wilderness,
when your ancestors tested me, and put me to · **the** proof,
though they had seen · **my** work. R.

Fourth Sunday of Lent – C

Psalm 34

I will bless the Lord at all · **times;**
his praise shall continually be in · **my** mouth.
My soul makes its boast in the · **Lord;**
let the humble hear and · **be** glad. R.

O magnify the Lord with · **me,**
and let us exalt his name · **to**-gether.
I sought the Lord, and he · **answered_me,**
and delivered me from all · **my** fears. R.

Look to him, and be · **radiant;**
so your faces shall never · **be_a**-shamed.
The poor one called, and the Lord · **heard,**
and saved that person from ev·-**ery** trouble. R.

Fourth Sunday of Lent – C

Psalm 34

Guitar

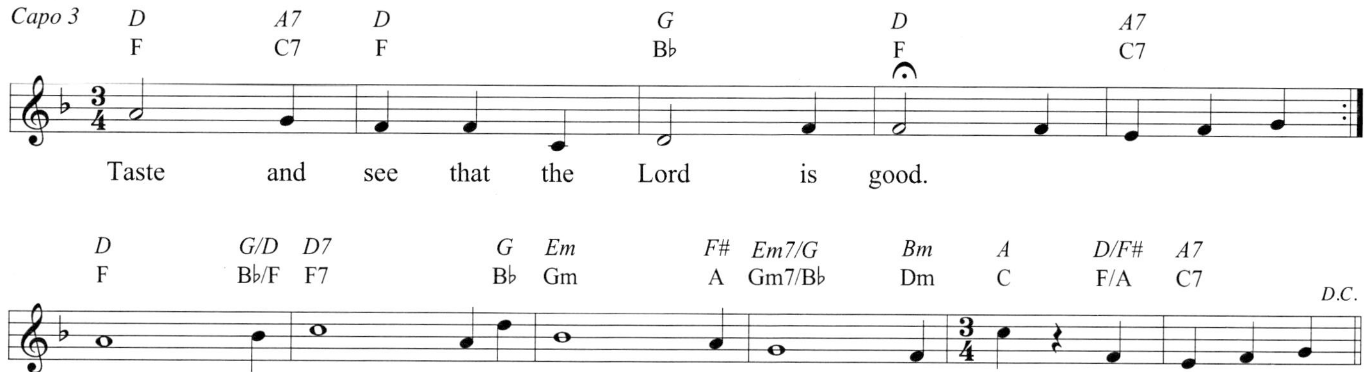

I will bless the Lord at all · **times;**
his praise shall continually be in · **my** mouth.
My soul makes its boast in the · **Lord;**
let the humble hear and · **be** glad. R.

O magnify the Lord with · **me,**
and let us exalt his name · **to**-gether.
I sought the Lord, and he · **answered_me,**
and delivered me from all · **my** fears. R.

Look to him, and be · **radiant;**
so your faces shall never · **be_a**-shamed.
The poor one called, and the Lord · **heard,**
and saved that person from ev·-**ery** trouble. R.

C Instrument

B♭ Instrument

63

Fourth Sunday of Lent (Christian Initiation)

Psalm 23

The Lord is my shepherd, I shall · **not** want.
He makes me lie down in · **green** pastures;
he leads me be·-**side** still waters;
he re·-**stores** my soul. R.

He leads me in right paths for his · **name's** sake.
Even though I walk through the darkest valley, I fear · **no** evil;
for · **you** are with_me;
your rod and your · **staff**—they comfort_me. R.

You prepare a table · **be**-fore_me
in the presence · **of_my** enemies;
you anoint my · **head** with oil;
my · **cup** over-flows. R.

Surely goodness and mercy · **shall** follow_me
all the days of · **my** life,
and I shall dwell in the · **house_of** the Lord
my · **whole** life long. R.

Fourth Sunday of Lent (Christian Initiation)

Psalm 23

Guitar

The Lord is my shepherd, I shall · **not** want.
He makes me lie down in · **green** pastures;
he leads me be·-**side** still waters;
he re·-**stores** my soul. R.

He leads me in right paths for his · **name's** sake.
Even though I walk through the darkest valley, I fear · **no** evil;
for · **you** are with_me;
your rod and your · **staff**—they comfort_me. R.

You prepare a table · **be**-fore_me
in the presence · **of_my** enemies;
you anoint my · **head** with oil;
my · **cup** over-flows. R.

Surely goodness and mercy · **shall** follow_me
all the days of · **my** life,
and I shall dwell in the · **house_of** the Lord
my · **whole** life long. R.

C Instrument

B♭ Instrument

65

Fifth Sunday of Lent – C

Psalm 126

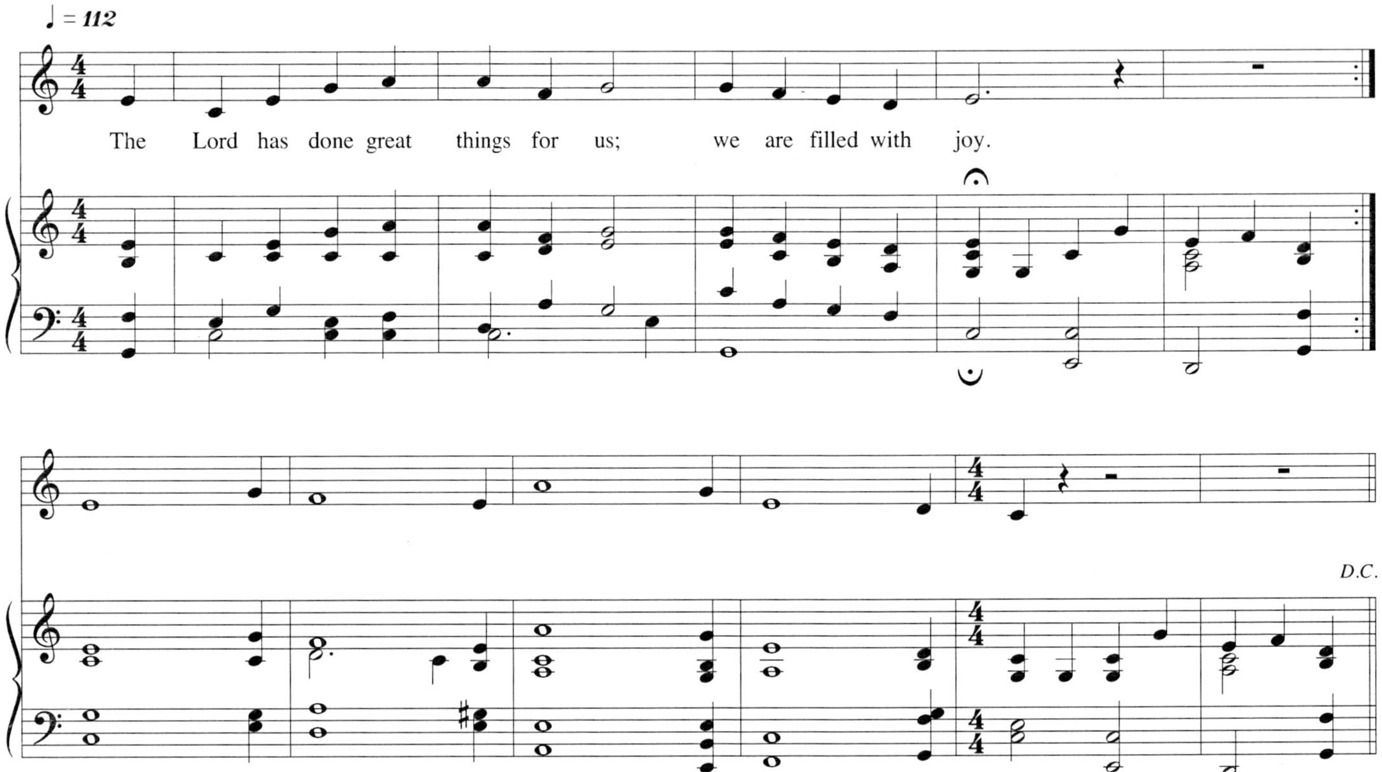

When the Lord restored the fortunes of · **Zion,**
we were like those who · **dream.**
Then our mouth was filled with · **laughter,**
and our tongue with shouts · **of** joy. R.

Then it was said among the · **nations,**
"The Lord has done great things for · **them."**
The Lord has done great things for · **us,**
and we · **re**-joiced. R.

Restore our fortunes, O · **Lord,**
like the watercourses in the desert of the · **Negev.**
May those who sow in · **tears**
reap with shouts · **of** joy. R.

Those who go out · **weeping,**
bearing the seed for · **sowing,**
shall come home with shouts of · **joy,**
carrying · **their** sheaves. R.

Fifth Sunday of Lent – C

Psalm 126

Guitar

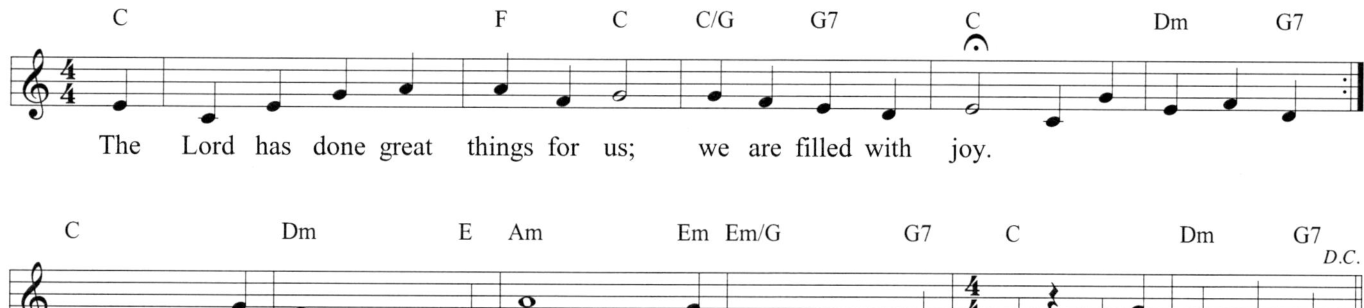

When the Lord restored the fortunes of · **Zion,**
we were like those who · **dream.**
Then our mouth was filled with · **laughter,**
and our tongue with shouts · **of** joy. R.

Then it was said among the · **nations,**
"The Lord has done great things for · **them."**
The Lord has done great things for · **us,**
and we · **re**-joiced. R.

Restore our fortunes, O · **Lord,**
like the watercourses in the desert of the · **Negev.**
May those who sow in · **tears**
reap with shouts · **of** joy. R.

Those who go out · **weeping,**
bearing the seed for · **sowing,**
shall come home with shouts of · **joy,**
carrying · **their** sheaves. R.

C Instrument

B♭ Instrument

67

Fifth Sunday of Lent (Christian Initiation)

Psalm 130

Out of the depths I cry to you, O · **Lord.**
Lord, hear · **my** voice!
Let your ears be at·-**tentive**
to the voice of my sup·-**pli**-cations! R.

If you, O Lord, should mark in·-**iquities,**
Lord, who · **could** stand?
But there is forgiveness with · **you,**
so that you may be · **re**-vered. R.

I wait for the · **Lord,**
my soul waits, and in his word · **I** hope;
my soul waits for the · **Lord**
more than watchmen for · **the** morning. R.

For with the Lord there is steadfast · **love,**
and with him is great power to · **re**-deem.
It is he who will redeem · **Israel**
from all its · **in**-iquities. R.

Fifth Sunday of Lent (Christian Initiation)

Psalm 130

Guitar

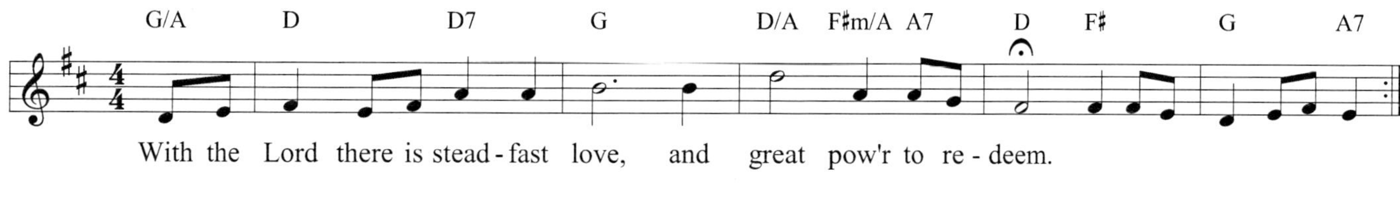

Out of the depths I cry to you, O · **Lord.**
Lord, hear · **my** voice!
Let your ears be at·-**tentive**
to the voice of my sup·-**pli**-cations! R.

If you, O Lord, should mark in·-**iquities,**
Lord, who · **could** stand?
But there is forgiveness with · **you,**
so that you may be · **re**-vered. R.

I wait for the · **Lord,**
my soul waits, and in his word · **I** hope;
my soul waits for the · **Lord**
more than watchmen for · **the** morning. R.

For with the Lord there is steadfast · **love,**
and with him is great power to · **re**-deem.
It is he who will redeem · **Israel**
from all its · **in**-iquities. R.

C Instrument

B♭ Instrument

69

Passion Sunday – C

Psalm 22

All who see me · **mock_at_me;**
they make mouths at me, they shake · **their** heads;
"Commit your cause to the Lord; let him de··**liver;**
let him rescue the one in whom he · **de**-lights!" R.

For dogs are all a··**round_me;**
a company of evildoers · **en**-circles_me.
My hands and feet have · **shrivelled;**
I can count all · **my** bones. R.

They divide my clothes a··**mong_themselves,**
and for my clothing they · **cast** lots.
But you, O Lord, do not be far a··**way!**
O my help, come quickly · **to_my** aid! R.

I will tell of your name to my brothers and sisters;
    in the midst of the congregation I will · **praise_you:**
You who fear the · **Lord,** praise_him!
All you offspring of Jacob, · **glorify_him;**
stand in awe of him, all you offspring · **of** Israel! R.

Passion Sunday – C

Psalm 22

Guitar

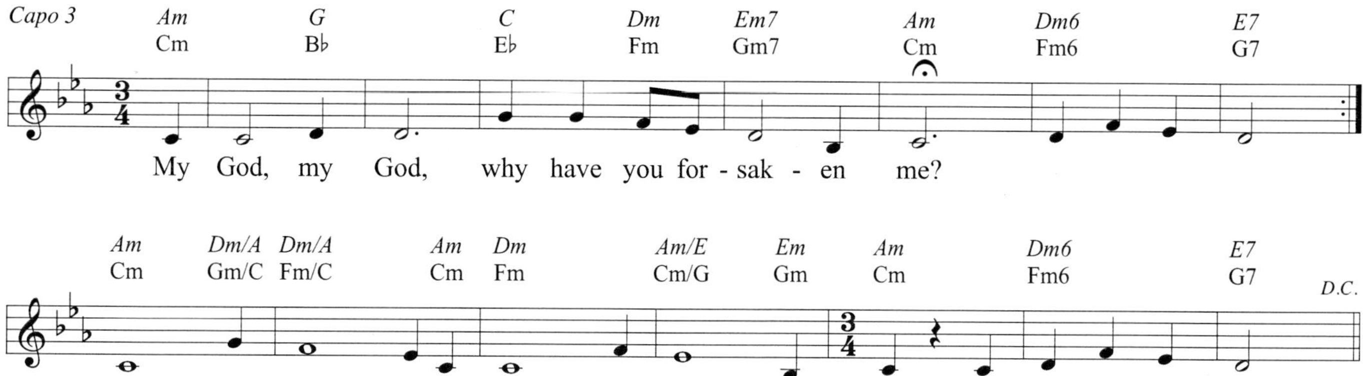

All who see me · **mock_at_me;**
they make mouths at me, they shake · **their** heads;
"Commit your cause to the Lord; let him de·-**liver;**
let him rescue the one in whom he · **de**-lights!" R.

For dogs are all a·-**round_me;**
a company of evildoers · **en**-circles_me.
My hands and feet have · **shrivelled;**
I can count all · **my** bones. R.

They divide my clothes a·-**mong_themselves,**
and for my clothing they · **cast** lots.
But you, O Lord, do not be far a·-**way!**
O my help, come quickly · **to_my** aid! R.

I will tell of your name to my brothers and sisters;
    in the midst of the congregation I will · **praise_you:**
You who fear the · **Lord,** praise_him!
All you offspring of Jacob, · **glorify_him;**
stand in awe of him, all you offspring · **of** Israel! R.

C Instrument

B♭ Instrument

Mass of Chrism – ABC

Psalm 89

I have found my servant · **David;**
with my holy oil I have a·-**nointed_him;**
my hand shall always re·-**main_with_him;**
my arm also · **shall** strengthen_him. R.

My faithfulness and steadfast love shall be · **with_him;**
and in my name his name shall be ex·-**alted.**
He shall cry to me, "You are my · **Father,**
my God, and the Rock of my · **sal**-vation!" R.

I will make him the · **firstborn,**
the highest of the kings of the · **earth.**
Forever I will keep my steadfast love for · **him,**
and my covenant with him will · **stand** firm. R.

Mass of Chrism – ABC

Psalm 89

Guitar

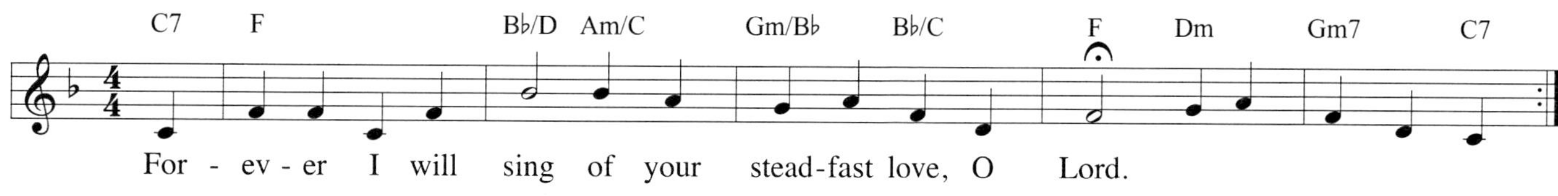

I have found my servant · **David;**
with my holy oil I have a·-**nointed_him;**
my hand shall always re·-**main_with_him;**
my arm also · **shall** strengthen_him. R.

My faithfulness and steadfast love shall be · **with_him;**
and in my name his name shall be ex·-**alted.**
He shall cry to me, "You are my · **Father,**
my God, and the Rock of my · **sal**-vation!" R.

I will make him the · **firstborn,**
the highest of the kings of the · **earth.**
Forever I will keep my steadfast love for · **him,**
and my covenant with him will · **stand** firm. R.

C Instrument

Bb Instrument

Mass of the Lord's Supper – ABC

Psalm 116

What shall I return to the · **Lord**
for all his bounty to · **me?**
I will lift up the cup of sal·-**vation**
and call on the name · **of_the** Lord. R.

Precious in the sight of the · **Lord**
is the death of his · **faithful_ones.**
I am your servant, the son of your · **serving_girl.**
You have loosed · **my** bonds. R.

I will offer to you a thanksgiving · **sacrifice**
and call on the name of the · **Lord.**
I will pay my vows to the · **Lord**
in the presence of all · **his** people. R.

Mass of the Lord's Supper – ABC

Psalm 116

Guitar

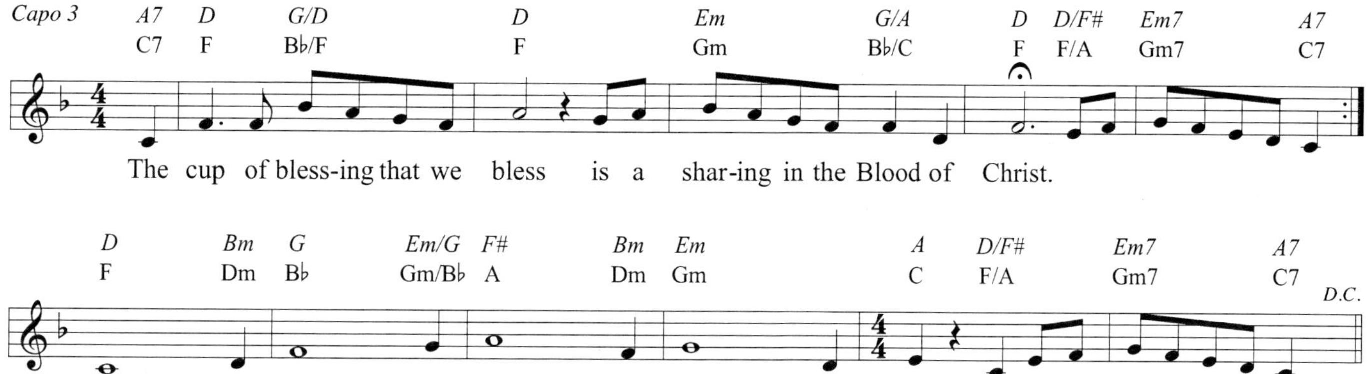

What shall I return to the · **Lord**
for all his bounty to · **me?**
I will lift up the cup of sal·-**vation**
and call on the name · **of_the** Lord. R.

Precious in the sight of the · **Lord**
is the death of his · **faithful_ones.**
I am your servant, the son of your · **serving_girl.**
You have loosed · **my** bonds. R.

I will offer to you a thanksgiving · **sacrifice**
and call on the name of the · **Lord.**
I will pay my vows to the · **Lord**
in the presence of all · **his** people. R.

C Instrument

B♭ Instrument

75

Celebration of the Lord's Passion – ABC

Psalm 31

In you, O Lord, I seek refuge; do not let me ever be put · **to** shame;
in your righteousness · **de**-liver_me.
Into your hand I commit · **my** spirit;
you have redeemed me, O Lord, · **faith**-ful God. R.

I am the scorn of all my adversaries, a horror to my neighbours, an object of dread to my · **ac**-quaintances.
Those who see me in the · **street** flee_from_me.
I have passed out of mind like one who · **is** dead;
I have become like a · **bro**-ken vessel. R.

But I trust in you, · **O** Lord;
I say, "You are · **my** God."
My times are in · **your** hand;
deliver me from the hand of my · **enemies** and persecutors. R.

Let your face shine upon · **your** servant;
save me in your stead·-**fast** love.
Be strong, and let your heart · **take** courage,
all you who wait · **for** the Lord. R.

Celebration of the Lord's Passion – ABC

Psalm 31

Guitar

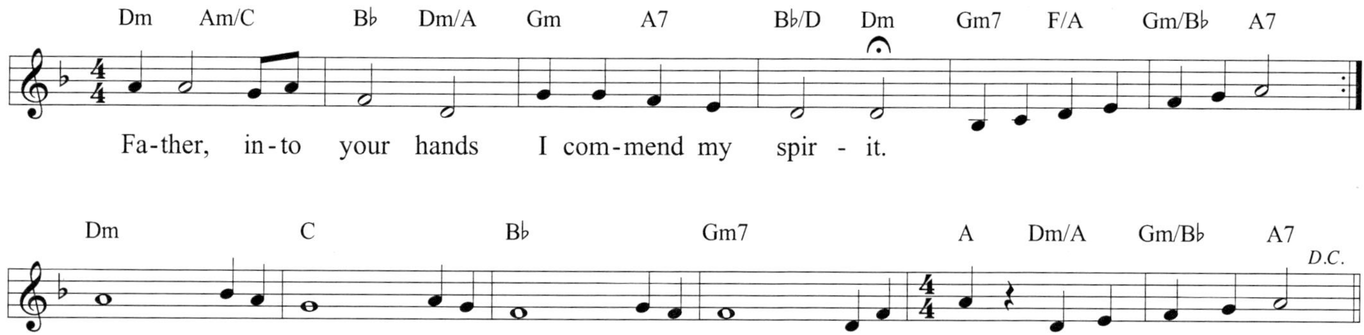

In you, O Lord, I seek refuge; do not let me ever be put · **to** shame;
in your righteousness · **de**-liver_me.
Into your hand I commit · **my** spirit;
you have redeemed me, O Lord, · **faith**-ful God. R.

I am the scorn of all my adversaries, a horror to my neighbours, an object of dread to my · **ac**-quaintances.
Those who see me in the · **street** flee_from_me.
I have passed out of mind like one who · **is** dead;
I have become like a · **bro**-ken vessel. R.

But I trust in you, · **O** Lord;
I say, "You are · **my** God."
My times are in · **your** hand;
deliver me from the hand of my · **enemies** and persecutors. R.

Let your face shine upon · **your** servant;
save me in your stead·-**fast** love.
Be strong, and let your heart · **take** courage,
all you who wait · **for** the Lord. R.

C Instrument

Bb Instrument

© 2009 GORDON JOHNSTON — NOVALIS

Resurrection of the Lord – Easter Vigil (1.1) – ABC

Psalm 104

Bless the Lord, O · **my** soul.
O Lord my God, you are very · **great.**
You are clothed with · **honour** and majesty,
wrapped in light as with · **a** garment. R.

You set the earth on its · **foun**-dations,
so that it shall never be · **shaken.**
You cover it with the deep as · **with** a garment;
the waters stood above · **the** mountains. R.

You make springs gush forth in · **the** valleys;
they flow between the · **hills.**
By the streams the birds of the air have their · **ha**-bi-tation;
they sing among · **the** branches. R.

From your lofty abode you water · **the** mountains;
the earth is satisfied with the fruit of your · **work.**
You cause the grass to · **grow_for** the cattle,
and plants for people to use, to bring forth food from · **thc** earth. R.

O Lord, how manifold are · **your** works!
In wisdom you have made them · **all;**
the earth is · **full_of** your creatures.
Bless the Lord, O · **my** soul. R.

Resurrection of the Lord – Easter Vigil (1.1) – ABC

Psalm 104

Guitar

Bless the Lord, O · **my** soul.
O Lord my God, you are very · **great.**
You are clothed with · **honour** and majesty,
wrapped in light as with · **a** garment. R.

You set the earth on its · **foun**-dations,
so that it shall never be · **shaken.**
You cover it with the deep as · **with** a garment;
the waters stood above · **the** mountains. R.

You make springs gush forth in · **the** valleys;
they flow between the · **hills.**
By the streams the birds of the air have their · **ha**-bi-tation;
they sing among · **the** branches. R.

From your lofty abode you water · **the** mountains;
the earth is satisfied with the fruit of your · **work.**
You cause the grass to · **grow_for** the cattle,
and plants for people to use, to bring forth food from · **the** earth. R.

O Lord, how manifold are · **your** works!
In wisdom you have made them · **all;**
the earth is · **full_of** your creatures.
Bless the Lord, O · **my** soul. R.

C Instrument

B♭ Instrument

Resurrection of the Lord – Easter Vigil (1.2) – ABC

Psalm 33

The word of the Lord · **is** upright,
and all his work is done · **in** faithfulness.
He loves righteousness · **and** justice;
the earth is full of the steadfast love of · **the** Lord. R.

By the word of the Lord the heavens · **were** made,
and all their host by the breath of · **his** mouth.
He gathered the waters of the sea as in · **a** bottle;
he put the deeps · **in** storehouses. R.

Blessed is the nation whose God is · **the** Lord,
the people whom he has chosen as · **his** heritage.
The Lord looks down · **from** heaven;
he sees all · **human** beings. R.

Our soul waits for · **the** Lord;
he is our help · **and** shield.
Let your steadfast love, O Lord, be · **up**-on_us,
even as we hope · **in** you. R.

Resurrection of the Lord – Easter Vigil (1.2) – ABC

Psalm 33

Guitar

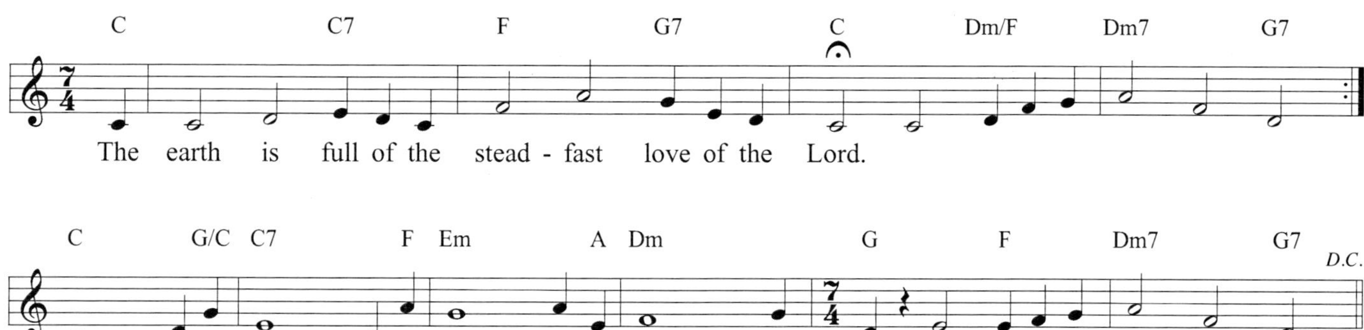

The word of the Lord · **is** upright,
and all his work is done · **in** faithfulness.
He loves righteousness · **and** justice;
the earth is full of the steadfast love of · **the** Lord. R.

By the word of the Lord the heavens · **were** made,
and all their host by the breath of · **his** mouth.
He gathered the waters of the sea as in · **a** bottle;
he put the deeps · **in** storehouses. R.

Blessed is the nation whose God is · **the** Lord,
the people whom he has chosen as · **his** heritage.
The Lord looks down · **from** heaven;
he sees all · **human** beings. R.

Our soul waits for · **the** Lord;
he is our help · **and** shield.
Let your steadfast love, O Lord, be · **up-on_us**,
even as we hope · **in** you. R.

C Instrument

B♭ Instrument

Resurrection of the Lord – Easter Vigil (2) – ABC

Psalm 16

The Lord is my chosen portion · **and_my** cup;
you hold · **my** lot.
I keep the Lord always · **be**-fore_me;
because he is at my right hand, I shall · **not** be moved. R.

Therefore my heart is glad, and my soul · **re**-joices;
my body also rests · **se**-cure.
For you do not give me up · **to** Sheol,
or let your faithful one · **see** the Pit. R.

You show me the path · **of** life.
In your presence there is fullness · **of** joy;
in your right hand · **are** pleasures
for·-**ev**-er-more. R.

Resurrection of the Lord – Easter Vigil (2) – ABC

Psalm 16

Guitar

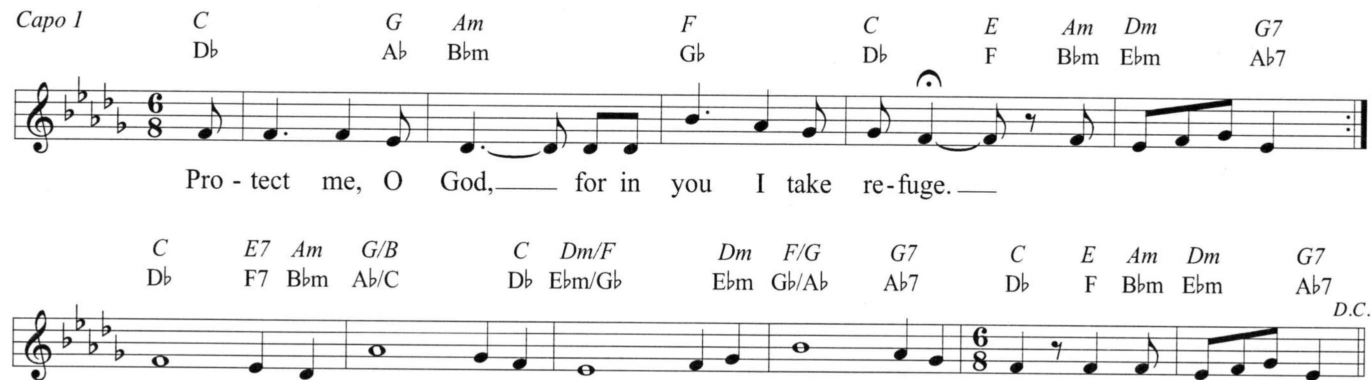

The Lord is my chosen portion · **and_my** cup;
you hold · **my** lot.
I keep the Lord always · **be**-fore_me;
because he is at my right hand, I shall · **not** be moved. R.

Therefore my heart is glad, and my soul · **re**-joices;
my body also rests · **se**-cure.
For you do not give me up · **to** Sheol,
or let your faithful one · **see** the Pit. R.

You show me the path · **of** life.
In your presence there is fullness · **of** joy;
in your right hand · **are** pleasures
for·-**ev**-er-more. R.

C Instrument

B♭ Instrument

83

Resurrection of the Lord – Easter Vigil (3) – ABC

Exodus 15

I will sing to the Lord, for he has triumphed · **gloriously;**
horse and rider he has thrown into · **the** sea.
The Lord is my strength and my · **might,**
and he has become my · **sal**-vation;
this is my God, and I will · **praise_him,**
my father's God, and I will · **ex**-alt_him. R.

The Lord is a · **warrior;**
the Lord is · **his** name.
Pharaoh's chariots and his army he cast into the · **sea;**
his picked officers were sunk in the · **Red** Sea.
The floods · **covered_them;**
they went down into the depths · **like_a** stone. R.

Your right hand, O Lord, glorious in · **power;** / your right hand, O Lord, shattered · **the** enemy.
In the greatness of your · **majesty** / you overthrew · **your** adversaries;
you sent out your · **fury,** / it consumed them · **like** stubble. R.

You brought your people · **in** / and plant·-**ed** them
on the mountain of your own pos·-**session,** / the place, O Lord, that you made your · **a**-bode,
the sanctuary, O Lord, that your hands have es·-**tablished.** / The Lord will reign forever · **and** ever. R.

Resurrection of the Lord – Easter Vigil (3) – ABC

Exodus 15

Guitar

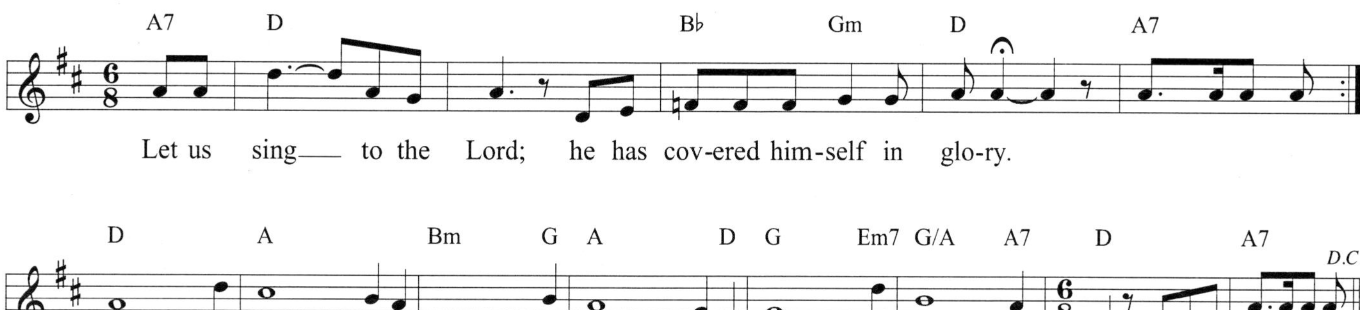

I will sing to the Lord, for he has triumphed · **gloriously;**
horse and rider he has thrown into · **the** sea.
The Lord is my strength and my · **might,**
and he has become my · **sal**-vation;
this is my God, and I will · **praise_him,**
my father's God, and I will · **ex**-alt_him. R.

The Lord is a · **warrior;** / the Lord is · **his** name.
Pharaoh's chariots and his army he cast into the · **sea;** / his picked officers were sunk in the · **Red** Sea.
The floods · **covered_them;** / they went down into the depths · **like_a** stone. R.

Your right hand, O Lord, glorious in · **power;** / your right hand, O Lord, shattered · **the** enemy.
In the greatness of your · **majesty** / you overthrew · **your** adversaries;
you sent out your · **fury,** / it consumed them · **like** stubble. R.

You brought your people · **in** / and plant·-**ed** them
on the mountain of your own pos·-**session,** / the place, O Lord, that you made your · **a**-bode,
the sanctuary, O Lord, that your hands have es·-**tablished.** / The Lord will reign forever · **and** ever. R.

C Instrument

B♭ Instrument

Resurrection of the Lord – Easter Vigil (4) – ABC

Psalm 30

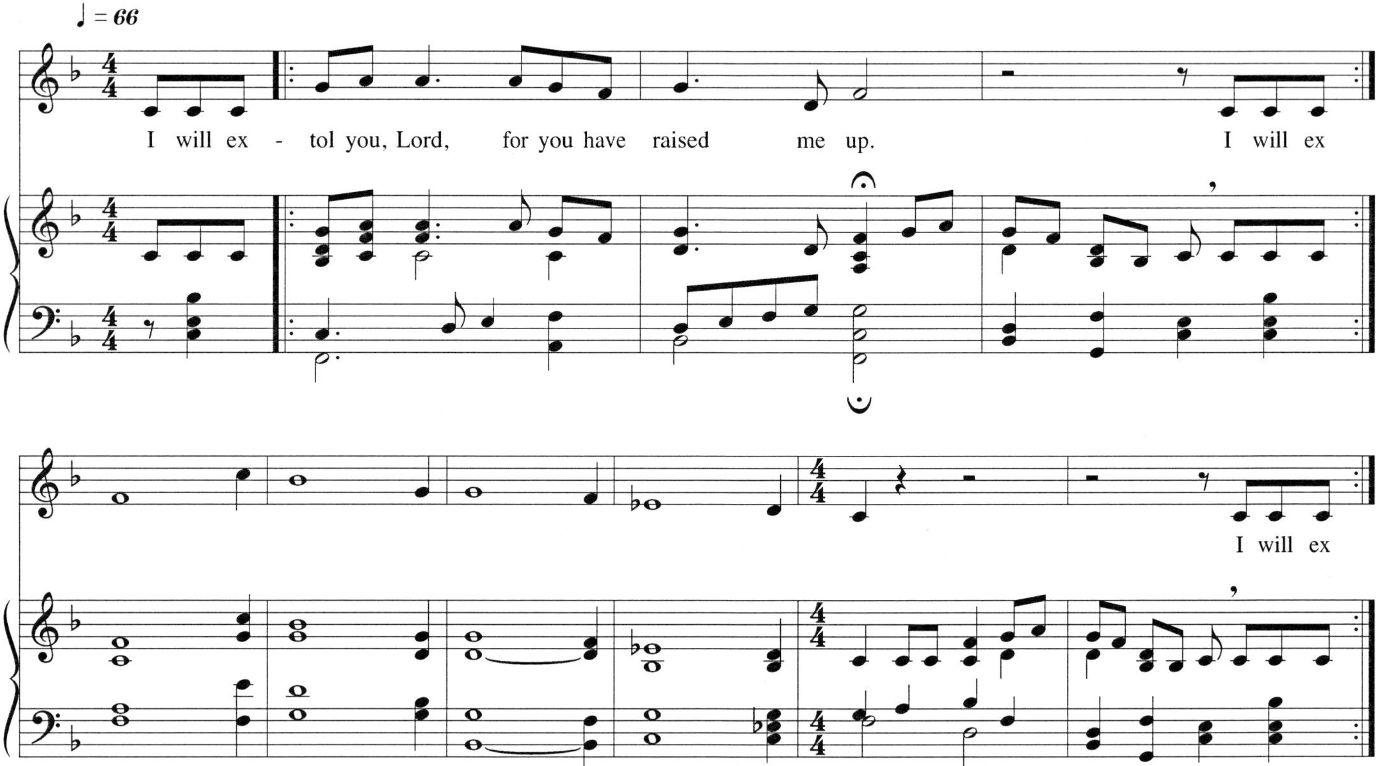

I will extol you, O Lord, for you have drawn me · **up,**
and did not let my foes rejoice · **over_me.**
O Lord, you brought up my soul from · **Sheol,**
restored me to life from among those gone down · **to_the** Pit. R.

Sing praises to the Lord, O you his · **faithful_ones,**
and give thanks to his holy · **name.**
For his anger is but for a moment; his favour is for a · **lifetime.**
Weeping may linger for the night, but joy comes · **with_the** morning. R.

Hear, O Lord, and be gracious to · **me!**
O Lord, be my · **helper!**
You have turned my mourning into · **dancing.**
O Lord my God, I will give thanks to you · **for**-ever. R.

Resurrection of the Lord – Easter Vigil (4) – ABC

Psalm 30

Guitar

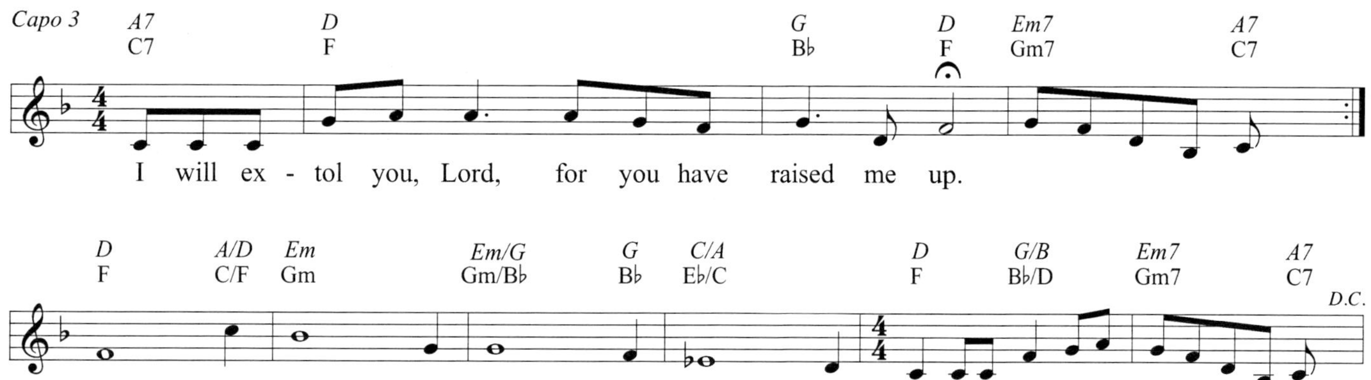

I will extol you, O Lord, for you have drawn me · **up,**
and did not let my foes rejoice · **over_me.**
O Lord, you brought up my soul from · **Sheol,**
restored me to life from among those gone down · **to_the** Pit. R.

Sing praises to the Lord, O you his · **faithful_ones,**
and give thanks to his holy · **name.**
For his anger is but for a moment; his favour is for a · **lifetime.**
Weeping may linger for the night, but joy comes · **with_the** morning. R.

Hear, O Lord, and be gracious to · **me!**
O Lord, be my · **helper!**
You have turned my mourning into · **dancing.**
O Lord my God, I will give thanks to you · **for**-ever. R.

C Instrument

Bb Instrument

Resurrection of the Lord – Easter Vigil (5) – ABC

Isaiah 12

Surely God is my salvation; I will trust, and will not · **be** a-fraid,
for the Lord God is my strength and my might; he has be·-**come_my** sal-vation.
With joy · **you_will** draw water
from the wells · **of** sal-vation. R.

Give thanks · **to** the Lord,
call · **on** his name;
make known his deeds a·-**mong** the nations;
proclaim that his · **name_is** ex-alted. R.

Sing praises to the Lord, for he · **has** done gloriously;
let this be known in · **all** the earth.
Shout aloud and sing for joy, O · **roy**-al Zion,
for great in your midst is the Holy · **One** of Israel. R.

Resurrection of the Lord – Easter Vigil (5) – ABC

Isaiah 12

Guitar

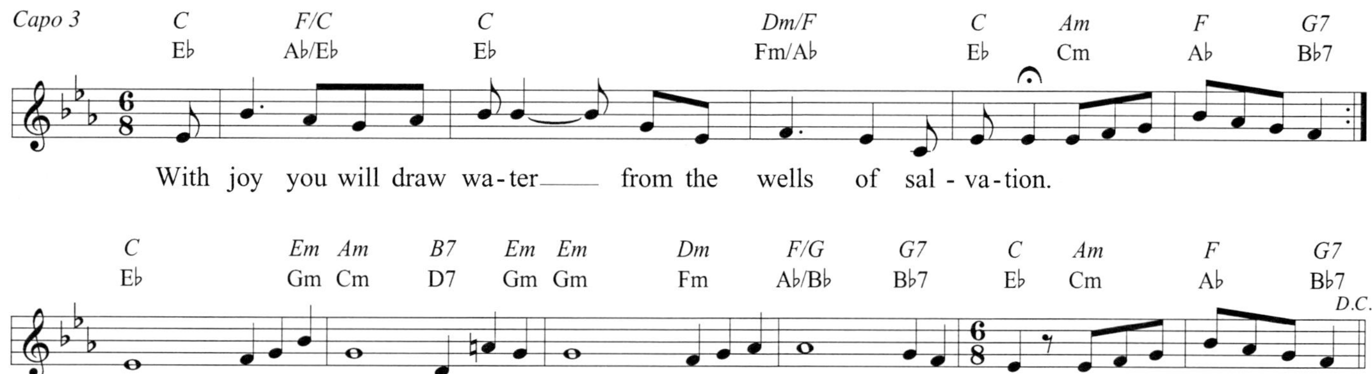

Surely God is my salvation; I will trust, and will not · **be** a-fraid,
for the Lord God is my strength and my might; he has be·-**come_my** sal-vation.
With joy · **you_will** draw water
from the wells · **of** sal-vation. R.

Give thanks · **to** the Lord,
call · **on** his name;
make known his deeds a·-**mong** the nations;
proclaim that his · **name_is** ex-alted. R.

Sing praises to the Lord, for he · **has** done gloriously;
let this be known in · **all** the earth.
Shout aloud and sing for joy, O · **roy**-al Zion,
for great in your midst is the Holy · **One** of Israel. R.

C Instrument

B♭ Instrument

89

Resurrection of the Lord – Easter Vigil (6) – ABC

Psalm 19

The law of the Lord is · **perfect,**
reviving the · **soul;**
the decrees of the Lord are · **sure,**
making · **wise** the simple. R.

The precepts of the Lord are · **right,**
rejoicing the · **heart;**
the commandment of the Lord is · **clear,**
en-·**lightening** the eyes. R.

The fear of the Lord is · **pure,**
enduring for-·**ever;**
the ordinances of the Lord are · **true**
and righteous · **al**-to-gether. R.

More to be desired are they than · **gold,**
even much fine · **gold;**
sweeter also than · **honey,**
and drippings · **of** the honeycomb. R.

Resurrection of the Lord – Easter Vigil (6) – ABC

Psalm 19

Guitar

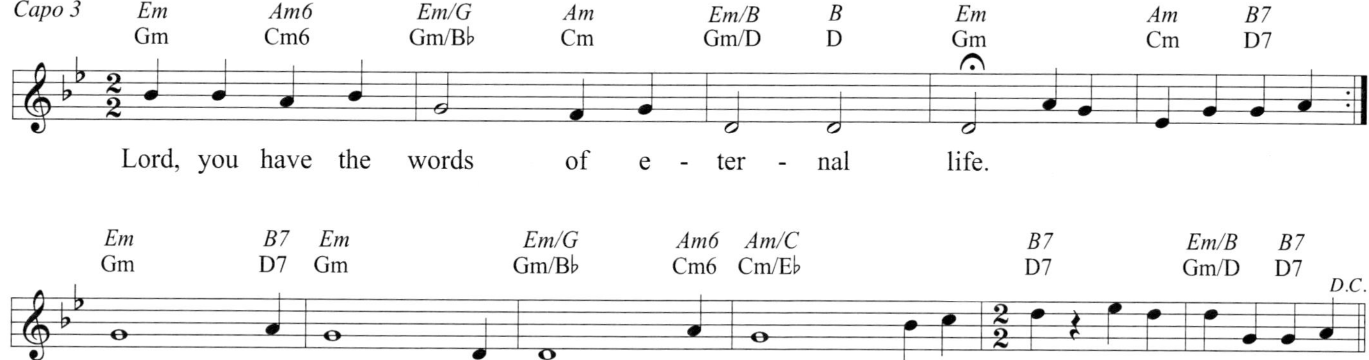

The law of the Lord is · **perfect,**
reviving the · **soul;**
the decrees of the Lord are · **sure,**
making · **wise** the simple. R.

The precepts of the Lord are · **right,**
rejoicing the · **heart;**
the commandment of the Lord is · **clear,**
en-·**lightening** the eyes. R.

The fear of the Lord is · **pure,**
enduring for-·**ever;**
the ordinances of the Lord are · **true**
and righteous · **al**-to-gether. R.

More to be desired are they than · **gold,**
even much fine · **gold;**
sweeter also than · **honey,**
and drippings · **of** the honeycomb. R.

C Instrument

B♭ Instrument

91

Resurrection of the Lord – Easter Vigil (7.1) – ABC

Psalm 42/43

My soul thirsts for · **God,**
for the living · **God.**
When shall I · **come**
and behold the face · **of** God? R.

I went with the · **throng,**
and led them in procession to the house of · **God,**
with glad shouts and songs of · **thanksgiving,**
a multitude · **keeping** festival. R.

O send out your light and your · **truth;**
let them · **lead_me;**
let them bring me to your holy · **mountain**
and to · **your** dwelling. R.

Then I will go to the altar of · **God,**
to God my exceeding · **joy;**
and I will praise you with the · **harp,**
O God, · **my** God. R.

Resurrection of the Lord – Easter Vigil (7.1) – ABC

Psalm 42/43

Guitar

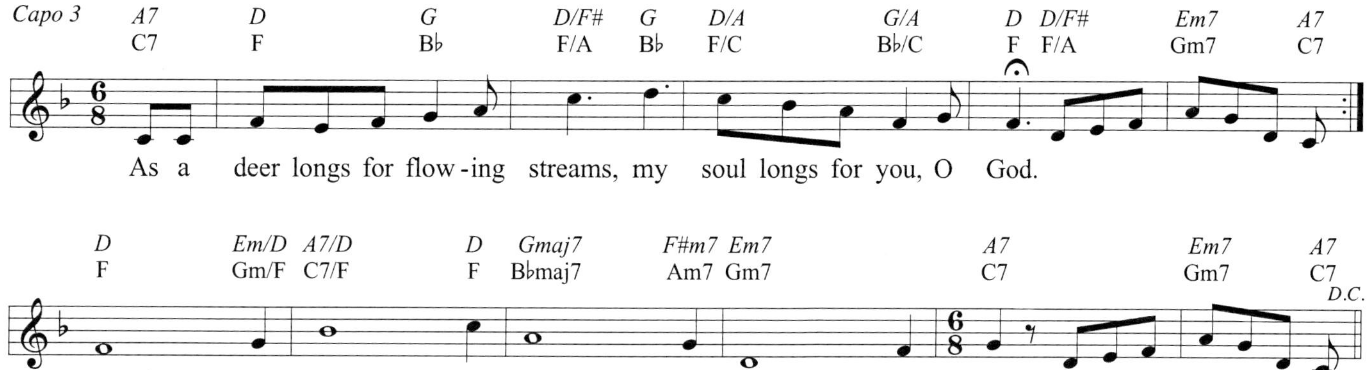

My soul thirsts for · **God,**
for the living · **God.**
When shall I · **come**
and behold the face · **of** God? R.

I went with the · **throng,**
and led them in procession to the house of · **God,**
with glad shouts and songs of · **thanksgiving,**
a multitude · **keeping** festival. R.

O send out your light and your · **truth;**
let them · **lead_me;**
let them bring me to your holy · **mountain**
and to · **your** dwelling. R.

Then I will go to the altar of · **God,**
to God my exceeding · **joy;**
and I will praise you with the · **harp,**
O God, · **my** God. R.

C Instrument

B♭ Instrument

© 2009 GORDON JOHNSTON — NOVALIS

Resurrection of the Lord – Easter Vigil (7.2) – ABC

Psalm 51

Create in me a clean heart, · **O** God,
and put a new and right spirit · **with**-in_me.
Do not cast me away from · **your** presence,
and do not take your holy · **spirit** from me. R.

Restore to me the joy of your · **sal**-vation,
and sustain in me a will·-**ing** spirit.
Then I will teach transgressors · **your** ways,
and sinners will re·-**turn** to you. R.

For you have no delight · **in** sacrifice;
if I were to give a burnt offering, you would not · **be** pleased.
The sacrifice acceptable to God is a bro·-**ken** spirit;
a broken and contrite heart, O God, you will · **not** de-spise. R.

Resurrection of the Lord – Easter Vigil (7.2) – ABC

Psalm 51

Guitar

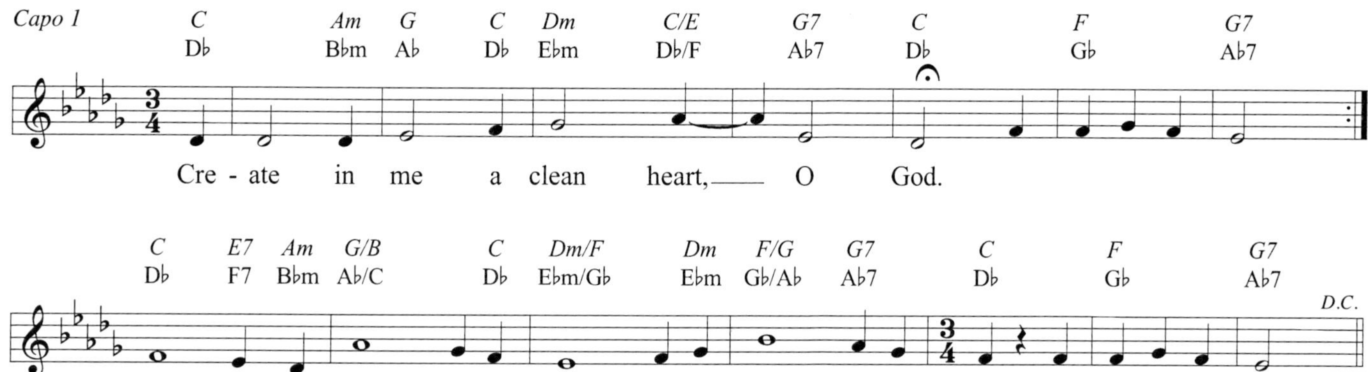

Create in me a clean heart, · **O** God,
and put a new and right spirit · **with**-in_me.
Do not cast me away from · **your** presence,
and do not take your holy · **spirit** from me. R.

Restore to me the joy of your · **sal**-vation,
and sustain in me a will·-**ing** spirit.
Then I will teach transgressors · **your** ways,
and sinners will re·-**turn** to you. R.

For you have no delight · **in** sacrifice;
if I were to give a burnt offering, you would not · **be** pleased.
The sacrifice acceptable to God is a bro·-**ken** spirit;
a broken and contrite heart, O God, you will · **not** de-spise. R.

C Instrument

B♭ Instrument

Resurrection of the Lord – Easter Vigil – Solemn Alleluia – ABC

Psalm 118

O give thanks to the Lord, for · **he** is good;
his steadfast love en·-**dures** for-ever.
Let Is·-**rael** say,
"His steadfast love en·-**dures** for-ever." R.

"The right hand of the Lord · **is** ex-alted;
the right hand of the · **Lord** does valiantly."
I shall not die, but · **I_shall** live,
and recount the · **deeds_of** the Lord. R.

The stone that the · **builders** re-jected
has become · **the** chief cornerstone.
This is the · **Lord's** doing;
it is marvellous · **in** our eyes. R.

Resurrection of the Lord – Easter Vigil – Solemn Alleluia – ABC

Psalm 118

Guitar

O give thanks to the Lord, for · **he** is good;
his steadfast love en·-**dures** for-ever.
Let Is·-**rael** say,
"His steadfast love en·-**dures** for-ever." R.

"The right hand of the Lord · **is** ex-alted;
the right hand of the · **Lord** does valiantly."
I shall not die, but · **I_shall** live,
and recount the · **deeds_of** the Lord. R.

The stone that the · **builders** re-jected
has become · **the** chief cornerstone.
This is the · **Lord's** doing;
it is marvellous · **in** our eyes. R.

C Instrument

B♭ Instrument

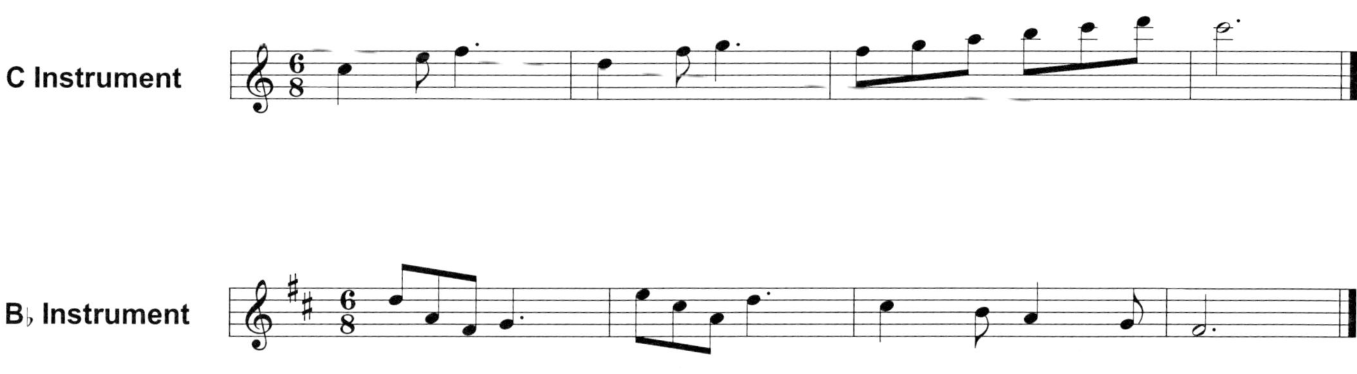

97

Resurrection of the Lord – Easter Sunday – ABC

Psalm 118

O give thanks to the Lord, for · **he** is good;
his steadfast love en·-**dures** for-ever.
Let Is·-**rael** say,
"His steadfast love en·-**dures** for-ever." R.

"The right hand of the Lord · **is** ex-alted;
the right hand of the · **Lord** does valiantly."
I shall not die, but · **I_shall** live,
and recount the · **deeds_of** the Lord. R.

The stone that the · **builders** re-jected
has become · **the** chief cornerstone.
This is the · **Lord's** doing;
it is marvellous · **in** our eyes. R.

Resurrection of the Lord – Easter Sunday – ABC

Psalm 118

Guitar

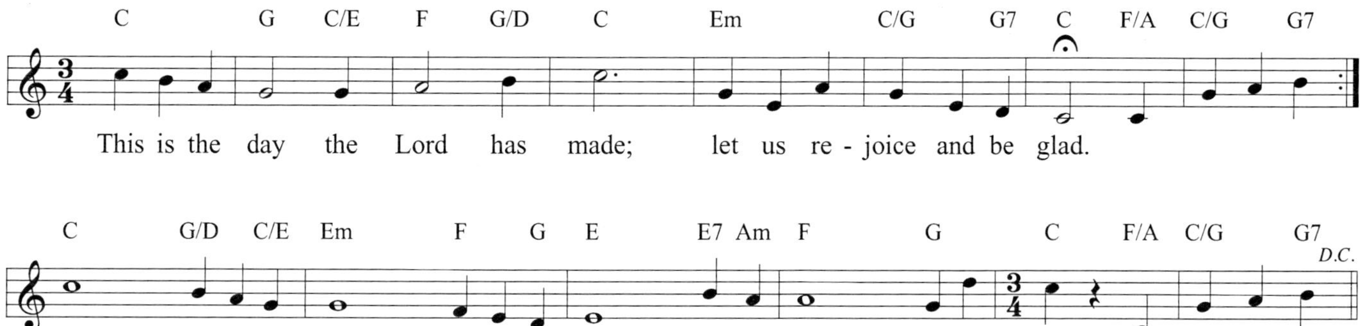

O give thanks to the Lord, for · **he** is good;
his steadfast love en·-**dures** for-ever.
Let Is·-**rael** say,
"His steadfast love en·-**dures** for-ever." R.

"The right hand of the Lord · **is** ex-alted;
the right hand of the · **Lord** does valiantly."
I shall not die, but · **I_shall** live,
and recount the · **deeds_of** the Lord. R.

The stone that the · **builders** re-jected
has become · **the** chief cornerstone.
This is the · **Lord's** doing;
it is marvellous · **in** our eyes. R.

C Instrument

B♭ Instrument

99

Common Psalm for Easter

Psalm 118

O give thanks to the Lord, for · **he** is good;
his steadfast love en·-**dures** for-ever.
Let Is·-**rael** say,
"His steadfast love en·-**dures** for-ever." R.

"The right hand of the Lord · **is** ex-alted;
the right hand of the · **Lord** does valiantly."
I shall not die, but · **I_shall** live,
and recount the · **deeds_of** the Lord. R.

The stone that the · **builders** re-jected
has become · **the** chief cornerstone.
This is the · **Lord's** doing;
it is marvellous · **in** our eyes. R.

Common Psalm for Easter

Psalm 118

Guitar

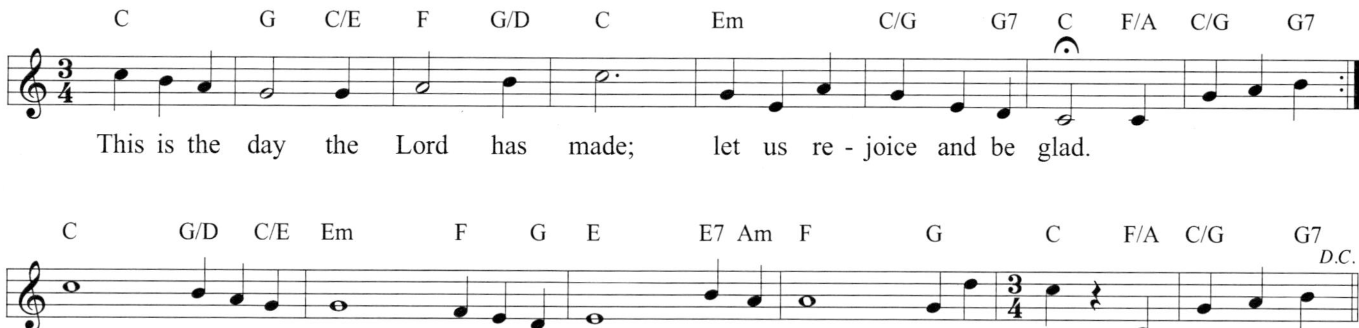

O give thanks to the Lord, for · **he** is good;
his steadfast love en·-**dures** for-ever.
Let Is·-**rael** say,
"His steadfast love en·-**dures** for-ever." R.

"The right hand of the Lord · **is** ex-alted;
the right hand of the · **Lord** does valiantly."
I shall not die, but · **I_shall** live,
and recount the · **deeds_of** the Lord. R.

The stone that the · **builders** re-jected
has become · **the** chief cornerstone.
This is the · **Lord's** doing;
it is marvellous · **in** our eyes. R.

C Instrument

B♭ Instrument

Common Psalm for Easter

Psalm 66

Make a joyful noise to God, all · **the** earth;
sing the glory · **of_his** name;
give to him · **glorious** praise.
Say to God, "How awesome are your · **deeds!**" R.

"All the earth · **worships** you;
they sing praises to you, sing praises · **to_your** name."
Come and see what God · **has** done:
he is awesome in his deeds among the children of · **Adam.** R.

He turned the sea into · **dry** land;
they passed through the river · **on** foot.
There we rejoiced · **in** him,
who rules by his might for·-**ever.** R.

Come and hear, all you who · **fear** God,
and I will tell what he · **has** done_for_me.
Blessed be God, because he has not rejected · **my** prayer
or removed his steadfast love from · **me.** R.

Common Psalm for Easter

Psalm 66

Guitar

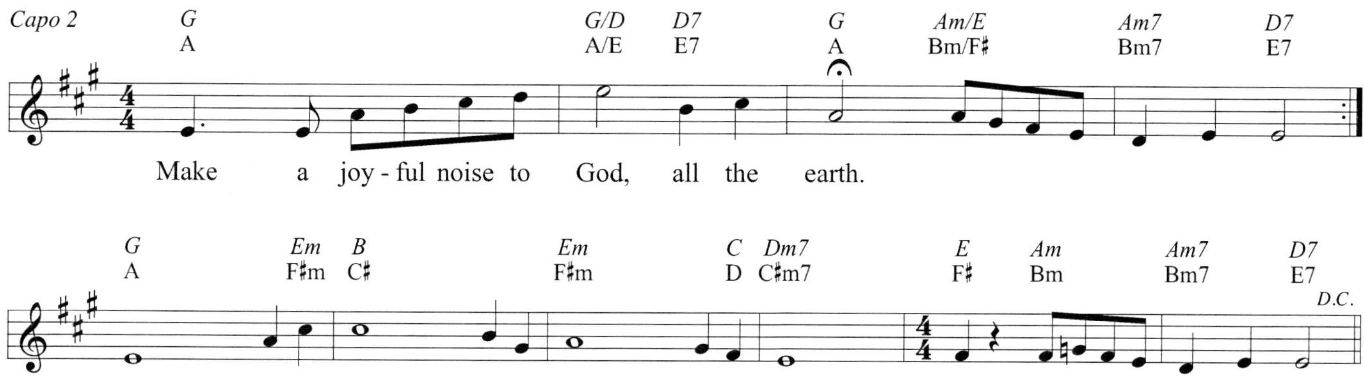

Make a joyful noise to God, all · **the** earth;
sing the glory · **of_his** name;
give to him · **glorious** praise.
Say to God, "How awesome are your · **deeds!**" R.

"All the earth · **worships** you;
they sing praises to you, sing praises · **to_your** name."
Come and see what God · **has** done:
he is awesome in his deeds among the children of · **Adam.** R.

He turned the sea into · **dry** land;
they passed through the river · **on** foot.
There we rejoiced · **in** him,
who rules by his might for·-**ever.** R.

Come and hear, all you who · **fear** God,
and I will tell what he · **has** done_for_me.
Blessed be God, because he has not rejected · **my** prayer
or removed his steadfast love from · **me.** R.

C Instrument

B♭ Instrument

103

Common Psalm for after Ascension

Psalm 47

Clap your hands, all · **you** peoples;
shout to God with loud songs · **of** joy.
For the Lord, the Most High, · **is** awesome,
a great king over · **all** the earth. R.

God has gone up · **with_a** shout,
the Lord with the sound of · **a** trumpet.
Sing praises to God, · **sing** praises;
sing praises to our · **King,** sing praises. R.

For God is the king of all · **the** earth;
sing praises · **with_a** Psalm.
God is king over · **the** nations;
God sits on his · **ho**-ly throne. R.

Common Psalm for after Ascension

Psalm 47

Guitar

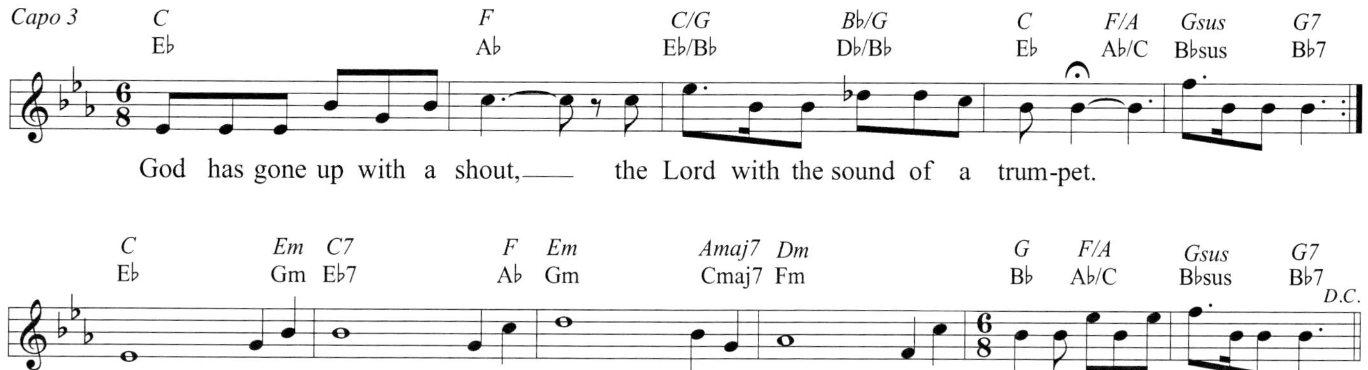

Clap your hands, all · **you** peoples;
shout to God with loud songs · **of** joy.
For the Lord, the Most High, · **is** awesome,
a great king over · **all** the earth. R.

God has gone up · **with_a** shout,
the Lord with the sound of · **a** trumpet.
Sing praises to God, · **sing** praises;
sing praises to our · **King,** sing praises. R.

For God is the king of all · **the** earth;
sing praises · **with_a** Psalm.
God is king over · **the** nations;
God sits on his · **ho**-ly throne. R.

C Instrument

B♭ Instrument

105

Common Psalm for Pentecost

Psalm 104

Bless the Lord, O · **my** soul.
O Lord my God, you are very · **great.**
O Lord, how manifold · **are** your works!
The earth is full of · **your** creatures. R.

When you take away · **their** breath,
they die and return to their · **dust.**
When you send forth your spirit, they · **are** cre-ated;
and you renew the face of · **the** earth. R.

May the glory of the Lord endure · **for-**ever;
may the Lord rejoice in his · **works.**
May my meditation be · **pleasing** to him,
for I rejoice in · **the** Lord. R.

Common Psalm for Pentecost

Psalm 104

Guitar

Bless the Lord, O · **my** soul.
O Lord my God, you are very · **great.**
O Lord, how manifold · **are** your works!
The earth is full of · **your** creatures. R.

When you take away · **their** breath,
they die and return to their · **dust.**
When you send forth your spirit, they · **are** cre-ated;
and you renew the face of · **the** earth. R.

May the glory of the Lord endure · **for-**ever;
may the Lord rejoice in his · **works.**
May my meditation be · **pleasing** to him,
for I rejoice in · **the** Lord. R.

C Instrument

Second Sunday of Easter – C

Psalm 118

Let Israel · **say,**
"His steadfast love endures for·-**ever.**"
Let the house of Aaron · **say,**
"His steadfast love endures for·-**ever.**"
Let those who fear the Lord · **say,**
"His steadfast love endures for·-**ever.**" R.

The stone that the builders re·-**jected**
has become the chief · **cornerstone.**
This is the Lord's · **doing;**
it is marvellous in our · **eyes.**
This is the day that the Lord has · **made;**
let us rejoice and be glad in · **it.** R.

Save us, we beseech you, O · **Lord!**
O Lord, we beseech you, give us suc·-**cess!**
Blessed is the one who comes in the name of the · **Lord.**
We bless you from the house of the · **Lord.**
The Lord is · **God,**
and he has given us · **light.** R.

Second Sunday of Easter – C

Psalm 118

Guitar

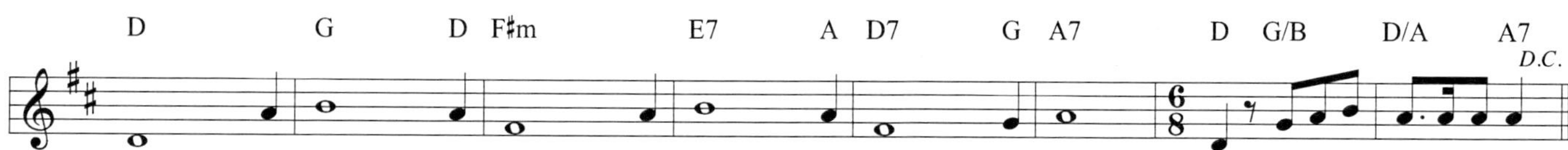

Let Israel · **say,**
"His steadfast love endures for·-**ever."**
Let the house of Aaron · **say,**
"His steadfast love endures for·-**ever."**
Let those who fear the Lord · **say,**
"His steadfast love endures for·-**ever."** R.

The stone that the builders re·-**jected**
has become the chief · **cornerstone.**
This is the Lord's · **doing;**
it is marvellous in our · **eyes.**
This is the day that the Lord has · **made;**
let us rejoice and be glad in · **it.** R.

Save us, we beseech you, O · **Lord!**
O Lord, we beseech you, give us suc·-**cess!**
Blessed is the one who comes in the name of the · **Lord.**
We bless you from the house of the · **Lord.**
The Lord is · **God,**
and he has given us · **light.** R.

C Instrument

B♭ Instrument

Third Sunday of Easter – C

Psalm 30

I will extol you, O Lord, for you have drawn me · **up,**
and did not let my foes rejoice · **over_me.**
O Lord, you brought up my soul from · **Sheol,**
restored me to life from among those gone down · **to_the** Pit. R.

Sing praises to the Lord, O you his · **faithful_ones,**
and give thanks to his holy · **name.**
For his anger is but for a moment; his favour is for a · **lifetime.**
Weeping may linger for the night, but joy comes · **with_the** morning. R.

Hear, O Lord, and be gracious to · **me!**
O Lord, be my · **helper!**
You have turned my mourning into · **dancing.**
O Lord my God, I will give thanks to you · **for**-ever. R.

Third Sunday of Easter – C

Psalm 30

Guitar

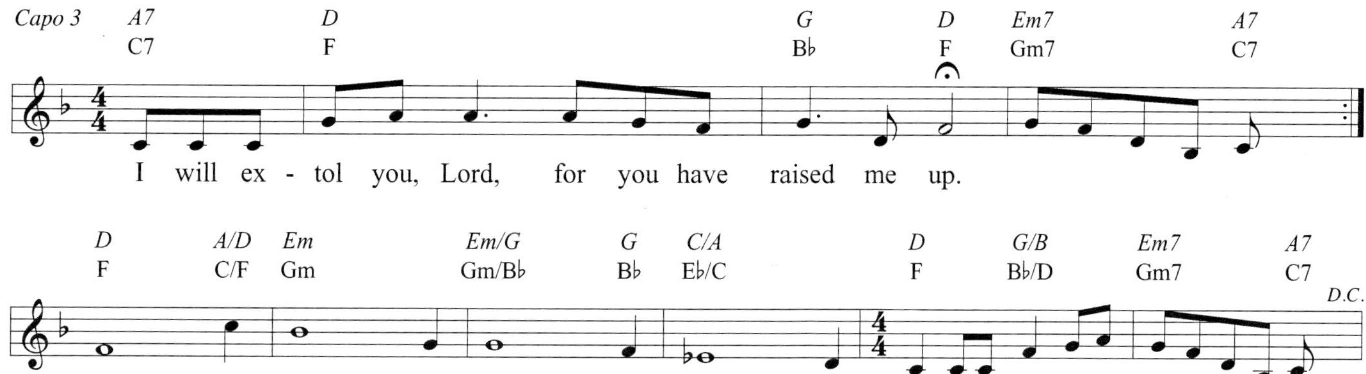

I will extol you, O Lord, for you have drawn me · **up,**
and did not let my foes rejoice · **over_me.**
O Lord, you brought up my soul from · **Sheol,**
restored me to life from among those gone down · **to_the** Pit. R.

Sing praises to the Lord, O you his · **faithful_ones,**
and give thanks to his holy · **name.**
For his anger is but for a moment; his favour is for a · **lifetime.**
Weeping may linger for the night, but joy comes · **with_the** morning. R.

Hear, O Lord, and be gracious to · **me!**
O Lord, be my · **helper!**
You have turned my mourning into · **dancing.**
O Lord my God, I will give thanks to you · **for**-ever. R.

C Instrument

B♭ Instrument

111

Fourth Sunday of Easter – C

Psalm 100

Make a joyful noise to the Lord, all · **the** earth.
Worship the Lord with · **gladness;**
come into his presence · **with** singing. R.

Know that the Lord · **is** God.
It is he that made us, and we are · **his;**
we are his people, and the sheep of · **his** pasture. R.

For the Lord · **is** good;
his steadfast love endures for·-**ever,**
and his faithfulness to all · **gener**-ations. R.

Fourth Sunday of Easter – C

Psalm 100

Guitar

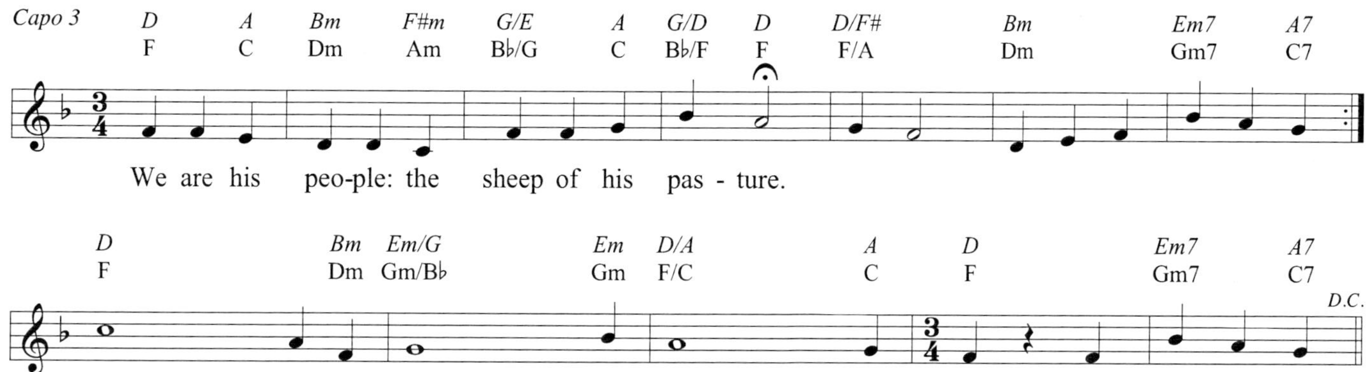

Make a joyful noise to the Lord, all · **the** earth.
Worship the Lord with · **gladness;**
come into his presence · **with** singing. R.

Know that the Lord · **is** God.
It is he that made us, and we are · **his;**
we are his people, and the sheep of · **his** pasture. R.

For the Lord · **is** good;
his steadfast love endures for·-**ever,**
and his faithfulness to all · **gener**-ations. R.

C Instrument

B♭ Instrument

Fifth Sunday of Easter – C

Psalm 145

The Lord is gracious and · **merciful,**
slow to anger and abounding in steadfast · **love.**
The Lord is good to · **all,**
and his compassion is over all that he · **has** made. R.

All your works shall give thanks to you, O · **Lord,**
and all your faithful shall · **bless_you.**
They shall speak of the glory of your · **kingdom,**
and tell of · **your** power. R.

To make known to human beings your mighty · **deeds,**
and the glorious splendour of your · **kingdom.**
Your kingdom is an everlasting · **kingdom,**
and your dominion endures throughout all · **gener**-ations. R.

Fifth Sunday of Easter – C

Psalm 145

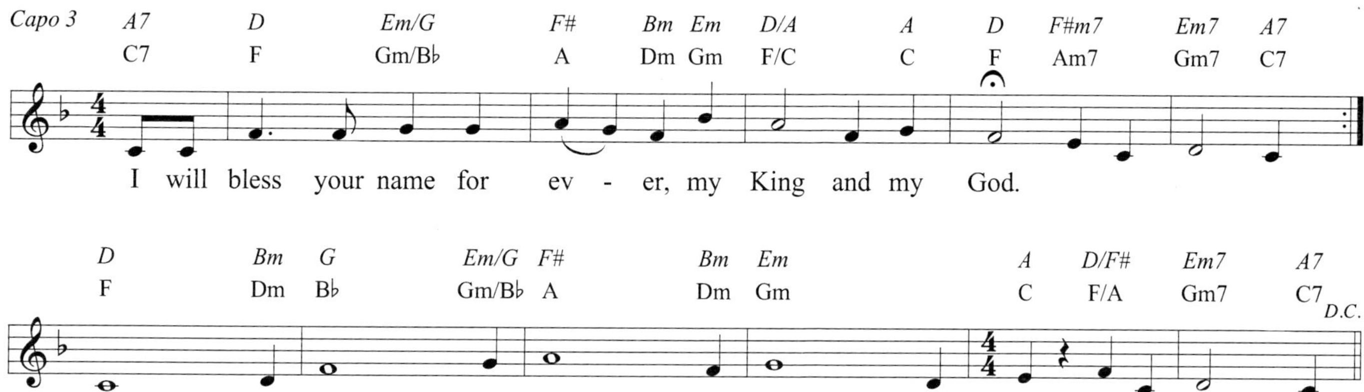

The Lord is gracious and · **merciful,**
slow to anger and abounding in steadfast · **love.**
The Lord is good to · **all,**
and his compassion is over all that he · **has** made. R.

All your works shall give thanks to you, O · **Lord,**
and all your faithful shall · **bless_you.**
They shall speak of the glory of your · **kingdom,**
and tell of · **your** power. R.

To make known to human beings your mighty · **deeds,**
and the glorious splendour of your · **kingdom.**
Your kingdom is an everlasting · **kingdom,**
and your dominion endures throughout all · **gener**-ations. R.

115

Sixth Sunday of Easter – C

Psalm 67

May God be gracious to us · **and** bless_us
and make his face to shine · **up**-on_us,
that your way may be known up·-**on** earth,
your saving power a·-**mong** all nations. R.

Let the nations be glad and sing · **for** joy,
for you judge the peoples with equity and guide the nations · **upon** earth.
Let the peoples praise you, · **O** God;
let all the · **peo**-ples praise_you. R.

The earth has yielded · **its** increase;
God, our God, · **has** blessed_us.
May God continue · **to** bless_us;
let all the ends of the · **earth** re-vere_him. R.

Sixth Sunday of Easter – C

Psalm 67

Guitar

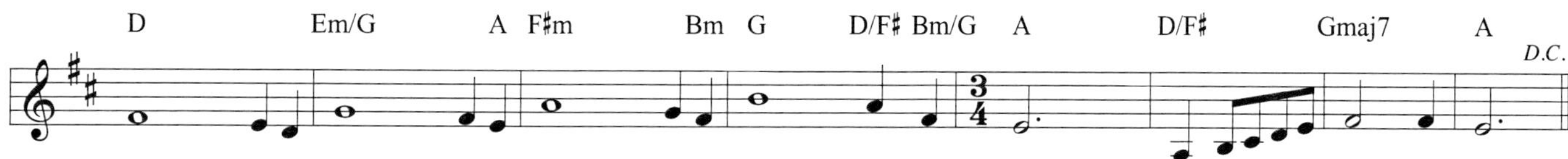

May God be gracious to us · **and** bless_us
and make his face to shine · **up**-on_us,
that your way may be known up·-**on** earth,
your saving power a·-**mong** all nations. R.

Let the nations be glad and sing · **for** joy,
for you judge the peoples with equity and guide the nations · **upon** earth.
Let the peoples praise you, · **O** God;
let all the · **peo**-ples praise_you. R.

The earth has yielded · **its** increase;
God, our God, · **has** blessed_us.
May God continue · **to** bless_us;
let all the ends of the · **earth** re-vere_him. R.

C Instrument

B♭ Instrument

Ascension of the Lord – C

Psalm 47

Clap your hands, all · **you** peoples;
shout to God with loud songs · **of** joy.
For the Lord, the Most High, · **is** awesome,
a great king over · **all** the earth. R.

God has gone up · **with_a** shout,
the Lord with the sound of · **a** trumpet.
Sing praises to God, · **sing** praises;
sing praises to our · **King,** sing praises. R.

For God is the king of all · **the** earth;
sing praises · **with_a** Psalm.
God is king over · **the** nations;
God sits on his · **ho**-ly throne. R.

Ascension of the Lord – C

Psalm 47

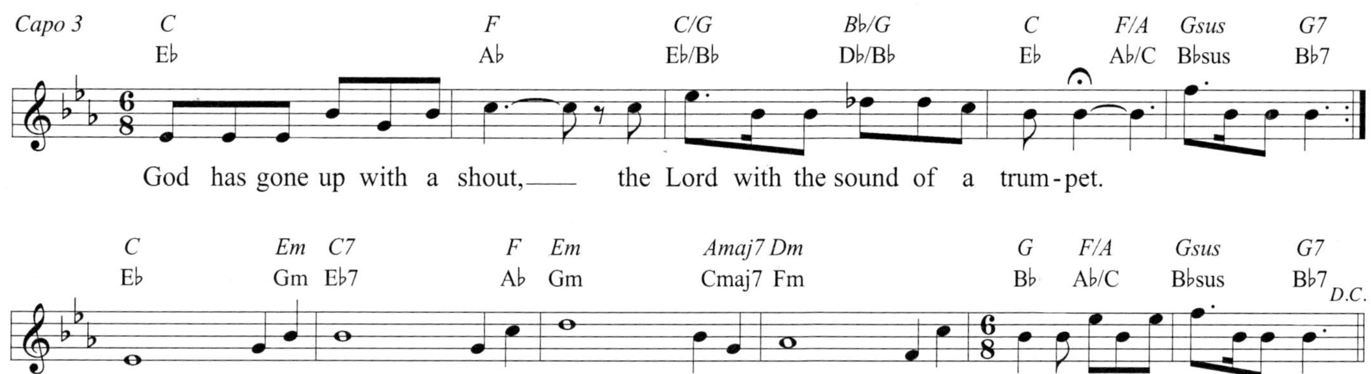

Clap your hands, all · **you** peoples;
shout to God with loud songs · **of** joy.
For the Lord, the Most High, · **is** awesome,
a great king over · **all** the earth. R.

God has gone up · **with_a** shout,
the Lord with the sound of · **a** trumpet.
Sing praises to God, · **sing** praises;
sing praises to our · **King,** sing praises. R.

For God is the king of all · **the** earth;
sing praises · **with_a** Psalm.
God is king over · **the** nations;
God sits on his · **ho**-ly throne. R.

119

Seventh Sunday of Easter – C

Psalm 97

The Lord is king! Let the earth re·-**joice;**
let the many coastlands · **be** glad!
Clouds and thick darkness are · **all** around him;
righteousness and justice are the foundation · **of** his throne. R.

The heavens proclaim his · **righteousness;**
and all the peoples be·-**hold_his** glory.
All worshippers of images are · **put** to shame;
all Angels bow · **down** be-fore_him. R.

For you, O Lord, are most high over all the · **earth;**
you are exalted far a· -**bove_all** gods.
Light dawns · **for** the righteous,
and joy for the · **upright** in heart. R.

Seventh Sunday of Easter – C

Psalm 97

Guitar

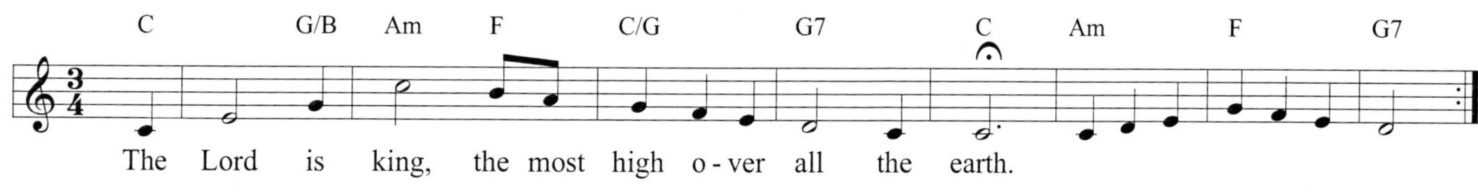

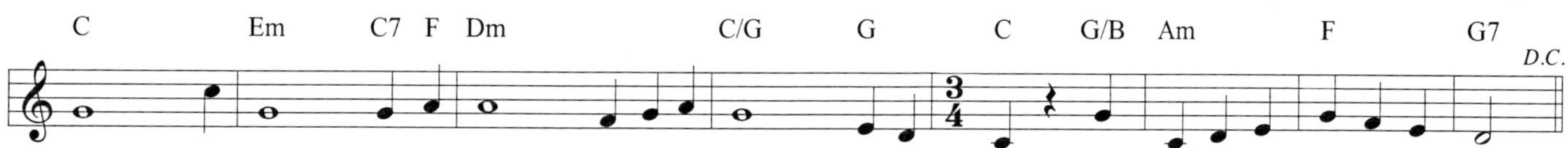

The Lord is king! Let the earth re·-**joice;**
let the many coastlands · **be** glad!
Clouds and thick darkness are · **all** around him;
righteousness and justice are the foundation · **of** his throne. R.

The heavens proclaim his · **righteousness;**
and all the peoples be·-**hold_his** glory.
All worshippers of images are · **put** to shame;
all Angels bow · **down** be-fore_him. R.

For you, O Lord, are most high over all the · **earth;**
you are exalted far a· -**bove_all** gods.
Light dawns · **for** the righteous,
and joy for the · **upright** in heart. R.

C Instrument

B♭ Instrument

121

Pentecost (Vigil) – ABC

Psalm 104

Bless the Lord, O · **my** soul.
O Lord my God, you are very · **great.**
You are clothed with · **honour** and majesty,
wrapped in light as with · **a** garment. R.

O Lord, how manifold are · **your** works!
In wisdom you have made them · **all;**
the earth is · **full_of** your creatures,
living things both small · **and** great. R.

These all look · **to** you
to give them their food in due · **season;**
when you give to them, they · **gather** it up;
when you open your hand, they are filled with · **good** things. R.

When you take away · **their** breath,
they die and return to their · **dust.**
When you send forth your spirit, they · **are** cre-ated;
and you renew the face of · **the** earth. R.

For Pentecost Sunday, turn to page 138.

Pentecost (Vigil) – ABC

Psalm 104

Guitar

Bless the Lord, O · **my** soul.
O Lord my God, you are very · **great.**
You are clothed with · **honour** and majesty,
wrapped in light as with · **a** garment. R.

O Lord, how manifold are · **your** works!
In wisdom you have made them · **all;**
the earth is · **full_of** your creatures,
living things both small · **and** great. R.

These all look · **to** you
to give them their food in due · **season;**
when you give to them, they · **gather** it up;
when you open your hand, they are filled with · **good** things. R.

When you take away · **their** breath,
they die and return to their · **dust.**
When you send forth your spirit, they · **are** cre-ated;
and you renew the face of · **the** earth. R.

C Instrument

Bb Instrument

123

Extended Vigil of Pentecost (1) – ABC

Psalm 8

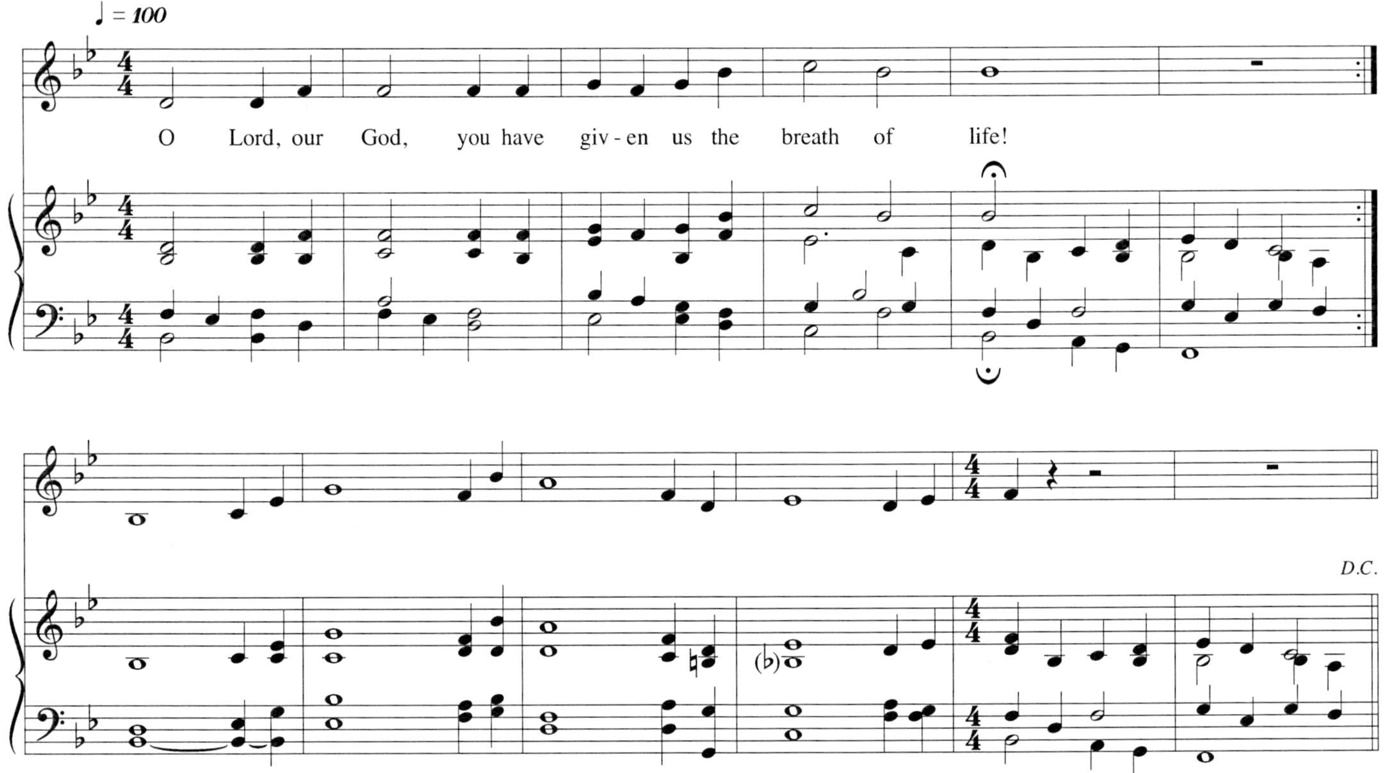

When I look at your heavens, the work of · **your** fingers,
the moon and the stars that you have · **es**-tablished;
what is a man that you · **are** mindful_of_him,
or the son of man · **that** you care_for_him? R.

Yet you have made him a little lower · **than_the** Angels,
and crowned him with glory · **and** honour.
You have given him dominion over the works of · **your** hands;
you have put all things · **under** his feet. R.

All sheep · **and** oxen,
and also the beasts of · **the** field,
the birds of the air, and the fish of · **the** sea,
whatever passes along the · **paths_of** the seas. R.

Extended Vigil of Pentecost (1) – ABC

Psalm 8

Guitar

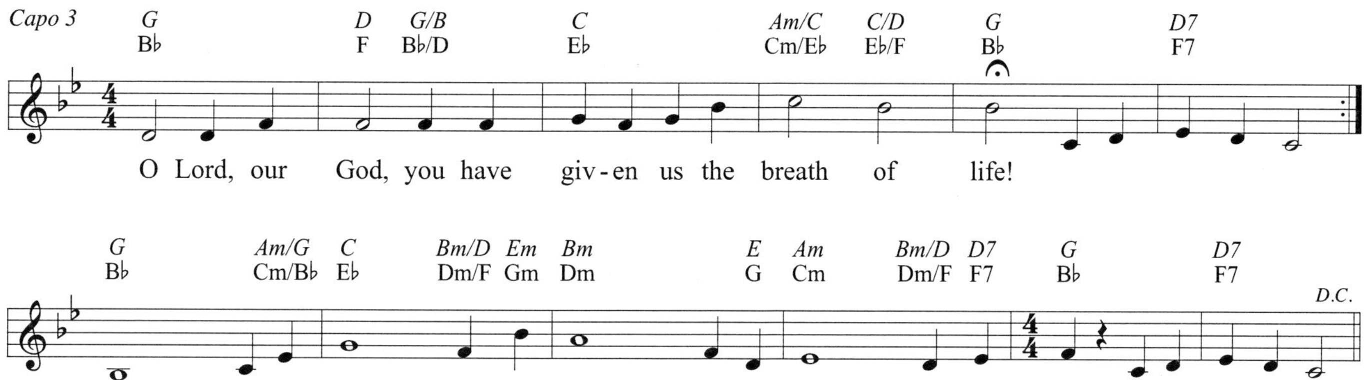

When I look at your heavens, the work of · **your** fingers,
the moon and the stars that you have · **es**-tablished;
what is a man that you · **are** mindful_of_him,
or the son of man · **that** you care_for_him? R.

Yet you have made him a little lower · **than_the** Angels,
and crowned him with glory · **and** honour.
You have given him dominion over the works of · **your** hands;
you have put all things · **under** his feet. R.

All sheep · **and** oxen,
and also the beasts of · **the** field,
the birds of the air, and the fish of · **the** sea,
whatever passes along the · **paths_of** the seas. R.

C Instrument

B♭ Instrument

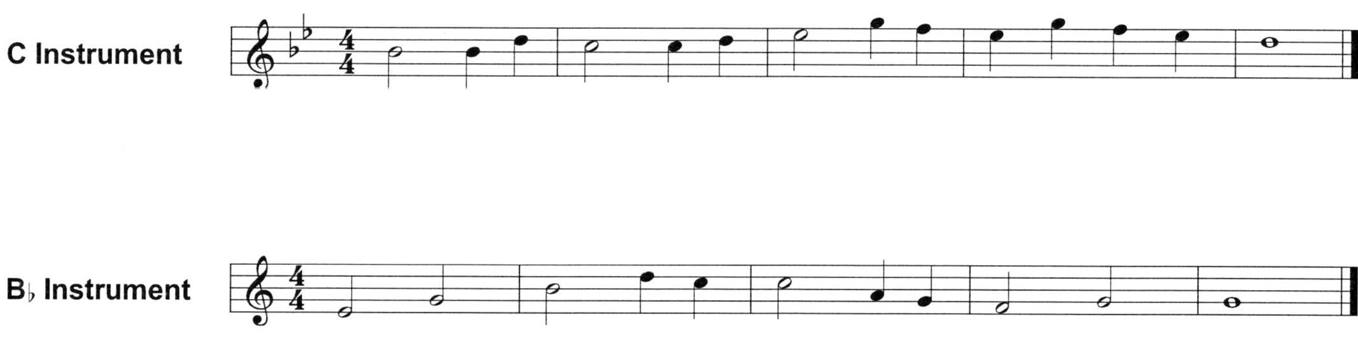

125

Extended Vigil of Pentecost (2) – ABC

Psalm 80

Give ear, O Shepherd · **of** Israel,
you who are enthroned upon the cherubim, shine · **forth.**
Stir up your · **might,**
and come to · **save_us.** R.

Restore us, · **O** God;
let your face shine, that we may be · **saved.**
O Lord God of · **hosts,**
how long will you be angry with your people's · **prayers?** R.

Turn again, O God · **of** hosts;
look down from heaven, and · **see.**
Then we will never turn · **back_from_you;**
give us life, and we will call on your · **name.** R.

Extended Vigil of Pentecost (2) – ABC

Psalm 80

Guitar

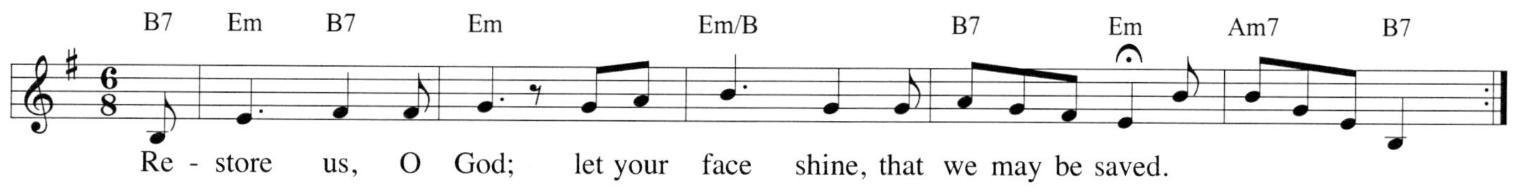

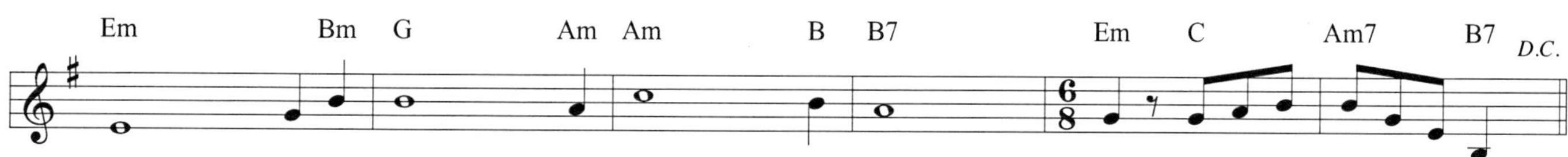

Give ear, O Shepherd · **of** Israel,
you who are enthroned upon the cherubim, shine · **forth.**
Stir up your · **might,**
and come to · **save_us.** R.

Restore us, · **O** God;
let your face shine, that we may be · **saved.**
O Lord God of · **hosts,**
how long will you be angry with your people's · **prayers?** R.

Turn again, O God · **of** hosts;
look down from heaven, and · **see.**
Then we will never turn · **back_from_you;**
give us life, and we will call on your · **name.** R.

C Instrument

B♭ Instrument

Extended Vigil of Pentecost (3) – ABC

Psalm 97

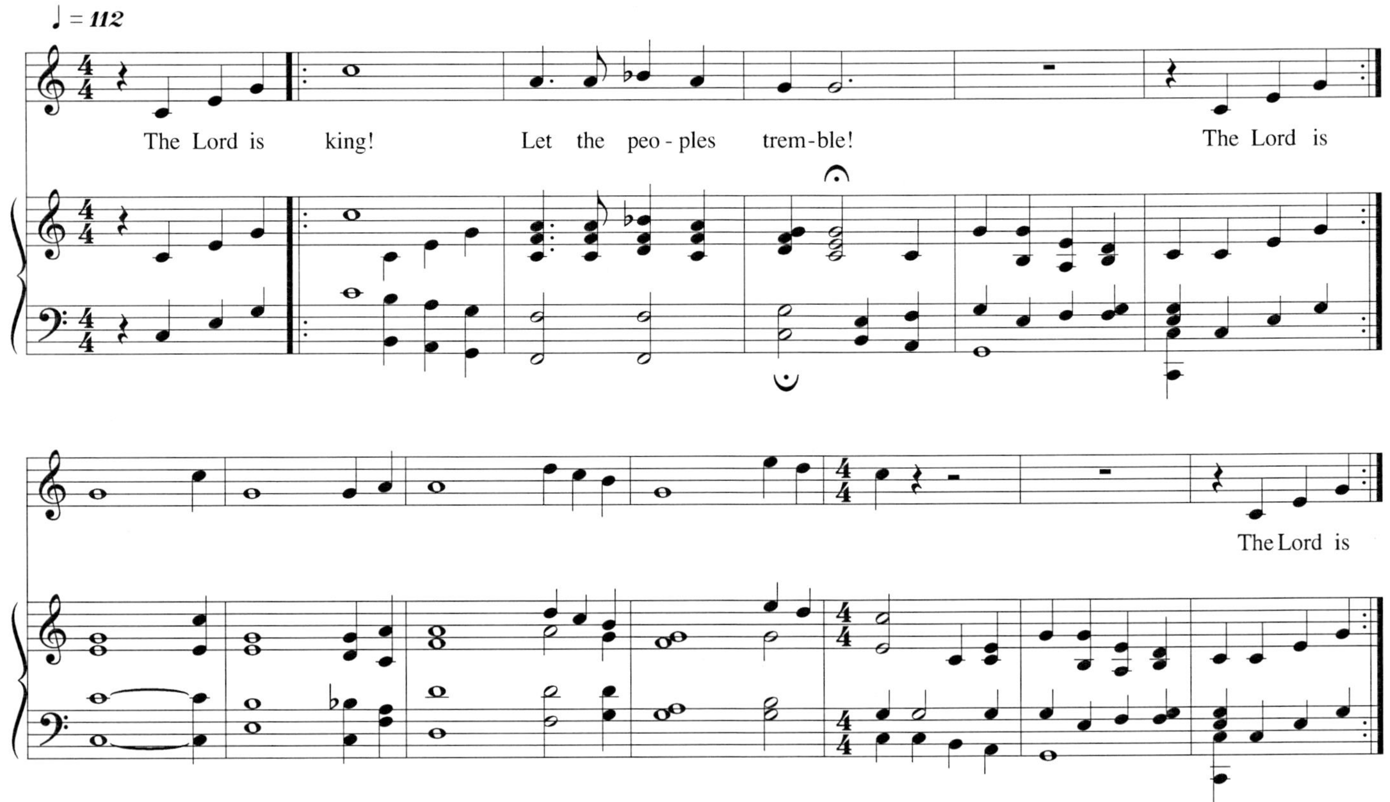

The Lord is king! Let the earth re·-**joice;**
let the many coastlands · **be** glad!
Clouds and thick darkness are · **all** a-round_him;
righteousness and justice are the foundation · **of** his throne. R.

Fire goes be·-**fore_him,**
and consumes his adversaries on · **every** side.
His lightnings light · **up** the world;
the earth · **sees** and trembles. R.

The mountains melt like wax before the · **Lord,**
before the Lord of · **all_the** earth.
The heavens pro·-**claim** his righteousness;
and all the peoples be·-**hold** his glory. R.

Light dawns for the · **righteous,**
and joy for the upright · **in** heart.
Rejoice in the Lord, · **O** you righteous,
and give thanks to his · **ho**-ly name! R.

Extended Vigil of Pentecost (3) – ABC

Psalm 97

Guitar

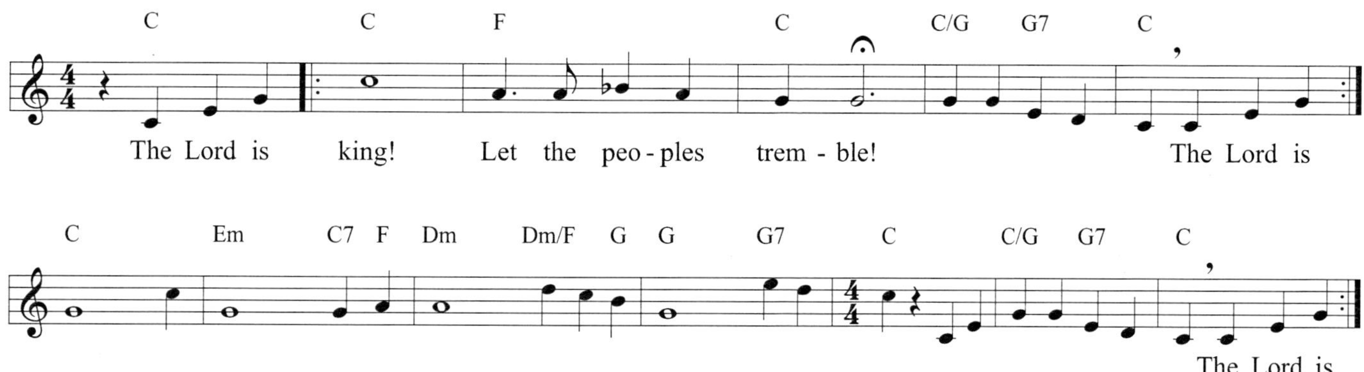

The Lord is king! Let the earth re·-**joice;**
let the many coastlands · **be** glad!
Clouds and thick darkness are · **all** a-round_him;
righteousness and justice are the foundation · **of** his throne. R.

Fire goes be·-**fore_him,**
and consumes his adversaries on · **every** side.
His lightnings light · **up** the world;
the earth · **sees** and trembles. R.

The mountains melt like wax before the · **Lord,**
before the Lord of · **all_the** earth.
The heavens pro·-**claim** his righteousness;
and all the peoples be·-**hold** his glory. R.

Light dawns for the · **righteous,**
and joy for the upright · **in** heart.
Rejoice in the Lord, · **O** you righteous,
and give thanks to his · **ho**-ly name! R.

C Instrument

B♭ Instrument

129

Extended Vigil of Pentecost (4) – ABC

Psalm 139

O Lord, you have searched me and · **known_me.**
You know when I sit down and when I · **rise** up;
you discern my thoughts from far a·-**way.**
You search out my path and my lying down, and are acquainted with all · **my** ways. R.

Even before a word is on my · **tongue,**
O Lord, you know it · **com**-pletely.
Such knowledge is too · **wonderful_for_me;**
it is so high that I cannot · **at**-tain_it. R.

Where can I go from your · **spirit?**
Or where can I flee from · **your** presence?
If I ascend to heaven, you are · **there;**
if I make my bed in Sheol, you · **are** there. R.

Even there your hand shall · **lead_me,**
and your right hand shall · **hold_me** fast.
How weighty to me are your thoughts, O · **God!**
How vast is · **the** sum_of_them! R.

Extended Vigil of Pentecost (4) – ABC

Psalm 139

Guitar

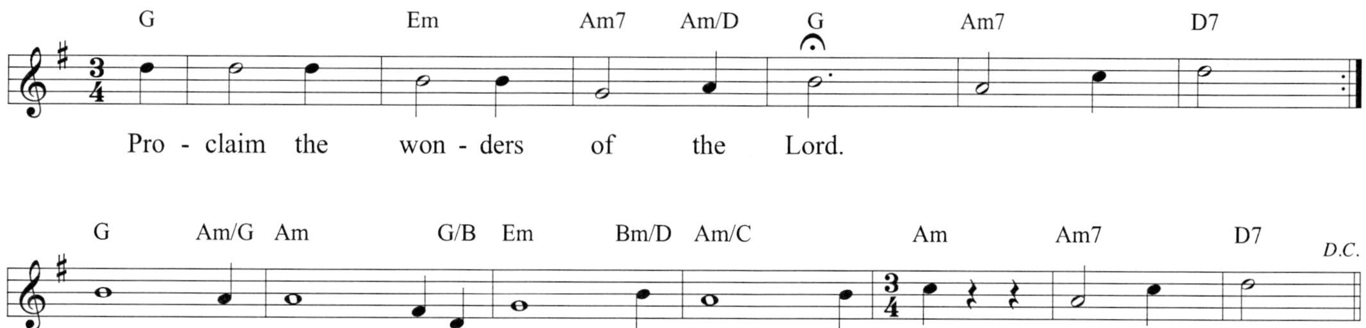

O Lord, you have searched me and · **known_me.**
You know when I sit down and when I · **rise** up;
you discern my thoughts from far a·-**way.**
You search out my path and my lying down, and are acquainted with all · **my** ways. R.

Even before a word is on my · **tongue,**
O Lord, you know it · **com**-pletely.
Such knowledge is too · **wonderful_for_me;**
it is so high that I cannot · **at**-tain_it. R.

Where can I go from your · **spirit?**
Or where can I flee from · **your** presence?
If I ascend to heaven, you are · **there;**
if I make my bed in Sheol, you · **are** there. R.

Even there your hand shall · **lead_me,**
and your right hand shall · **hold_me** fast.
How weighty to me are your thoughts, O · **God!**
How vast is · **the** sum_of_them! R.

131

Extended Vigil of Pentecost (5) – ABC

Psalm 105

O give thanks to the Lord, call · **on_his** name,
make known his deeds a·-**mong_the** peoples.
Sing to him, sing · **praises** to him;
tell of all his · **wonderful** works. R.

Remember the wonderful works he · **has** done,
his miracles, and the judgments · **he** uttered,
O offspring of his · **ser**-vant Abraham,
children of Jacob, · **his** chosen_ones. R.

He is the Lord · **our** God;
his judgments are in all · **the** earth.
He is mindful of his · **covenant** for-ever,
the covenant that he made with Abraham, to Israel as an ever·-**lasting** covenant. R.

For he remembered his · **holy** promise,
and Abraham, · **his** servant,
that they might · **keep** his statutes
and observe · **his** laws. R.

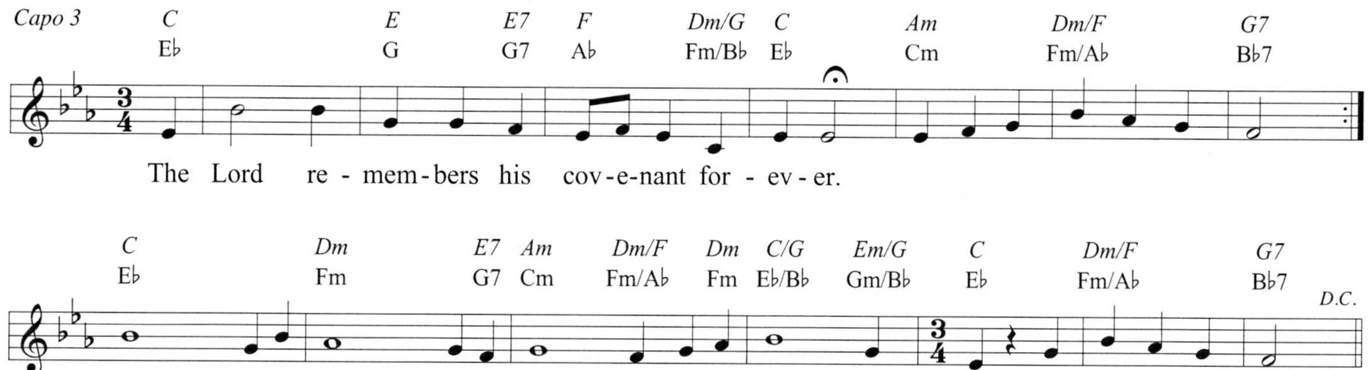

Extended Vigil of Pentecost (5) – ABC

Psalm 105

O give thanks to the Lord, call · **on_his** name,
make known his deeds a·-**mong_the** peoples.
Sing to him, sing · **praises** to him;
tell of all his · **wonderful** works. R.

Remember the wonderful works he · **has** done,
his miracles, and the judgments · **he** uttered,
O offspring of his · **ser**-vant Abraham,
children of Jacob, · **his** chosen_ones. R.

He is the Lord · **our** God;
his judgments are in all · **the** earth.
He is mindful of his · **covenant** for-ever,
the covenant that he made with Abraham, to Israel as an ever·-**lasting** covenant. R.

For he remembered his · **holy** promise,
and Abraham, · **his** servant,
that they might · **keep** his statutes
and observe · **his** laws. R.

133

Extended Vigil of Pentecost (6) – ABC

Psalm 90

Lord, you have been our dwelling place in · **all** gene-rations.
Before the mountains · **were** brought forth,
or ever you had formed the · **earth_and** the world,
from everlasting to everlasting · **you** are God. R.

You turn man back to · **dust,** and say,
"Turn back, you · **children** of Adam."
For a thousand years in your sight are like yesterday when · **it** is past,
or like a watch · **in** the night. R.

You sweep them away; they are · **like** a dream,
like grass that is renewed · **in** the morning;
in the morning it flourishes and · **is** re-newed;
in the evening it · **fades** and withers. R.

Satisfy us in the morning with your · **stead**-fast love,
so that we may rejoice and be glad · **all** our days.
Let your work be manifest · **to** your servants,
and your glorious power · **to** their children. R.

Extended Vigil of Pentecost (6) – ABC

Psalm 90

Guitar

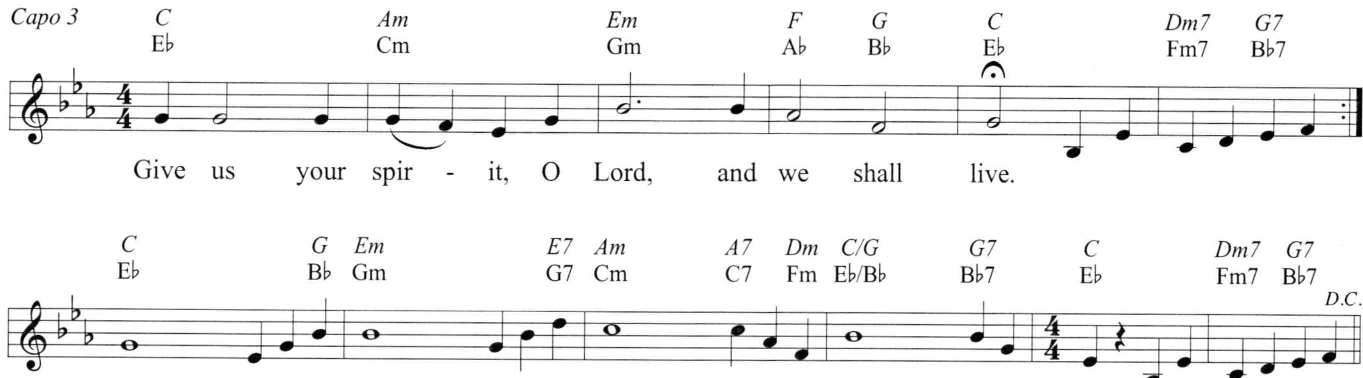

Lord, you have been our dwelling place in · **all** gene-rations.
Before the mountains · **were** brought forth,
or ever you had formed the · **earth_and** the world,
from everlasting to everlasting · **you** are God. R.

You turn man back to · **dust,** and say,
"Turn back, you · **children** of Adam."
For a thousand years in your sight are like yesterday when · **it** is past,
or like a watch · **in** the night. R.

You sweep them away; they are · **like** a dream,
like grass that is renewed · **in** the morning;
in the morning it flourishes and · **is** re-newed;
in the evening it · **fades** and withers. R.

Satisfy us in the morning with your · **stead**-fast love,
so that we may rejoice and be glad · **all** our days.
Let your work be manifest · **to** your servants,
and your glorious power · **to** their children. R.

C Instrument

B♭ Instrument

135

Extended Vigil of Pentecost (7) – ABC

Psalm 104

Bless the Lord, O · **my** soul.
O Lord my God, you are very · **great.**
You are clothed with · **honour** and majesty,
wrapped in light as with · **a** garment. R.

O Lord, how manifold are · **your** works!
In wisdom you have made them · **all;**
the earth is · **full_of** your creatures,
living things both small · **and** great. R.

These all look · **to** you
to give them their food in due · **season;**
when you give to them, they · **gather** it up;
when you open your hand, they are filled with · **good** things. R.

When you take away · **their** breath,
they die and return to their · **dust.**
When you send forth your spirit, they · **are** cre-ated;
and you renew the face of · **the** earth. R.

Extended Vigil of Pentecost (7) – ABC

Psalm 104

Guitar

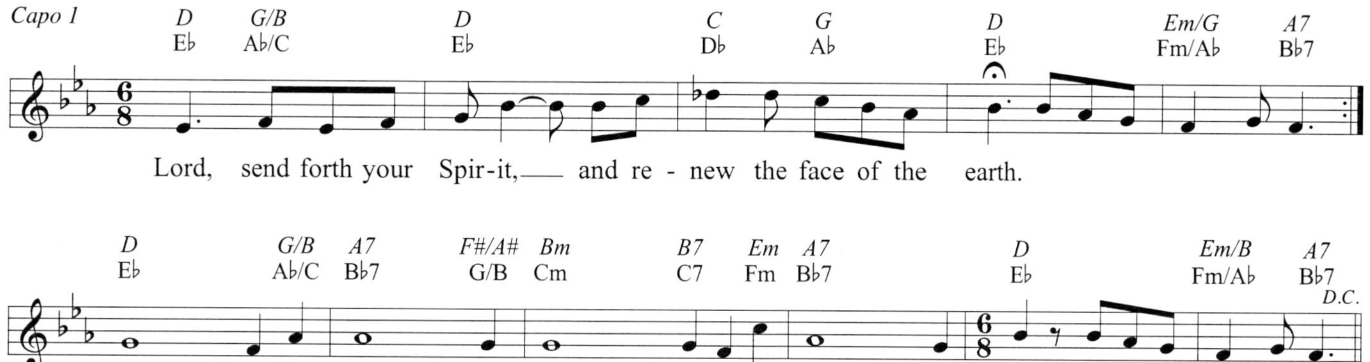

Bless the Lord, O · **my** soul.
O Lord my God, you are very · **great.**
You are clothed with · **honour** and majesty,
wrapped in light as with · **a** garment. R.

O Lord, how manifold are · **your** works!
In wisdom you have made them · **all;**
the earth is · **full_of** your creatures,
living things both small · **and** great. R.

These all look · **to** you
to give them their food in due · **season;**
when you give to them, they · **gather** it up;
when you open your hand, they are filled with · **good** things. R.

When you take away · **their** breath,
they die and return to their · **dust.**
When you send forth your spirit, they · **are** cre-ated;
and you renew the face of · **the** earth. R.

C Instrument

B♭ Instrument

© 2009 GORDON JOHNSTON — NOVALIS

Pentecost Sunday – C

Psalm 104

Bless the Lord, O · **my** soul.
O Lord my God, you are very · **great.**
O Lord, how manifold · **are** your works!
The earth is full of · **your** creatures. R.

When you take away · **their** breath,
they die and return to their · **dust.**
When you send forth your spirit, they · **are** cre-ated;
and you renew the face of · **the** earth. R.

May the glory of the Lord endure · **for**-ever;
may the Lord rejoice in his · **works.**
May my meditation be · **pleasing** to him,
for I rejoice in · **the** Lord. R.

Pentecost Sunday – C

Psalm 104

Guitar

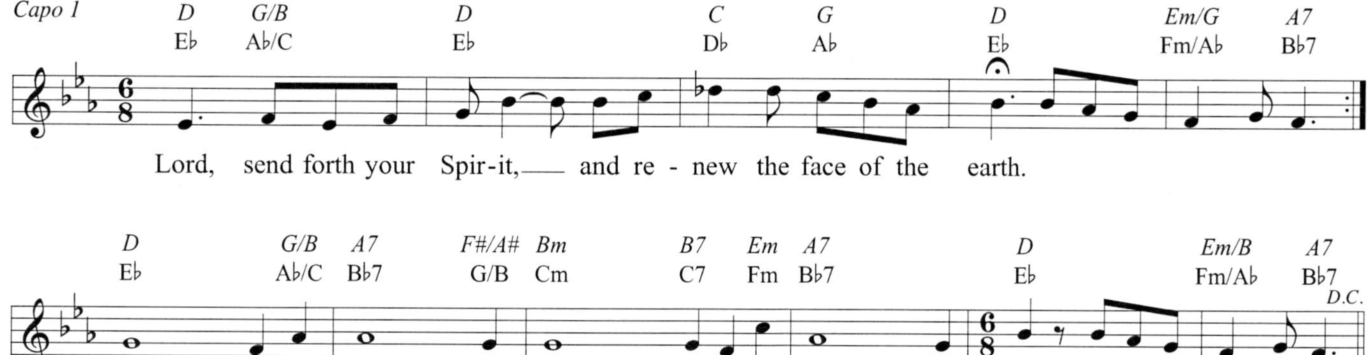

Bless the Lord, O · **my** soul.
O Lord my God, you are very · **great.**
O Lord, how manifold · **are** your works!
The earth is full of · **your** creatures. R.

When you take away · **their** breath,
they die and return to their · **dust.**
When you send forth your spirit, they · **are** cre-ated;
and you renew the face of · **the** earth. R.

May the glory of the Lord endure · **for-**ever;
may the Lord rejoice in his · **works.**
May my meditation be · **pleasing** to him,
for I rejoice in · **the** Lord. R.

C Instrument

B♭ Instrument

139

Solemnity of the Most Holy Trinity – C

Psalm 8

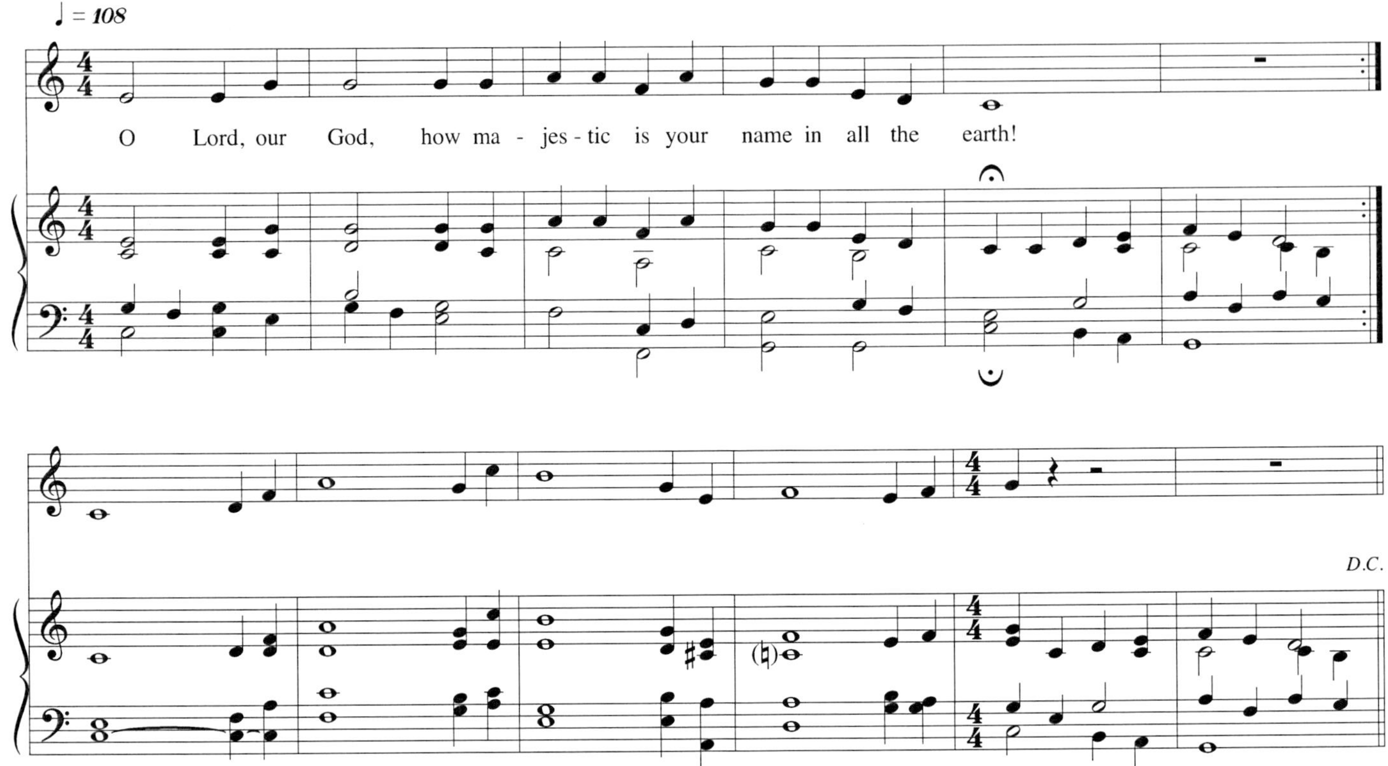

When I look at your heavens, the work of · **your** fingers,
the moon and the stars that you have · **es**-tablished;
what is a man that you · **are** mindful_of_him,
or the son of man · **that** you care_for_him? R.

Yet you have made him a little lower · **than_the** Angels,
and crowned him with glory · **and** honour.
You have given him dominion over the works of · **your** hands;
you have put all things · **under** his feet. R.

All sheep · **and** oxen,
and also the beasts of · **the** field,
the birds of the air, and the fish of · **the** sea,
whatever passes along the · **paths_of** the seas. R.

Solemnity of the Most Holy Trinity – C

Psalm 8

Guitar

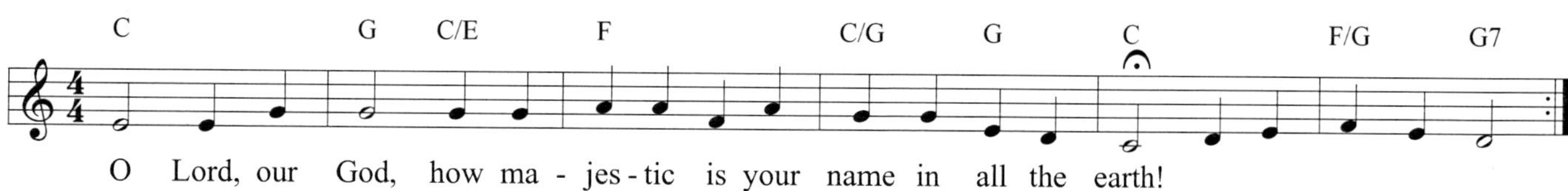

When I look at your heavens, the work of · **your** fingers,
the moon and the stars that you have · **es**-tablished;
what is a man that you · **are** mindful_of_him,
or the son of man · **that** you care_for_him? R.

Yet you have made him a little lower · **than_the** Angels,
and crowned him with glory · **and** honour.
You have given him dominion over the works of · **your** hands;
you have put all things · **under** his feet. R.

All sheep · **and** oxen,
and also the beasts of · **the** field,
the birds of the air, and the fish of · **the** sea,
whatever passes along the · **paths_of** the seas. R.

C Instrument

B♭ Instrument

141

Solemnity of the Most Holy Body and Blood of Christ – C

Psalm 110

The Lord says to · **my** lord,
"Sit at my · **right** hand
until I make your enemies · **your** footstool." R.

The Lord sends out · **from** Zion
your might·-**y** sceptre.
Rule in the midst of · **your** foes. R.

Your people will offer them·-**selves** willingly
on the day you lead your forces on the · **holy** mountains.
From the womb of the morning, like dew, your youth · **will** come_to_you. R.

The Lord has sworn and will not change · **his** mind,
"You are a priest · **for**-ever
according to the order of · **Mel**-chizedek." R.

Solemnity of the Most Holy Body and Blood of Christ – C

Psalm 110

Guitar

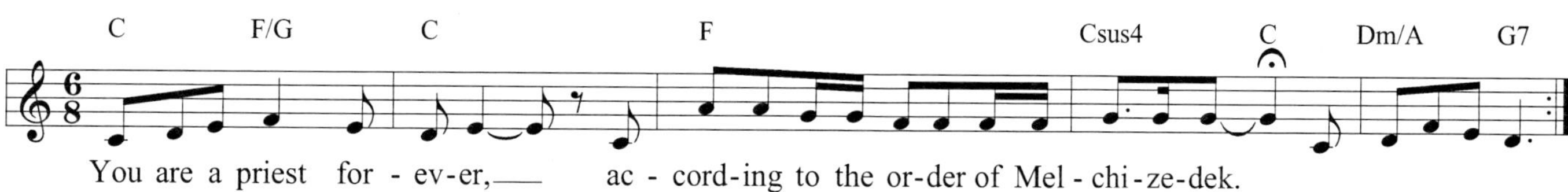

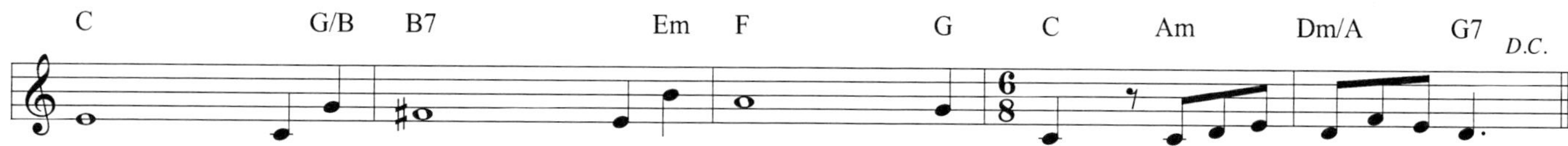

The Lord says to · **my** lord,
"Sit at my · **right** hand
until I make your enemies · **your** footstool." R.

The Lord sends out · **from** Zion
your might·-**y** sceptre.
Rule in the midst of · **your** foes. R.

Your people will offer them·-**selves** willingly
on the day you lead your forces on the · **holy** mountains.
From the womb of the morning, like dew, your youth · **will** come_to_you. R.

The Lord has sworn and will not change · **his** mind,
"You are a priest · **for**-ever
according to the order of · **Mel**-chizedek." R.

C Instrument

B♭ Instrument

143

Solemnity of the Most Sacred Heart of Jesus – C

Psalm 23

The Lord is my shepherd, I shall · **not** want.
He makes me lie down in · **green** pastures;
he leads me be·-**side** still waters;
he re·-**stores** my soul. R.

He leads me in right paths for his · **name's** sake.
Even though I walk through the darkest valley, I fear · **no** evil;
for · **you** are with_me;
your rod and your · **staff**—they comfort_me. R.

You prepare a table · **be**-fore_me
in the presence · **of_my** enemies;
you anoint my · **head** with oil;
my · **cup** over-flows. R.

Surely goodness and mercy · **shall** follow_me
all the days of · **my** life,
and I shall dwell in the · **house_of** the Lord
my · **whole** life long. R.

Solemnity of the Most Sacred Heart of Jesus – C

Psalm 23

Guitar

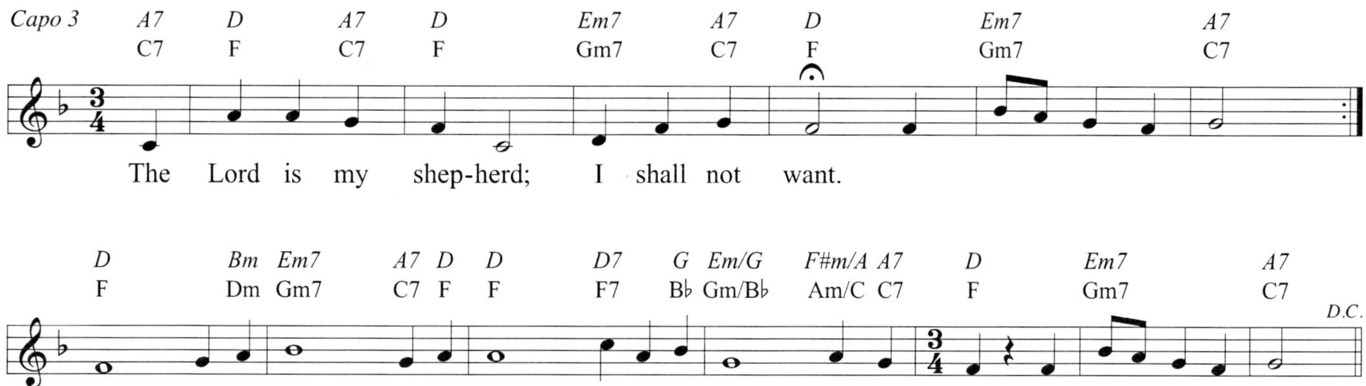

The Lord is my shepherd, I shall · **not** want.
He makes me lie down in · **green** pastures;
he leads me be·-**side** still waters;
he re·-**stores** my soul. R.

He leads me in right paths for his · **name's** sake.
Even though I walk through the darkest valley, I fear · **no** evil;
for · **you** are with_me;
your rod and your · **staff**—they comfort_me. R.

You prepare a table · **be**-fore_me
in the presence · **of_my** enemies;
you anoint my · **head** with oil;
my · **cup** over-flows. R.

Surely goodness and mercy · **shall** follow_me
all the days of · **my** life,
and I shall dwell in the · **house_of** the Lord
my · **whole** life long. R.

Common Psalm for Ordinary Time

Psalm 19

The law of the Lord is · **perfect,**
reviving the · **soul;**
the decrees of the Lord are · **sure,**
making · **wise** the simple. R.

The precepts of the Lord are · **right,**
rejoicing the · **heart;**
the commandment of the Lord is · **clear,**
en-·**lightening** the eyes. R.

The fear of the Lord is · **pure,**
enduring for-·**ever;**
the ordinances of the Lord are · **true**
and righteous · **al**-to-gether. R.

More to be desired are they than · **gold,**
even much fine · **gold;**
sweeter also than · **honey,**
and drippings · **of** the honeycomb. R.

Common Psalm for Ordinary Time

Psalm 19

Guitar

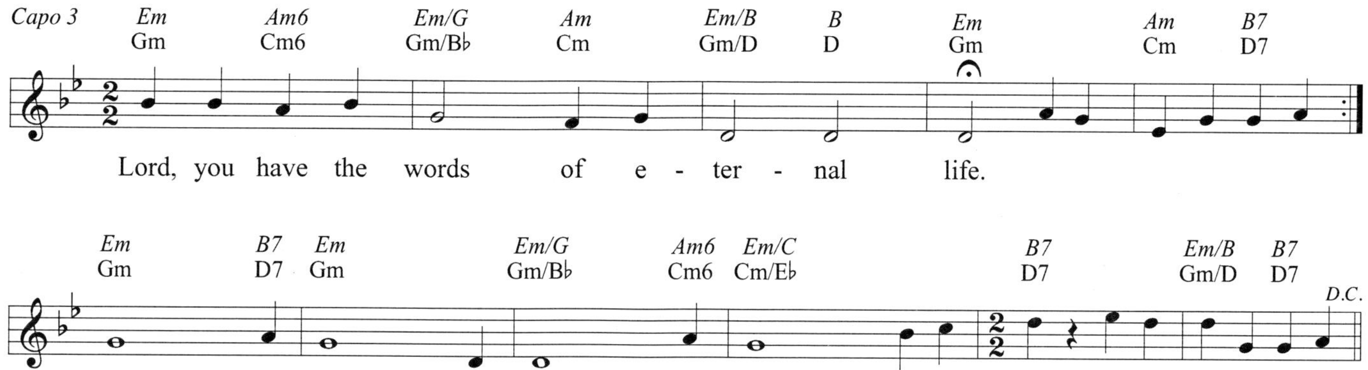

The law of the Lord is · **perfect,**
reviving the · **soul;**
the decrees of the Lord are · **sure,**
making · **wise** the simple. R.

The precepts of the Lord are · **right,**
rejoicing the · **heart;**
the commandment of the Lord is · **clear,**
en-·**lightening** the eyes. R.

The fear of the Lord is · **pure,**
enduring for-·**ever;**
the ordinances of the Lord are · **true**
and righteous · **al**-to-gether. R.

More to be desired are they than · **gold,**
even much fine · **gold;**
sweeter also than · **honey,**
and drippings · **of** the honeycomb. R.

C Instrument

B♭ Instrument

Common Psalm for Ordinary Time

Psalm 27

The Lord is my light and my sal·-**vation;**
whom shall · **I** fear?
The Lord is the stronghold of my · **life;**
of whom shall I be · **a**-fraid? R.

One thing I asked of the Lord, that will I · **seek_after:**
to live in the house of the Lord all the days of · **my** life,
to behold the beauty of the · **Lord,**
and to inquire in · **his** temple. R.

I believe that I shall see the goodness of the · **Lord**
in the land of · **the** living.
Wait for the Lord; be · **strong,**
and let your heart take courage; wait · **for_the** Lord! R.

Common Psalm for Ordinary Time

Psalm 27

Guitar

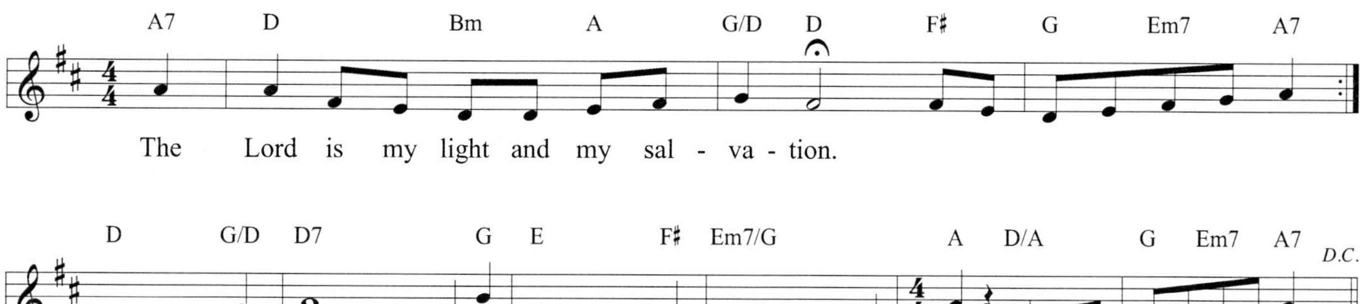

The Lord is my light and my sal·-**vation;**
whom shall · **I** fear?
The Lord is the stronghold of my · **life;**
of whom shall I be · **a**-fraid? R.

One thing I asked of the Lord, that will I · **seek_after:**
to live in the house of the Lord all the days of · **my** life,
to behold the beauty of the · **Lord,**
and to inquire in · **his** temple. R.

I believe that I shall see the goodness of the · **Lord**
in the land of · **the** living.
Wait for the Lord; be · **strong,**
and let your heart take courage; wait · **for_the** Lord! R.

C Instrument

B♭ Instrument

149

Common Psalm for Ordinary Time

Psalm 34

I will bless the Lord at all · **times;**
his praise shall continually be in · **my** mouth.
My soul makes its boast in the · **Lord;**
let the humble hear and · **be** glad. R.

O magnify the Lord with · **me,**
and let us exalt his name · **to**-gether.
I sought the Lord, and he · **answered_me,**
and delivered me from all · **my** fears. R.

Look to him, and be · **radiant;**
so your faces shall never · **be_a**-shamed.
The poor one called, and the Lord · **heard,**
and saved that person from ev·-**ery** trouble. R.

The Angel of the Lord en·-**camps**
around those who fear him, and · **de**-livers_them.
O taste and see that the Lord is · **good;**
blessed is the one who takes refuge · **in** him. R.

Common Psalm for Ordinary Time

Psalm 34

Guitar

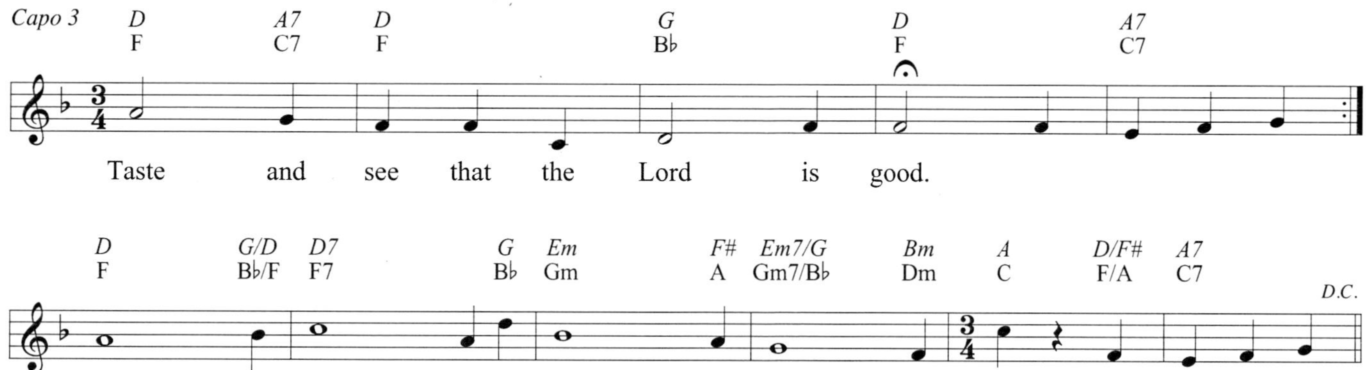

I will bless the Lord at all · **times;**
his praise shall continually be in · **my** mouth.
My soul makes its boast in the · **Lord;**
let the humble hear and · **be** glad. R.

O magnify the Lord with · **me,**
and let us exalt his name · **to**-gether.
I sought the Lord, and he · **answered_me,**
and delivered me from all · **my** fears. R.

Look to him, and be · **radiant;**
so your faces shall never · **be_a**-shamed.
The poor one called, and the Lord · **heard,**
and saved that person from ev·-**ery** trouble. R.

The Angel of the Lord en·-**camps**
around those who fear him, and · **de**-livers_them.
O taste and see that the Lord is · **good;**
blessed is the one who takes refuge · **in** him. R.

C Instrument

B♭ Instrument

151

Common Psalm for Ordinary Time

Psalm 63

O God, you are my God, I · **seek_you,**
my soul · **thirsts_for_you;**
my flesh · **faints_for_you,**
as in a dry and weary land where there · **is** no water. R.

So I have looked upon you in the · **sanctuary,**
beholding your power and · **glory.**
Because your steadfast love is better than · **life,**
my · **lips** will praise_you. R.

So I will bless you as long as I · **live;**
I will lift up my hands and call on your · **name.**
My soul is satisfied as with a rich · **feast,**
and my mouth praises you with · **joy**-ful lips. R.

For you have been my · **help,**
and in the shadow of your wings I sing for · **joy.**
My soul · **clings_to_you;**
your right · **hand** up-holds_me. R.

Common Psalm for Ordinary Time

Psalm 63

Guitar

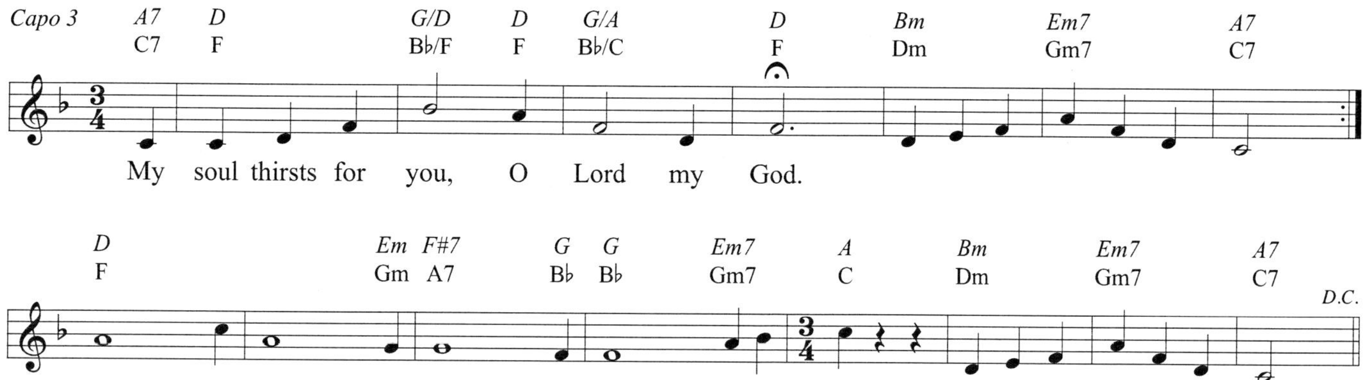

O God, you are my God, I · **seek_you,**
my soul · **thirsts_for_you;**
my flesh · **faints_for_you,**
as in a dry and weary land where there · **is** no water. R.

So I have looked upon you in the · **sanctuary,**
beholding your power and · **glory.**
Because your steadfast love is better than · **life,**
my · **lips** will praise_you. R.

So I will bless you as long as I · **live;**
I will lift up my hands and call on your · **name.**
My soul is satisfied as with a rich · **feast,**
and my mouth praises you with · **joy**-ful lips. R.

For you have been my · **help,**
and in the shadow of your wings I sing for · **joy.**
My soul · **clings_to_you;**
your right · **hand** up-holds_me. R.

C Instrument

B♭ Instrument

Common Psalm for Ordinary Time

Psalm 95

O come, let us sing to · **the** Lord;
let us make a joyful noise to the rock of our · **sal**-vation!
Let us come into his presence with · **thanks**-giving;
let us make a joyful noise to him with songs · **of** praise! R.

O come, let us worship and · **bow** down,
let us kneel before the Lord, · **our** Maker!
For he is our God, and we are the people of · **his** pasture,
and the sheep of · **his** hand. R.

O that today you would listen to · **his** voice!
Do not harden your hearts, as at Meribah, as on the day at Massah in · **the** wilderness,
when your ancestors tested me, and put me to · **the** proof,
though they had seen · **my** work. R.

Common Psalm for Ordinary Time

Psalm 95

Guitar

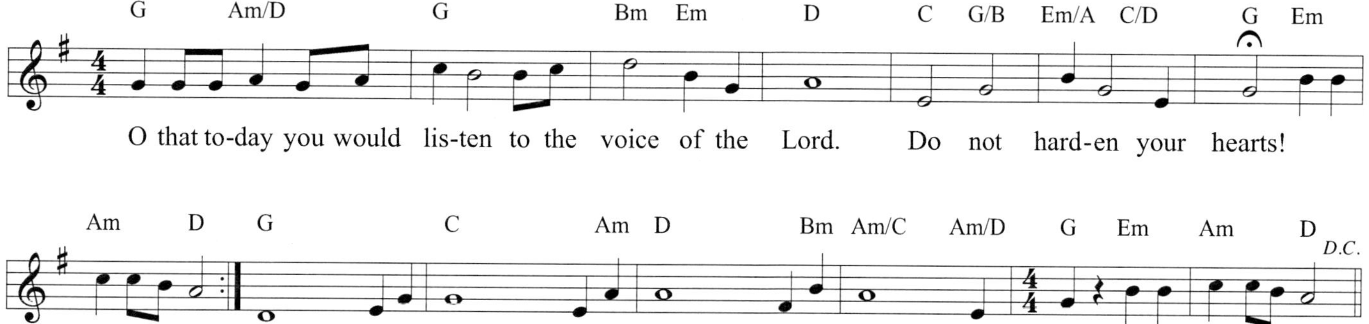

O come, let us sing to · **the** Lord;
let us make a joyful noise to the rock of our · **sal**-vation!
Let us come into his presence with · **thanks**-giving;
let us make a joyful noise to him with songs · **of** praise! R.

O come, let us worship and · **bow** down,
let us kneel before the Lord, · **our** Maker!
For he is our God, and we are the people of · **his** pasture,
and the sheep of · **his** hand. R.

O that today you would listen to · **his** voice!
Do not harden your hearts, as at Meribah, as on the day at Massah in · **the** wilderness,
when your ancestors tested me, and put me to · **the** proof,
though they had seen · **my** work. R.

C Instrument

B♭ Instrument

Common Psalm for Ordinary Time

Psalm 100

Make a joyful noise to the Lord, all · **the** earth.
Worship the Lord with · **gladness;**
come into his presence · **with** singing. R.

Know that the Lord · **is** God.
It is he that made us, and we are · **his;**
we are his people, and the sheep of · **his** pasture. R.

For the Lord · **is** good;
his steadfast love endures for·-**ever,**
and his faithfulness to all · **gener**-ations. R.

Common Psalm for Ordinary Time

Psalm 100

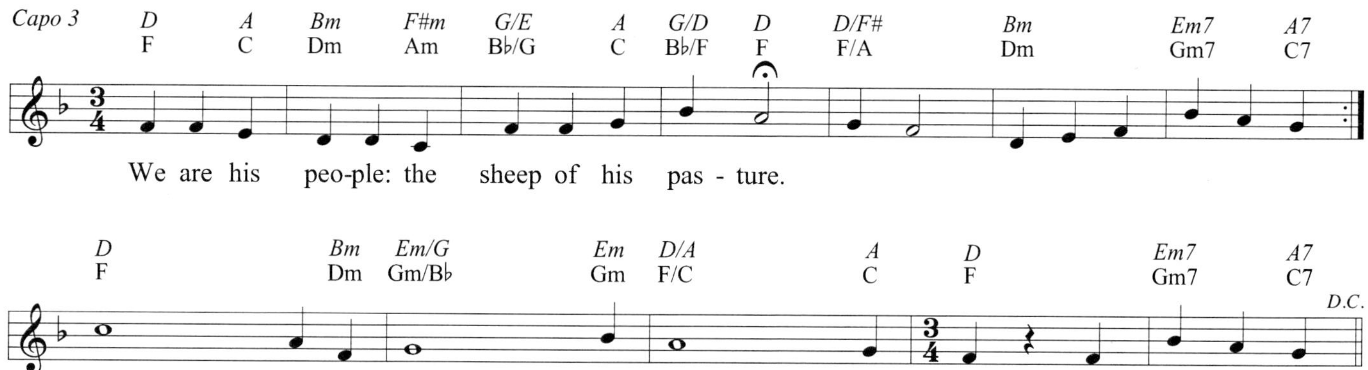

Make a joyful noise to the Lord, all · **the** earth.
Worship the Lord with · **gladness;**
come into his presence · **with** singing. R.

Know that the Lord · **is** God.
It is he that made us, and we are · **his;**
we are his people, and the sheep of · **his** pasture. R.

For the Lord · **is** good;
his steadfast love endures for·-**ever,**
and his faithfulness to all · **gener**-ations. R.

157

Common Psalm for Ordinary Time

Psalm 103

Bless the Lord, O my · **soul,**
and all that is within me, bless his · **holy** name.
Bless the Lord, O my · **soul,**
and do not forget all · **his** benefits. R.

It is the Lord who forgives all your in·-**iquity,**
who heals all your · **dis**-eases,
who redeems your life from the · **Pit,**
who crowns you with steadfast love · **and** mercy. R.

The Lord is merciful and · **gracious,**
slow to anger and abounding in stead·-**fast** love.
He does not deal with us according to our · **sins,**
nor repay us according to our · **in**-iquities. R.

As far as the east is from the · **west,**
so far he removes our transgressions · **from** us.
As a father has compassion for his · **children,**
so the Lord has compassion for those · **who** fear_him. R.

Common Psalm for Ordinary Time

Psalm 103

Guitar

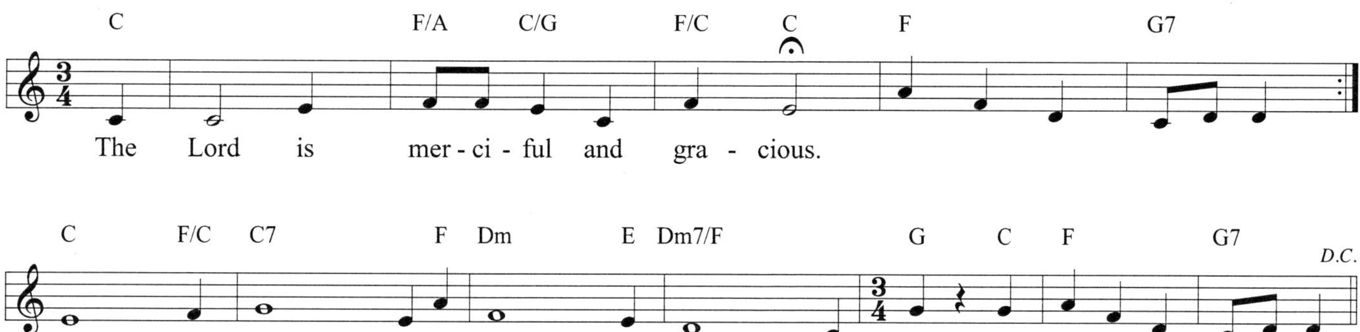

Bless the Lord, O my · **soul,**
and all that is within me, bless his · **holy** name.
Bless the Lord, O my · **soul,**
and do not forget all · **his** benefits. R.

It is the Lord who forgives all your in·-**iquity,**
who heals all your · **dis**-eases,
who redeems your life from the · **Pit,**
who crowns you with steadfast love · **and** mercy. R.

The Lord is merciful and · **gracious,**
slow to anger and abounding in stead·-**fast** love.
He does not deal with us according to our · **sins,**
nor repay us according to our · **in**-iquities. R.

As far as the east is from the · **west,**
so far he removes our transgressions · **from** us.
As a father has compassion for his · **children,**
so the Lord has compassion for those · **who** fear_him. R.

C Instrument

B♭ Instrument

Common Psalm for Ordinary Time

Psalm 145

I will extol you, my God and · **King,**
and bless your name forever and · **ever.**
Every day I will · **bless_you,**
and praise your name forever · **and** ever. R.

The Lord is gracious and · **merciful,**
slow to anger and abounding in steadfast · **love.**
The Lord is good to · **all,**
and his compassion is over all that he · **has** made. R.

All your works shall give thanks to you, O · **Lord,**
and all your faithful shall · **bless_you.**
They shall speak of the glory of your · **kingdom,**
and tell of · **your** power. R.

The Lord is faithful in all his · **words,**
and gracious in all his · **deeds.**
The Lord upholds all who are · **falling,**
and raises up all who are · **bowed** down. R.

Common Psalm for Ordinary Time

Psalm 145

Guitar

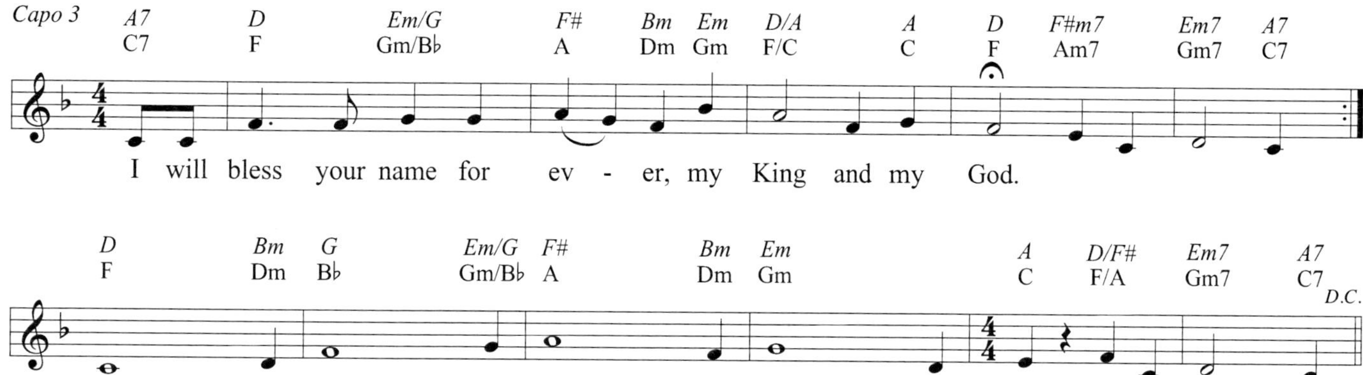

I will extol you, my God and · **King,**
and bless your name forever and · **ever.**
Every day I will · **bless_you,**
and praise your name forever · **and** ever. R.

The Lord is gracious and · **merciful,**
slow to anger and abounding in steadfast · **love.**
The Lord is good to · **all,**
and his compassion is over all that he · **has** made. R.

All your works shall give thanks to you, O · **Lord,**
and all your faithful shall · **bless_you.**
They shall speak of the glory of your · **kingdom,**
and tell of · **your** power. R.

The Lord is faithful in all his · **words,**
and gracious in all his · **deeds.**
The Lord upholds all who are · **falling,**
and raises up all who are · **bowed** down. R.

C Instrument

B♭ Instrument

161

Common Psalm for the Last Weeks of Ordinary Time

Psalm 122

I was glad when they said · **to** me,
"Let us go to the house of · **the** Lord!"
Our feet · **are** standing
within your gates, O · **Je**-rusalem. R.

Jerusalem—built as · **a** city
that is bound firmly · **to**-gether.
To it the tribes · **go** up,
the tribes · **of_the** Lord. R.

As was decreed · **for** Israel,
to give thanks to the name of · **the** Lord.
For there the thrones for judgment · **were_set** up,
the thrones of the · **house_of** David. R.

Pray for the peace of · **Je**-rusalem:
"May they prosper · **who** love_you.
Peace be within · **your** walls,
and security within · **your** towers." R.

For the sake of my relatives · **and** friends
I will say, "Peace be · **with**-in_you."
For the sake of the house of the Lord · **our** God,
I will seek · **your** good. R.

Common Psalm for the Last Weeks of Ordinary Time
Psalm 122

Guitar

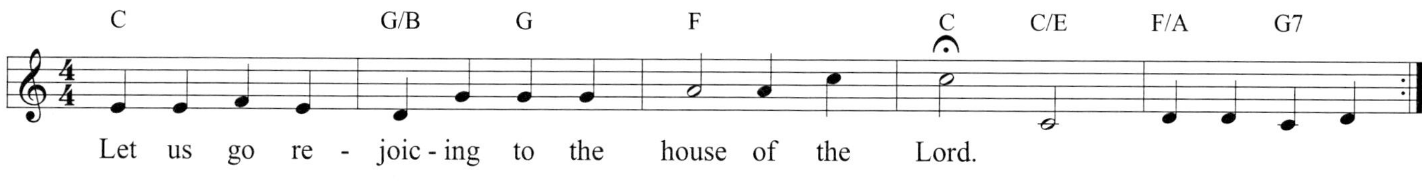

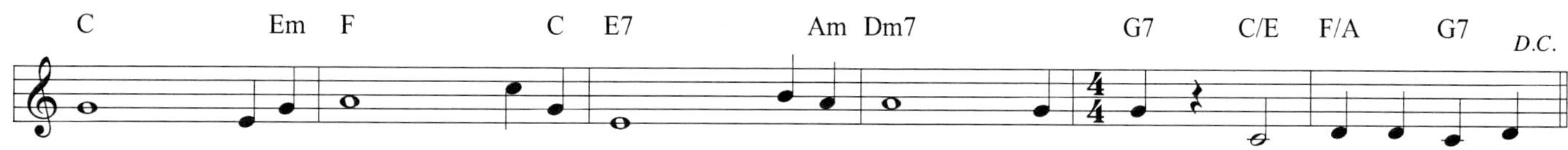

I was glad when they said · **to** me,
"Let us go to the house of · **the** Lord!"
Our feet · **are** standing
within your gates, O · **Je**-rusalem. R.

Jerusalem—built as · **a** city
that is bound firmly · **to**-gether.
To it the tribes · **go** up,
the tribes · **of_the** Lord. R.

As was decreed · **for** Israel,
to give thanks to the name of · **the** Lord.
For there the thrones for judgment · **were_set** up,
the thrones of the · **house_of** David. R.

Pray for the peace of · **Je**-rusalem:
"May they prosper · **who** love_you.
Peace be within · **your** walls,
and security within · **your** towers." R.

For the sake of my relatives · **and** friends
I will say, "Peace be · **with**-in_you."
For the sake of the house of the Lord · **our** God,
I will seek · **your** good. R.

C Instrument

B♭ Instrument

163

Second Sunday in Ordinary Time – C

Psalm 96

O sing to the Lord · **a** new song;
sing to the Lord, · **all** the earth.
Sing to the Lord, · **bless** his name;
tell of his salvation from · **day** to day. R.

Declare his glory a·-**mong** the nations,
his marvellous works among · **all** the peoples.
For great is the Lord, and greatly · **to** be praised;
he is to be revered a·-**bove** all gods. R.

Ascribe to the Lord, O families · **of** the peoples,
ascribe to the Lord · **glory** and strength.
Ascribe to the Lord the glory · **due** his name;
bring an offering, and come · **into** his courts. R.

Worship the Lord in · **ho**-ly splendour;
tremble before him, · **all** the earth.
Say among the nations, "The · **Lord** is king!
He will judge the · **peoples** with equity." R.

Second Sunday in Ordinary Time – C

Psalm 96

Guitar

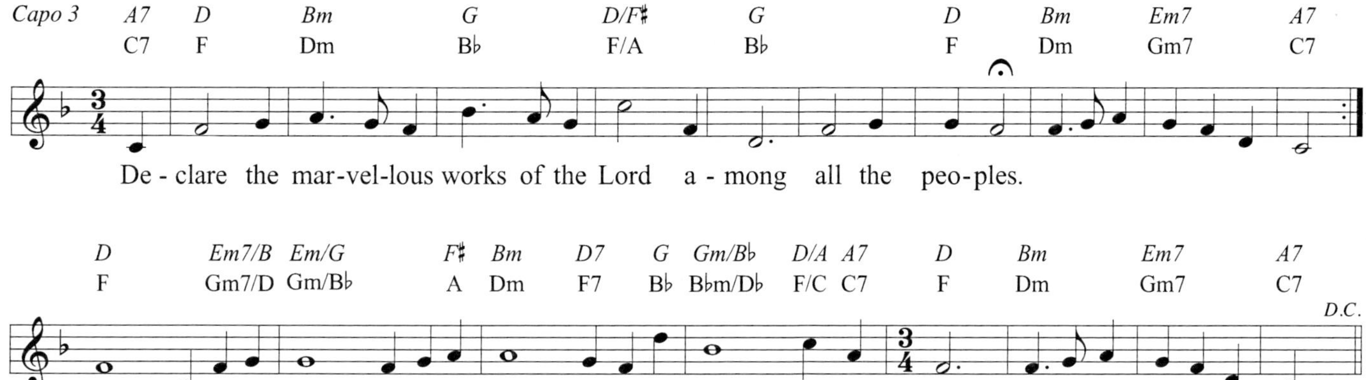

O sing to the Lord · **a** new song;
sing to the Lord, · **all** the earth.
Sing to the Lord, · **bless** his name;
tell of his salvation from · **day** to day. R.

Declare his glory a·-**mong** the nations,
his marvellous works among · **all** the peoples.
For great is the Lord, and greatly · **to** be praised;
he is to be revered a·-**bove** all gods. R.

Ascribe to the Lord, O families · **of** the peoples,
ascribe to the Lord · **glory** and strength.
Ascribe to the Lord the glory · **due** his name;
bring an offering, and come · **into** his courts. R.

Worship the Lord in · **ho**-ly splendour;
tremble before him, · **all** the earth.
Say among the nations, "The · **Lord** is king!
He will judge the · **peoples** with equity." R.

C Instrument

B♭ Instrument

165

Third Sunday in Ordinary Time – C

Psalm 19

The law of the Lord is · **perfect,**
reviving the · **soul;**
the decrees of the Lord are · **sure,**
making wise · **the** simple. R.

The precepts of the Lord are · **right,**
rejoicing the · **heart;**
the commandment of the Lord is · **clear,**
enlightening · **the** eyes. R.

The fear of the Lord is · **pure,**
enduring for·-**ever;**
the ordinances of the Lord are · **true**
and righteous · **alto**-gether. R.

Let the words of my · **mouth**
and the meditation of my · **heart**
be acceptable to · **you,**
O Lord, my rock and · **my_re**-deemer. R.

Guitar

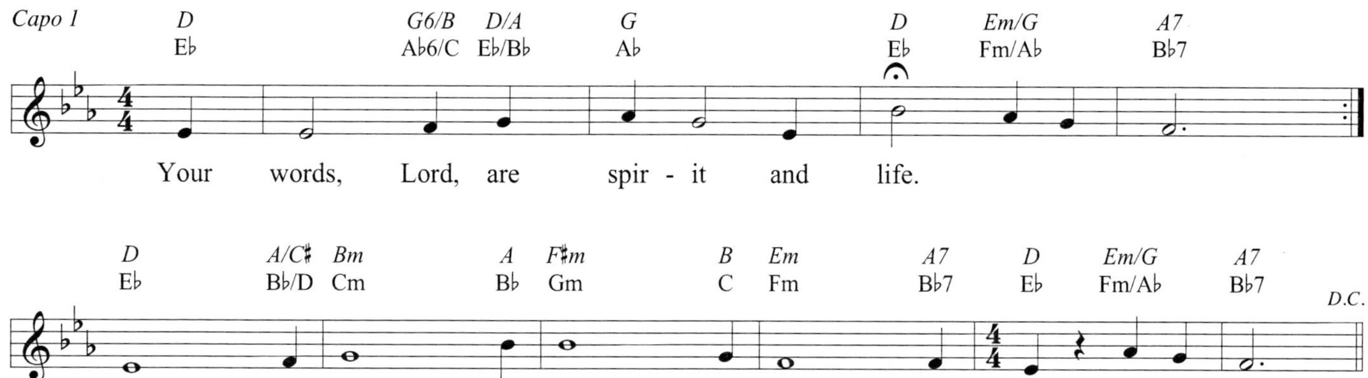

The law of the Lord is · **perfect,**
reviving the · **soul;**
the decrees of the Lord are · **sure,**
making wise · **the** simple. R.

The precepts of the Lord are · **right,**
rejoicing the · **heart;**
the commandment of the Lord is · **clear,**
enlightening · **the** eyes. R.

The fear of the Lord is · **pure,**
enduring for·-**ever;**
the ordinances of the Lord are · **true**
and righteous · **alto**-gether. R.

Let the words of my · **mouth**
and the meditation of my · **heart**
be acceptable to · **you,**
O Lord, my rock and · **my_re**-deemer. R.

C Instrument

B♭ Instrument

Fourth Sunday in Ordinary Time – C

Psalm 71

In you, O Lord, I · **take** refuge;
let me never be · **put** to shame.
In your righteousness de·-**liver_me** and rescue_me;
incline your ear to · **me** and save_me. R.

Be to me a rock · **of** refuge,
a strong · **fortress,** to save_me,
for you are my rock · **and** my fortress.
Rescue me, O my God, from the · **hand_of** the wicked. R.

For you, O Lord, are · **my** hope,
my trust, O Lord, · **from** my youth.
Upon you I have leaned · **from** my birth;
from my mother's womb you have · **been** my strength. R.

My mouth will tell of your right·-**eous** acts,
of your deeds of salvation · **all** day long.
O God, from my youth · **you** have taught_me,
and I still proclaim your · **won**-drous deeds. R.

Fourth Sunday in Ordinary Time – C

Psalm 71

Guitar

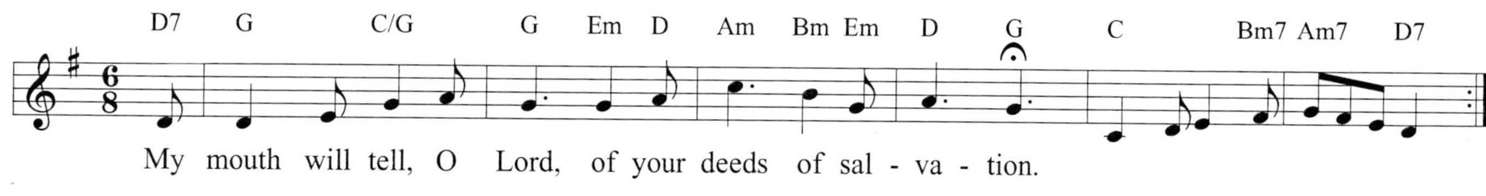

In you, O Lord, I · **take** refuge;
let me never be · **put** to shame.
In your righteousness de-·**liver_me** and rescue_me;
incline your ear to · **me** and save_me. R.

Be to me a rock · **of** refuge,
a strong · **fortress,** to save_me,
for you are my rock · **and** my fortress.
Rescue me, O my God, from the · **hand_of** the wicked. R.

For you, O Lord, are · **my** hope,
my trust, O Lord, · **from** my youth.
Upon you I have leaned · **from** my birth;
from my mother's womb you have · **been** my strength. R.

My mouth will tell of your right-·**eous** acts,
of your deeds of salvation · **all** day long.
O God, from my youth · **you** have taught_me,
and I still proclaim your · **won**-drous deeds. R.

C Instrument

B♭ Instrument

169

Fifth Sunday in Ordinary Time – C

Psalm 138

I give you thanks, O Lord, with my · **whole** heart;
before the Angels I sing · **your** praise;
I bow down toward your holy temple, and give thanks to · **your** name
for your steadfast · **love_and** your faithfulness. R.

For you have exalted · **your** name
and your word a·-**bove** everything.
On the day I called, · **you** answered_me,
you increased my · **strength** of soul. R.

All the kings of the earth shall praise you, · **O** Lord,
for they have heard the words of · **your** mouth.
They shall sing of the ways of · **the** Lord,
for great is the · **glory** of_the Lord. R.

You stretch out your hand, and your right hand · **de**-livers_me.
The Lord will fulfill his purpose · **for** me;
your steadfast love, O Lord, endures · **for**-ever.
Do not forsake the · **work_of** your hands. R.

Fifth Sunday in Ordinary Time – C

Psalm 138

Guitar

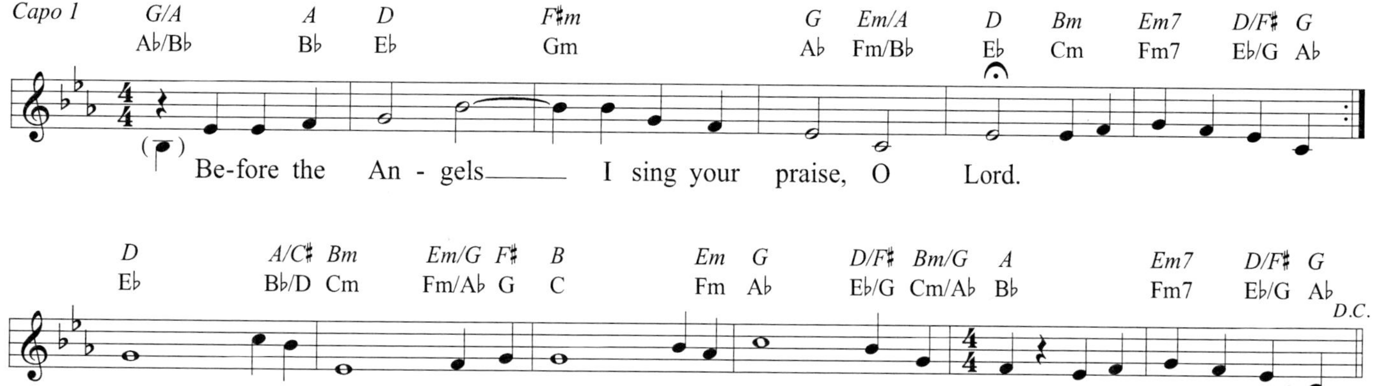

I give you thanks, O Lord, with my · **whole** heart;
before the Angels I sing · **your** praise;
I bow down toward your holy temple, and give thanks to · **your** name
for your steadfast · **love_and** your faithfulness. R.

For you have exalted · **your** name
and your word a·-**bove** everything.
On the day I called, · **you** answered_me,
you increased my · **strength** of soul. R.

All the kings of the earth shall praise you, · **O Lord,**
for they have heard the words of · **your** mouth.
They shall sing of the ways of · **the** Lord,
for great is the · **glory** of_the Lord. R.

You stretch out your hand, and your right hand · **de**-livers_me.
The Lord will fulfill his purpose · **for** me;
your steadfast love, O Lord, endures · **for**-ever.
Do not forsake the · **work_of** your hands. R.

C Instrument

B♭ Instrument

171

Sixth Sunday in Ordinary Time – C

Psalm 1

Blessed is the man who does not follow the advice of the · **wicked,**
or take the path that sinners tread, or sit in the seat of · **scoffers;**
but whose delight is in the law of the · **Lord,**
and on his law meditates day · **and** night. R.

He is like a tree planted by streams of · **water,**
which yields its fruit in its · **season,**
and its leaves do not · **wither.**
And everything he · **does,** prospers. R.

The wicked are not · **so,**
but are like chaff that the wind drives a·-**way,**
for the Lord watches over the way of the · **righteous,**
but the way of the wicked · **will** perish. R.

Sixth Sunday in Ordinary Time – C

Psalm 1

Guitar

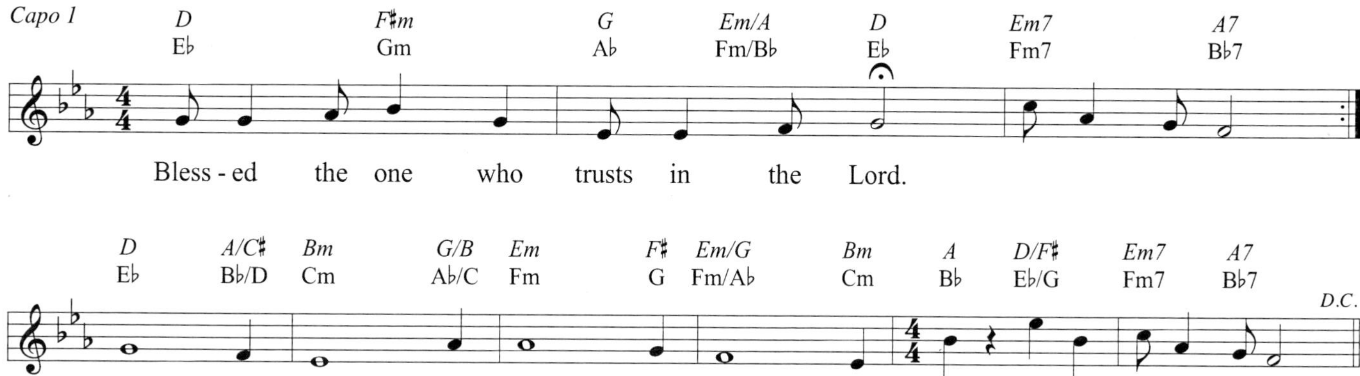

Blessed is the man who does not follow the advice of the · **wicked,**
or take the path that sinners tread, or sit in the seat of · **scoffers;**
but whose delight is in the law of the · **Lord,**
and on his law meditates day · **and** night. R.

He is like a tree planted by streams of · **water,**
which yields its fruit in its · **season,**
and its leaves do not · **wither.**
And everything he · **does,** prospers. R.

The wicked are not · **so,**
but are like chaff that the wind drives a·-**way,**
for the Lord watches over the way of the · **righteous,**
but the way of the wicked · **will** perish. R.

C Instrument

B♭ Instrument

173

Seventh Sunday in Ordinary Time – C

Psalm 103

Bless the Lord, O my · **soul,**
and all that is within me, bless his · **holy** name.
Bless the Lord, O my · **soul,**
and do not forget all · **his** benefits. R.

It is the Lord who forgives all your in·-**iquity,**
who heals all your · **dis**-eases,
who redeems your life from the · **Pit,**
who crowns you with steadfast love · **and** mercy. R.

The Lord is merciful and · **gracious,**
slow to anger and abounding in stead·-**fast** love.
He does not deal with us according to our · **sins,**
nor repay us according to our · **in**-iquities. R.

As far as the east is from the · **west,**
so far he removes our transgressions · **from** us.
As a father has compassion for his · **children,**
so the Lord has compassion for those · **who** fear_him. R.

Seventh Sunday in Ordinary Time – C

Psalm 103

Guitar

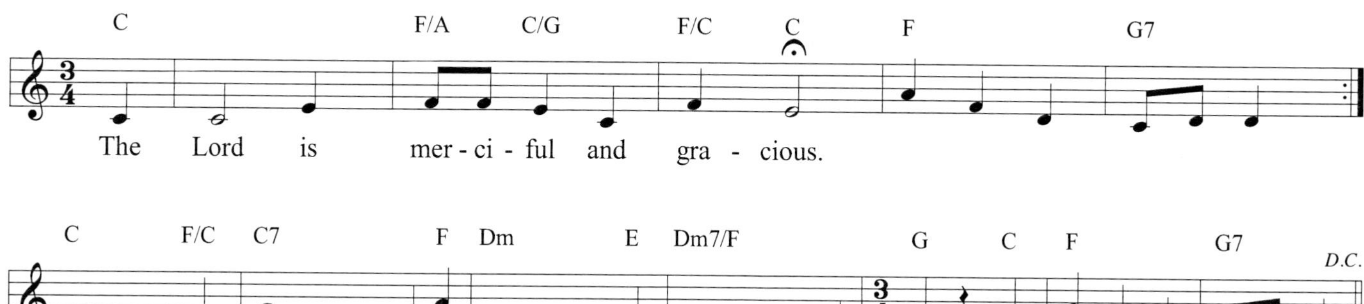

Bless the Lord, O my · **soul,**
and all that is within me, bless his · **holy** name.
Bless the Lord, O my · **soul,**
and do not forget all · **his** benefits. R.

It is the Lord who forgives all your in·-**iquity,**
who heals all your · **dis**-eases,
who redeems your life from the · **Pit,**
who crowns you with steadfast love · **and** mercy. R.

The Lord is merciful and · **gracious,**
slow to anger and abounding in stead·-**fast** love.
He does not deal with us according to our · **sins,**
nor repay us according to our · **in**-iquities. R.

As far as the east is from the · **west,**
so far he removes our transgressions · **from** us.
As a father has compassion for his · **children,**
so the Lord has compassion for those · **who** fear_him. R.

C Instrument

B♭ Instrument

Eighth Sunday in Ordinary Time – C

Psalm 92

It is good to give thanks · **to** the Lord,
to sing praises to your name, · **O** Most High;
to declare your steadfast love · **in** the morning,
and your · **faithfulness** by night. R.

The righteous flourish · **like** the palm_tree,
and grow like a · **cedar** in Lebanon.
They are planted in the house · **of** the Lord;
they flourish in the · **courts_of** our God. R.

In old age they · **still_pro**-duce fruit;
they are always green and · **full** of sap,
showing that the · **Lord** is upright;
he is my rock, and there is no un·-**righteousness** in him. R.

Eighth Sunday in Ordinary Time – C

Psalm 92

Guitar

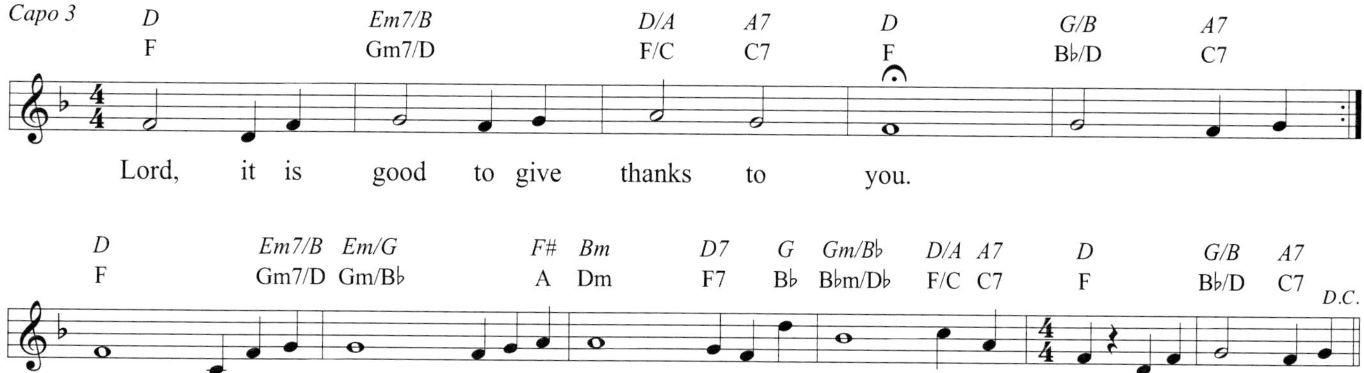

It is good to give thanks · **to** the Lord,
to sing praises to your name, · **O** Most High;
to declare your steadfast love · **in** the morning,
and your · **faithfulness** by night. R.

The righteous flourish · **like** the palm_tree,
and grow like a · **cedar** in Lebanon.
They are planted in the house · **of** the Lord;
they flourish in the · **courts_of** our God. R.

In old age they · **still_pro**-duce fruit;
they are always green and · **full** of sap,
showing that the · **Lord** is upright;
he is my rock, and there is no un·-**righteousness** in him. R.

C Instrument

B♭ Instrument

Ninth Sunday in Ordinary Time – C

Psalm 117

Praise the Lord, · **all** you nations!
Extol him, · **all** you peoples! R.

For great is his steadfast · **love** toward us,
and the faithfulness of the Lord en·-**dures** for-ever. R.

Ninth Sunday in Ordinary Time – C

Psalm 117

Guitar

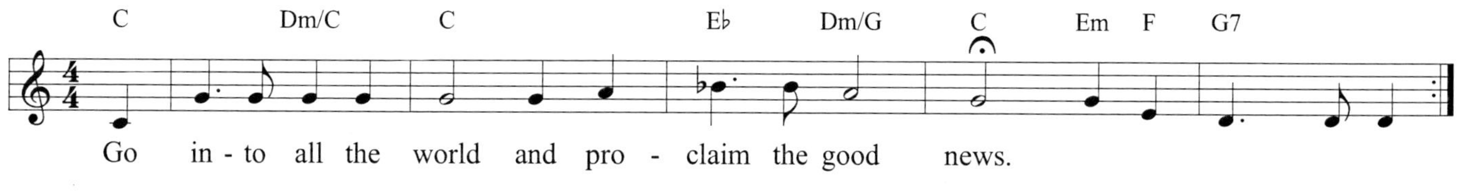

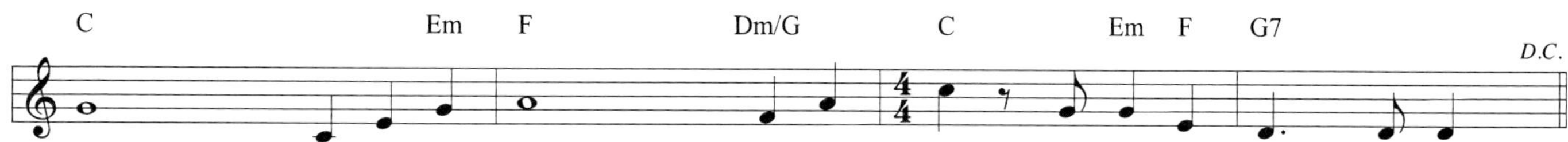

Praise the Lord, · **all** you nations!
Extol him, · **all** you peoples! R.

For great is his steadfast · **love** toward us,
and the faithfulness of the Lord en·-**dures** for-ever. R.

C Instrument

B♭ Instrument

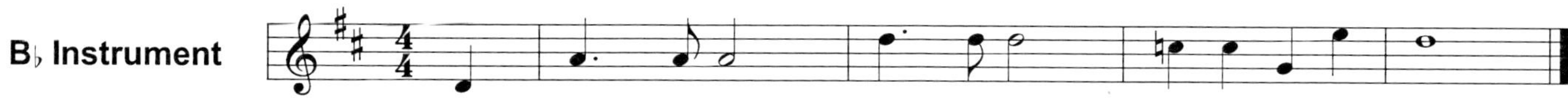

179

Tenth Sunday in Ordinary Time – C

Psalm 30

I will extol you, O Lord, for you have drawn me · **up,**
and did not let my foes rejoice · **over_me.**
O Lord, you brought up my soul from · **Sheol,**
restored me to life from among those gone down · **to_the** Pit. R.

Sing praises to the Lord, O you his · **faithful_ones,**
and give thanks to his holy · **name.**
For his anger is but for a moment; his favour is for a · **lifetime.**
Weeping may linger for the night, but joy comes · **with_the** morning. R.

Hear, O Lord, and be gracious to · **me!**
O Lord, be my · **helper!**
You have turned my mourning into · **dancing.**
O Lord my God, I will give thanks to you · **for**-ever. R.

Tenth Sunday in Ordinary Time – C

Psalm 30

Guitar

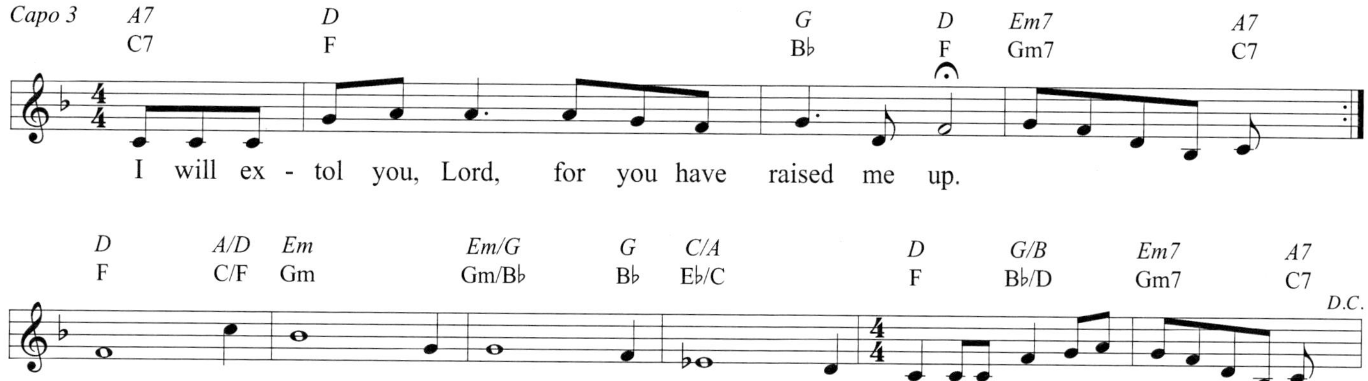

I will extol you, O Lord, for you have drawn me · **up,**
and did not let my foes rejoice · **over_me.**
O Lord, you brought up my soul from · **Sheol,**
restored me to life from among those gone down · **to_the** Pit. R.

Sing praises to the Lord, O you his · **faithful_ones,**
and give thanks to his holy · **name.**
For his anger is but for a moment; his favour is for a · **lifetime.**
Weeping may linger for the night, but joy comes · **with_the** morning. R.

Hear, O Lord, and be gracious to · **me!**
O Lord, be my · **helper!**
You have turned my mourning into · **dancing.**
O Lord my God, I will give thanks to you · **for**-ever. R.

C Instrument

B♭ Instrument

181

Eleventh Sunday in Ordinary Time – C

Psalm 32

Blessed is the one whose transgression is for·-**given,**
whose sin is · **covered.**
Blessed is the one to whom the Lord imputes no · in-**iquity,**
and in whose spirit there is no · de-**ceit.** R.

I acknowledged my sin to · **you,**
and I did not hide my in·-**iquity;**
I said, "I will confess my transgressions to the · **Lord,"**
and you forgave the guilt of my · **sin.** R.

1 - You are a hiding place for · **me;**
2 - you preserve me from · **trouble;**
4 - you surround me with glad cries of de·-**liverance.** R.

1 - Be glad in the Lord and rejoice, O · **righteous,**
4 - and shout for joy, all you upright in · **heart.** R.

Eleventh Sunday in Ordinary Time – C

Psalm 32

Guitar

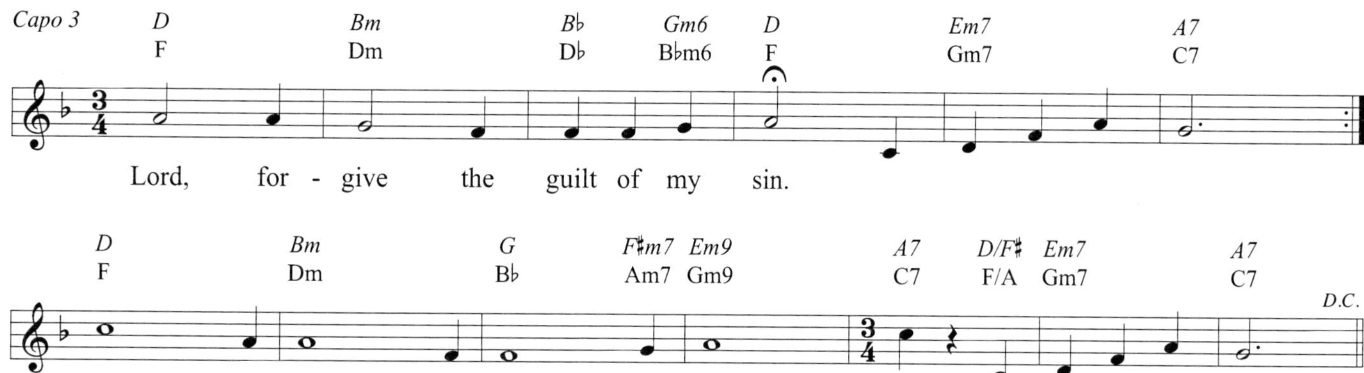

Blessed is the one whose transgression is for·-**given,**
whose sin is · **covered.**
Blessed is the one to whom the Lord imputes no · in-**iquity,**
and in whose spirit there is no · de-**ceit.** R.

I acknowledged my sin to · **you,**
and I did not hide my in·-**iquity;**
I said, "I will confess my transgressions to the · **Lord,"**
and you forgave the guilt of my · **sin.** R.

1 - You are a hiding place for · **me;**
2 - you preserve me from · **trouble;**
4 - you surround me with glad cries of de·-**liverance.** R.

1 - Be glad in the Lord and rejoice, O · **righteous,**
4 - and shout for joy, all you upright in · **heart.** R.

C Instrument

B♭ Instrument

183

Twelfth Sunday in Ordinary Time – C

Psalm 63

O God, you are my God, I · **seek_you,**
my soul · **thirsts_for_you;**
my flesh · **faints_for_you,**
as in a dry and weary land where there · **is** no water. R.

So I have looked upon you in the · **sanctuary,**
beholding your power and · **glory.**
Because your steadfast love is better than · **life,**
my · **lips** will praise_you. R.

So I will bless you as long as I · **live;**
I will lift up my hands and call on your · **name.**
My soul is satisfied as with a rich · **feast,**
and my mouth praises you with · **joy**-ful lips. R.

For you have been my · **help,**
and in the shadow of your wings I sing for · **joy.**
My soul · **clings_to_you;**
your right · **hand** up-holds_me. R.

Twelfth Sunday in Ordinary Time – C

Psalm 63

Guitar

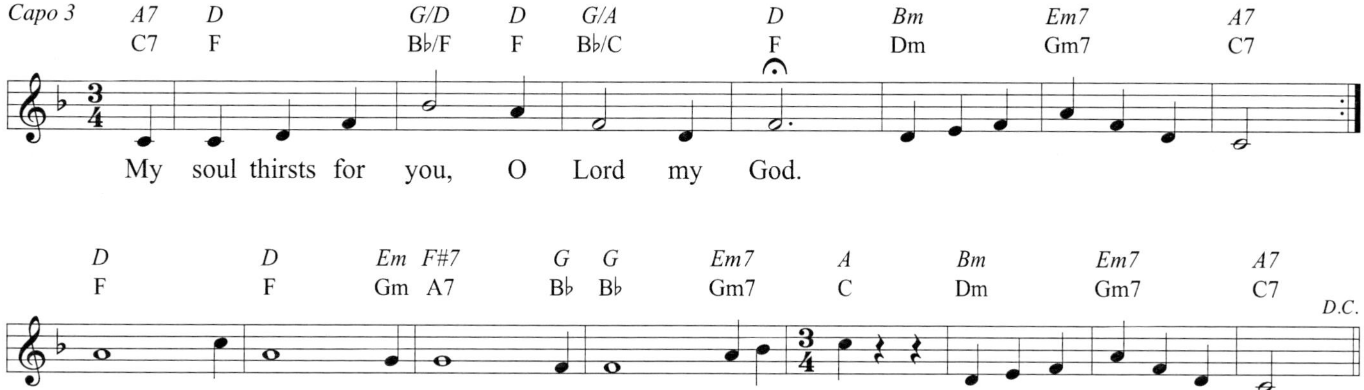

O God, you are my God, I · **seek_you,**
my soul · **thirsts_for_you;**
my flesh · **faints_for_you,**
as in a dry and weary land where there · **is** no water. R.

So I have looked upon you in the · **sanctuary,**
beholding your power and · **glory.**
Because your steadfast love is better than · **life,**
my · **lips** will praise_you. R.

So I will bless you as long as I · **live;**
I will lift up my hands and call on your · **name.**
My soul is satisfied as with a rich · **feast,**
and my mouth praises you with · **joy**-ful lips. R.

For you have been my · **help,**
and in the shadow of your wings I sing for · **joy.**
My soul · **clings_to_you;**
your right · **hand** up-holds_me. R.

185

Thirteenth Sunday in Ordinary Time – C

Psalm 16

Protect me, O God, for in you I · **take** refuge.
I say to the Lord, "You are · **my** Lord;
I have no good apart · **from** you."
The Lord is my chosen portion and my cup; you · **hold** my lot. R.

I bless the Lord who gives · **me** counsel;
in the night also my heart · **in**-structs_me.
I keep the Lord always · **be**-fore_me;
because he is at my right hand, I shall · **not** be moved. R.

Therefore my heart is glad, and my soul · **re**-joices;
my body also rests · **se**-cure.
For you do not give me up · **to** Sheol,
or let your faithful one · **see** the Pit. R.

1 - You show me the path · **of** life.
2 - In your presence there is fullness · **of** joy;
4 - in your right hand are pleasures for-·**ev**-er-more. R.

Thirteenth Sunday in Ordinary Time – C

Psalm 16

Guitar

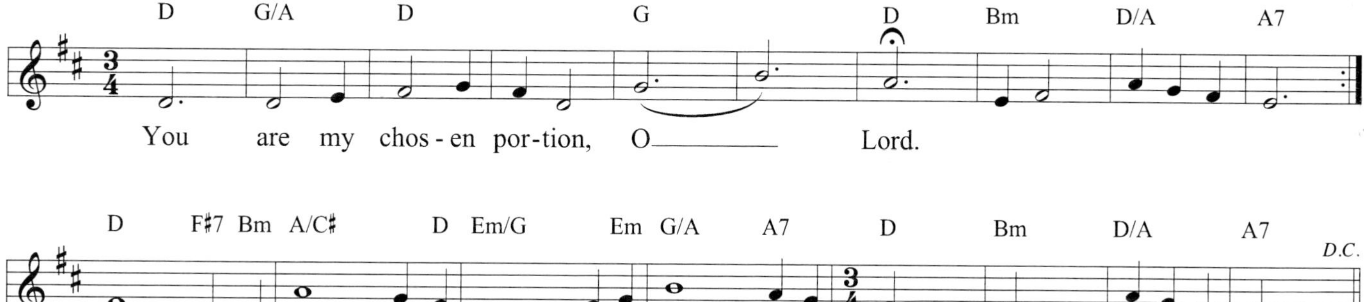

Protect me, O God, for in you I · **take** refuge.
I say to the Lord, "You are · **my** Lord;
I have no good apart · **from** you."
The Lord is my chosen portion and my cup; you · **hold** my lot. R.

I bless the Lord who gives · **me** counsel;
in the night also my heart · **in**-structs_me.
I keep the Lord always · **be**-fore_me;
because he is at my right hand, I shall · **not** be moved. R.

Therefore my heart is glad, and my soul · **re**-joices;
my body also rests · **se**-cure.
For you do not give me up · **to** Sheol,
or let your faithful one · **see** the Pit. R.

1 - You show me the path · **of** life.
2 - In your presence there is fullness · **of** joy;
4 - in your right hand are pleasures for·-**ev**-er-more. R.

C Instrument

B♭ Instrument

Fourteenth Sunday in Ordinary Time – C

Psalm 66

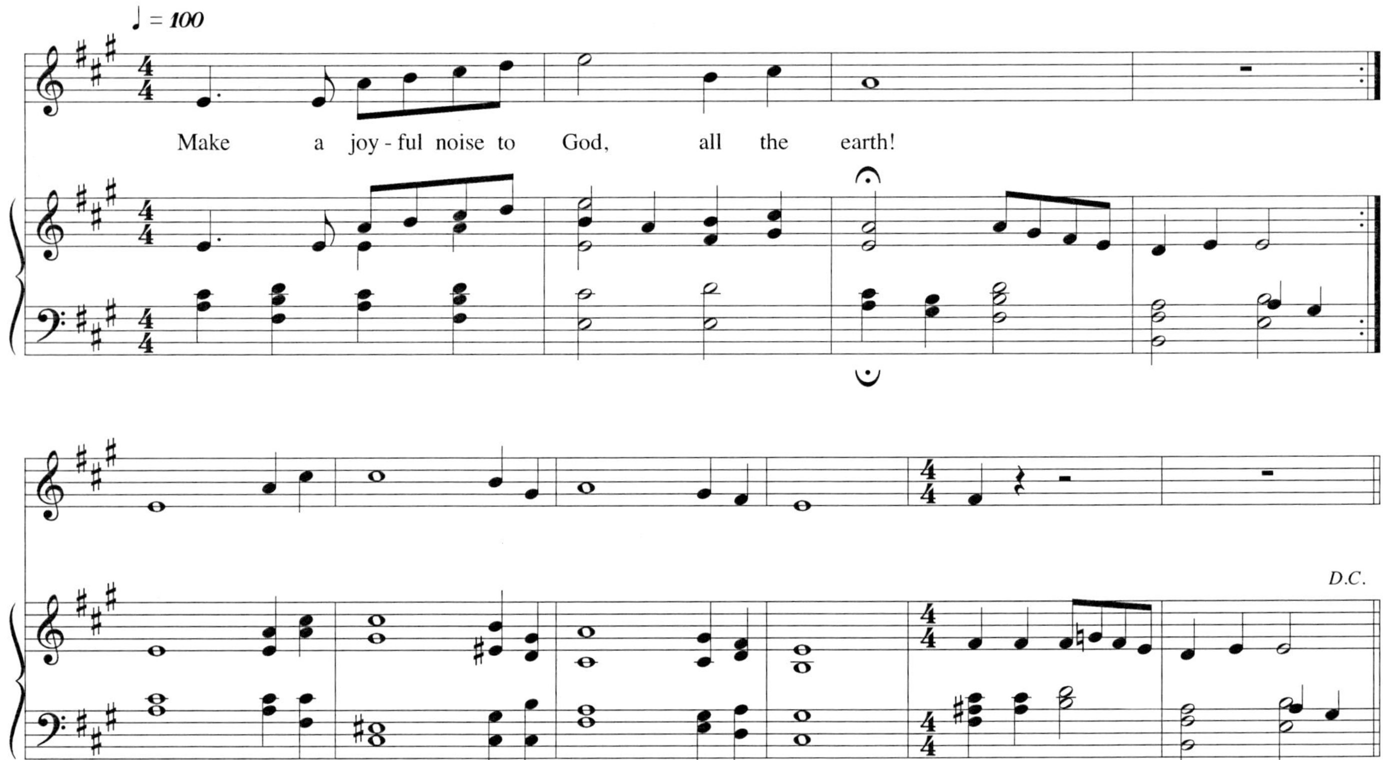

Make a joyful noise to God, all · **the** earth;
sing the glory · **of_his** name;
give to him · **glorious** praise.
Say to God, "How awesome are your · **deeds!**" R.

"All the earth · **worships** you;
they sing praises to you, sing praises · **to_your** name."
Come and see what God · **has** done:
he is awesome in his deeds among the children of · **Adam.** R.

He turned the sea into · **dry** land;
they passed through the river · **on** foot.
There we rejoiced · **in** him,
who rules by his might for-·**ever.** R.

Come and hear, all you who · **fear** God,
and I will tell what he · **has** done_for_me.
Blessed be God, because he has not rejected · **my** prayer
or removed his steadfast love from · **me.** R.

Fourteenth Sunday in Ordinary Time – C

Psalm 66

Guitar

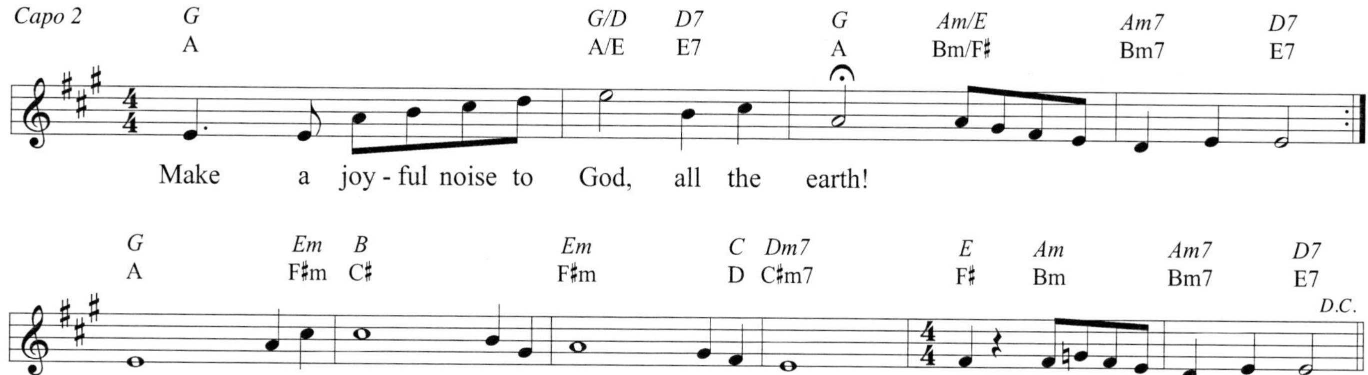

Make a joyful noise to God, all · **the** earth;
sing the glory · **of_his** name;
give to him · **glorious** praise.
Say to God, "How awesome are your · **deeds!"** R.

"All the earth · **worships** you;
they sing praises to you, sing praises · **to_your** name."
Come and see what God · **has** done:
he is awesome in his deeds among the children of · **Adam.** R.

He turned the sea into · **dry** land;
they passed through the river · **on** foot.
There we rejoiced · **in** him,
who rules by his might for-**ever.** R.

Come and hear, all you who · **fear** God,
and I will tell what he · **has** done_for_me.
Blessed be God, because he has not rejected · **my** prayer
or removed his steadfast love from · **me.** R.

C Instrument

B♭ Instrument

189

Fifteenth Sunday in Ordinary Time (1) – C

Psalm 69

As for me, my prayer is to you, · **O** Lord.
At an acceptable time, O God, in the abundance of your steadfast · **love**, answer_me.
With your · **steadfast** help, rescue_me.
Answer me, O Lord, for your steadfast love is good; according to your abundant mercy, · **turn** to me. R.

But I am lowly and · **in** pain;
let your salvation, O God, · **pro**-tect_me.
I will praise the name of God · **with** a song;
I will magnify him · **with** thanks-giving. R.

1 - Let the oppressed see it and · **be** glad;
3 - you · **who** seek God,
4 - let your · **hearts** re-vive. R.

For God will · **save** Zion
and rebuild the cities · **of** Judah;
the children of his servants · **shall** in-herit_it,
those who love his · **name** shall live_in_it. R.

Fifteenth Sunday in Ordinary Time (1) – C

Psalm 69

Guitar

As for me, my prayer is to you, · **O** Lord.
At an acceptable time, O God, in the abundance of your steadfast · **love**, answer_me.
With your · **steadfast** help, rescue_me.
Answer me, O Lord, for your steadfast love is good; according to your abundant mercy, · **turn** to me. R.

But I am lowly and · **in** pain;
let your salvation, O God, · **pro**-tect_me.
I will praise the name of God · **with** a song;
I will magnify him · **with** thanks-giving. R.

1 - Let the oppressed see it and · **be** glad;
3 - you · **who** seek God,
4 - let your · **hearts** re-vive. R.

For God will · **save** Zion
and rebuild the cities · **of** Judah;
the children of his servants · **shall** in-herit_it,
those who love his · **name** shall live_in_it. R.

C Instrument

B♭ Instrument

192

Fifteenth Sunday in Ordinary Time (2) – C

Psalm 19

The law of the Lord is · **perfect,**
reviving the · **soul;**
the decrees of the Lord are · **sure,**
making wise · **the** simple. R.

The precepts of the Lord are · **right,**
rejoicing the · **heart;**
the commandment of the Lord is · **clear,**
enlightening · **the** eyes. R.

The fear of the Lord is · **pure,**
enduring for·-**ever;**
the ordinances of the Lord are · **true**
and righteous · **alto**-gether. R.

More to be desired are they than · **gold,**
even much fine · **gold;**
sweeter also than · **honey,**
and drippings · **of_the** honeycomb. R.

Fifteenth Sunday in Ordinary Time (2) – C

Psalm 19

Guitar

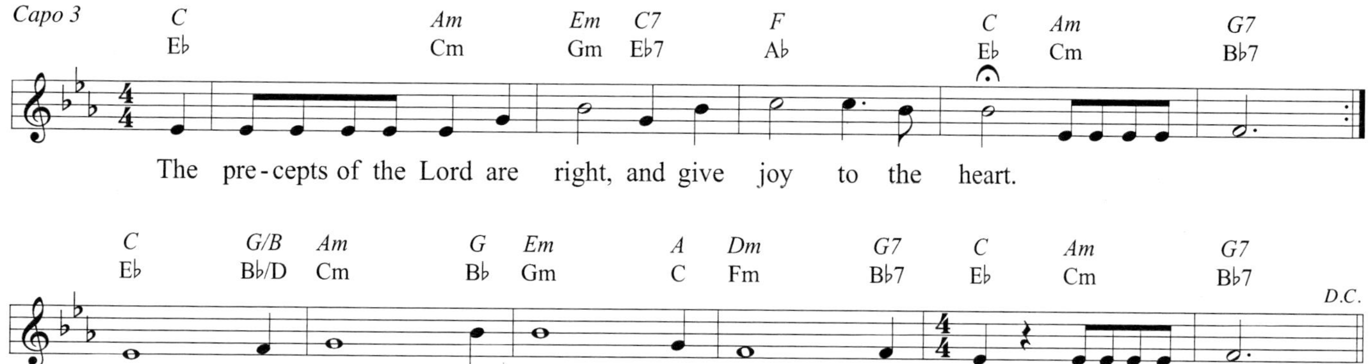

The law of the Lord is · **perfect,**
reviving the · **soul;**
the decrees of the Lord are · **sure,**
making wise · **the** simple. R.

The precepts of the Lord are · **right,**
rejoicing the · **heart;**
the commandment of the Lord is · **clear,**
enlightening · **the** eyes. R.

The fear of the Lord is · **pure,**
enduring for·-**ever;**
the ordinances of the Lord are · **true**
and righteous · **alto**-gether. R.

More to be desired are they than · **gold,**
even much fine · **gold;**
sweeter also than · **honey,**
and drippings · **of_the** honeycomb. R.

C Instrument

B♭ Instrument

Sixteenth Sunday in Ordinary Time – C

Psalm 15

Whoever walks · **blamelessly,**
and does what is · **right,**
and speaks the truth from their · **heart;**
whoever does not slander · **with_their** tongue. R.

Whoever does no evil to a · **friend,**
nor takes up a reproach against a · **neighbour;**
in whose eyes the wicked one is de·-**spised**,
but who honours those who fear · **the** Lord. R.

Whoever stands by their oath even to their · **hurt;**
who does not lend money at · **interest,**
and does not take a bribe against the · **innocent.**
One who does these things shall never · **be** moved. R.

Sixteenth Sunday in Ordinary Time – C

Psalm 15

Guitar

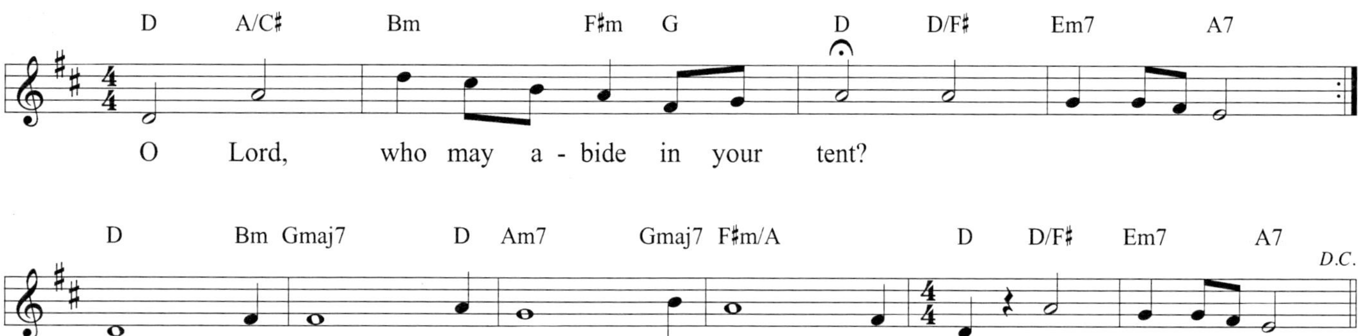

Whoever walks · **blamelessly,**
and does what is · **right,**
and speaks the truth from their · **heart;**
whoever does not slander · **with_their** tongue. R.

Whoever does no evil to a · **friend,**
nor takes up a reproach against a · **neighbour;**
in whose eyes the wicked one is de·-**spised**,
but who honours those who fear · **the** Lord. R.

Whoever stands by their oath even to their · **hurt;**
who does not lend money at · **interest,**
and does not take a bribe against the · **innocent.**
One who does these things shall never · **be** moved. R.

C Instrument

B♭ Instrument

Seventeenth Sunday in Ordinary Time – C

Psalm 138

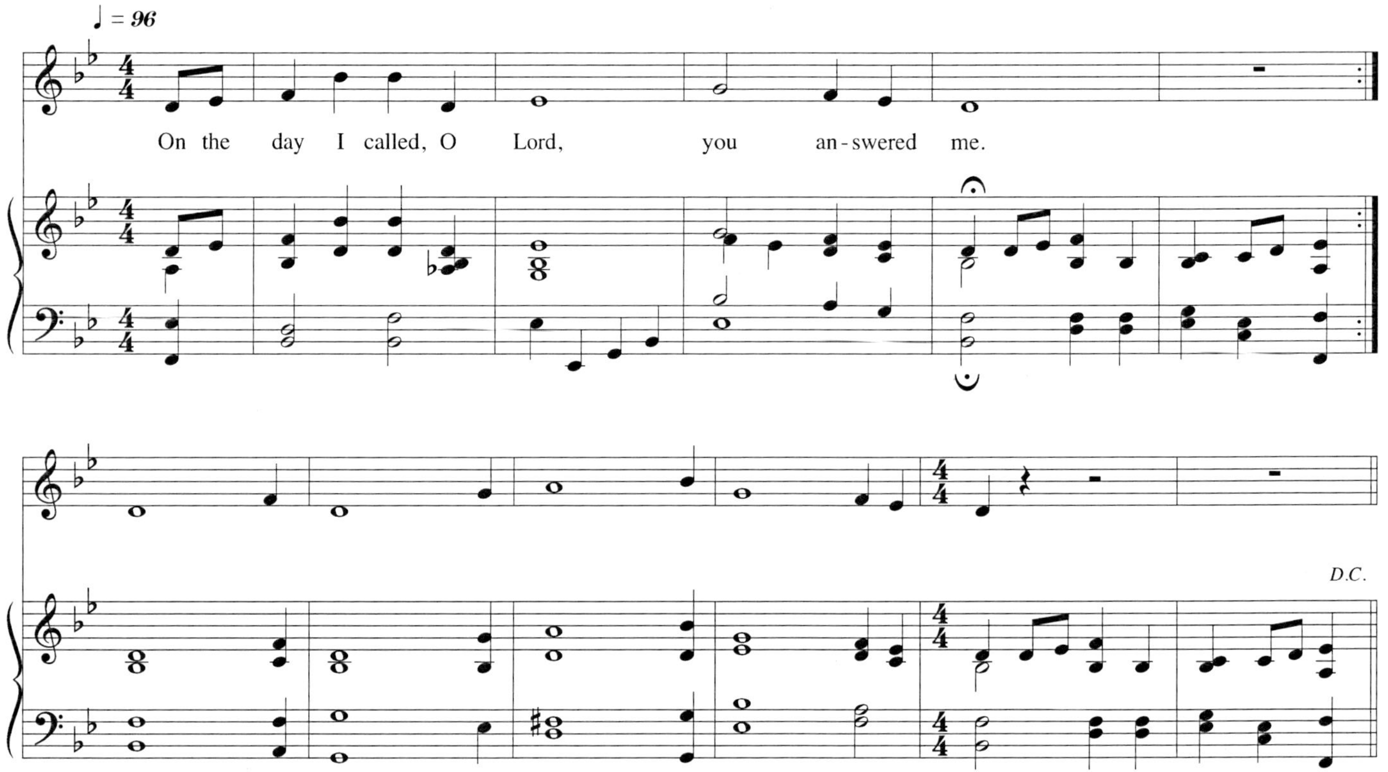

I give you thanks, O Lord, with my whole · **heart;**
before the Angels I sing your · **praise;**
I bow down toward your holy temple, and give thanks to your · **name**
for your steadfast love · **and** your faithfulness. R.

For you have exalted your · **name**
and your word above · **everything.**
On the day I called, you · **answered_me,**
you increased my · **strength** of soul. R.

For though the Lord is high, he regards the · **lowly;**
but the haughty he perceives from far a·-**way.**
Though I walk in the midst of · **trouble,**
you preserve me against the wrath · **of** my enemies. R.

You stretch out your hand and your right hand de·-**livers_me.**
The Lord will fulfill his purpose for · **me;**
your steadfast love, O Lord, endures for·-**ever.**
Do not forsake the · **work_of** your hands. R.

Seventeenth Sunday in Ordinary Time – C

Psalm 138

Guitar

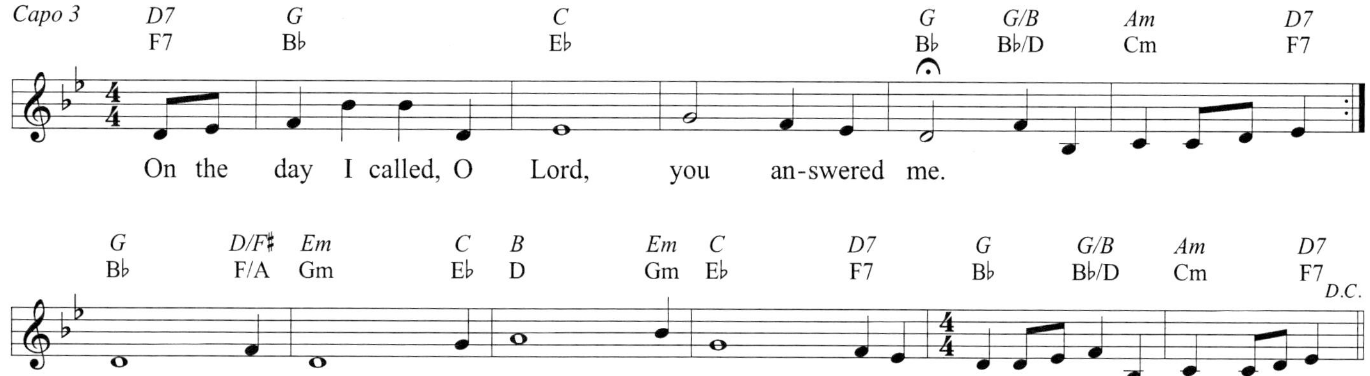

I give you thanks, O Lord, with my whole · **heart;**
before the Angels I sing your · **praise;**
I bow down toward your holy temple, and give thanks to your · **name**
for your steadfast love · **and** your faithfulness. R.

For you have exalted your · **name**
and your word above · **everything.**
On the day I called, you · **answered_me,**
you increased my · **strength** of soul. R.

For though the Lord is high, he regards the · **lowly;**
but the haughty he perceives from far a·-**way.**
Though I walk in the midst of · **trouble,**
you preserve me against the wrath · **of** my enemies. R.

You stretch out your hand and your right hand de·-**livers_me.**
The Lord will fulfill his purpose for · **me;**
your steadfast love, O Lord, endures for·-**ever.**
Do not forsake the · **work_of** your hands. R.

C Instrument

B♭ Instrument

197

Eighteenth Sunday in Ordinary Time – C

Psalm 90

You turn man back to · **dust**, and say,
"Turn back, you · **children** of Adam."
For a thousand years in your sight are like yesterday when · **it** is past,
or like a watch · **in** the night. R.

You sweep them away; they are · **like** a dream,
like grass that is re·-**newed_in** the morning;
in the morning it flourishes and · **is** re-newed;
in the evening it · **fades** and withers. R.

So teach us to · **count** our days
that we may gain · **a** wise heart.
Turn, O · **Lord**! How long?
Have compassion · **on** your servants! R.

Satisfy us in the morning with your · **stead**-fast love,
so that we may rejoice and be glad · **all** our days.
Let the favour of the Lord our · **God_be** up-on_us,
and prosper for us the · **work_of** our hands. R.

Eighteenth Sunday in Ordinary Time – C

Psalm 90

Guitar

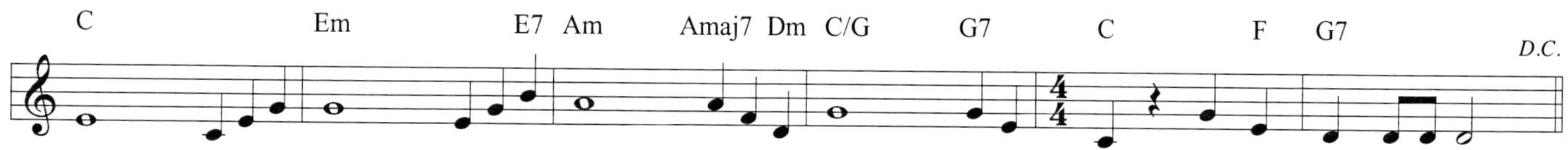

You turn man back to · **dust**, and say,
"Turn back, you · **children** of Adam."
For a thousand years in your sight are like yesterday when · **it** is past,
or like a watch · **in** the night. R.

You sweep them away; they are · **like** a dream,
like grass that is re-·**newed_in** the morning;
in the morning it flourishes and · **is** re-newed;
in the evening it · **fades** and withers. R.

So teach us to · **count** our days
that we may gain · **a** wise heart.
Turn, O · **Lord**! How long?
Have compassion · **on** your servants! R.

Satisfy us in the morning with your · **stead**-fast love,
so that we may rejoice and be glad · **all** our days.
Let the favour of the Lord our · **God_be** up-on_us,
and prosper for us the · **work_of** our hands. R.

C Instrument

B♭ Instrument

Nineteenth Sunday in Ordinary Time – C

Psalm 33

Rejoice in the Lord, · **O** you righteous.
Praise be·-**fits** the upright.
Blessed is the nation whose God · **is** the Lord,
the people whom he has · **chosen_as** his heritage. R.

Truly the eye of the Lord is on · **those** who fear_him,
on those who hope in his · **stead**-fast love,
to deliver their · **souls** from death,
and to keep them a·-**live** in famine. R.

Our soul waits · **for** the Lord;
he is our · **help** and shield.
Let your steadfast love, O Lord, · **be** up-on_us,
even as we · **hope** in you. R.

Nineteenth Sunday in Ordinary Time – C

Psalm 33

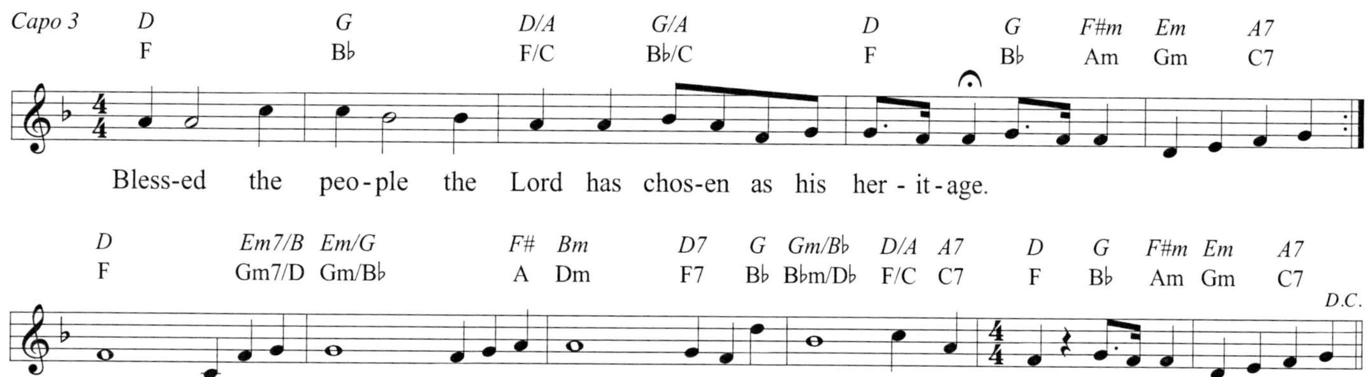

Rejoice in the Lord, · **O** you righteous.
Praise be·-**fits** the upright.
Blessed is the nation whose God · **is** the Lord,
the people whom he has · **chosen_as** his heritage. R.

Truly the eye of the Lord is on · **those** who fear_him,
on those who hope in his · **stead**-fast love,
to deliver their · **souls** from death,
and to keep them a·-**live** in famine. R.

Our soul waits · **for** the Lord;
he is our · **help** and shield.
Let your steadfast love, O Lord, · **be** up-on_us,
even as we · **hope** in you. R.

201

Twentieth Sunday in Ordinary Time – C

Psalm 40

1 - I waited patiently for the · **Lord;**
4 - he inclined to me and heard · **my** cry. R.

He drew me up from the desolate · **pit,**
out of the · **miry** bog,
and set my feet upon a · **rock,**
making my steps · **se**-cure. R.

He put a new song in my · **mouth,**
a song of praise to · **our** God.
Many will see and · **fear,**
and put their trust · **in_the** Lord. R.

As for me, I am poor and · **needy,**
but the Lord · **takes** thought_for_me.
You are my help and my de·-**liverer;**
do not delay, O · **my** God. R.

Twentieth Sunday in Ordinary Time – C

Psalm 40

Guitar

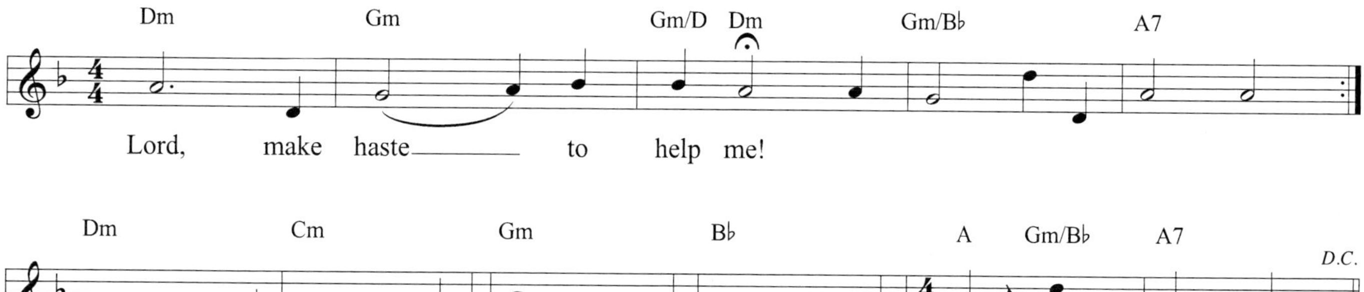

1 - I waited patiently for the · **Lord;**
4 - he inclined to me and heard · **my** cry. R.

He drew me up from the desolate · **pit,**
out of the · **miry** bog,
and set my feet upon a · **rock,**
making my steps · **se**-cure. R.

He put a new song in my · **mouth,**
a song of praise to · **our** God.
Many will see and · **fear,**
and put their trust · **in_the** Lord. R.

As for me, I am poor and · **needy,**
but the Lord · **takes** thought_for_me.
You are my help and my de·-**liverer;**
do not delay, O · **my** God. R.

C Instrument

B♭ Instrument

Twenty-first Sunday in Ordinary Time – C

Psalm 117

Praise the Lord, · **all** you nations!
Extol him, · **all** you peoples! R.

For great is his steadfast · **love** toward us,
and the faithfulness of the Lord en·-**dures** for-ever. R.

Twenty-first Sunday in Ordinary Time – C

Psalm 117

Guitar

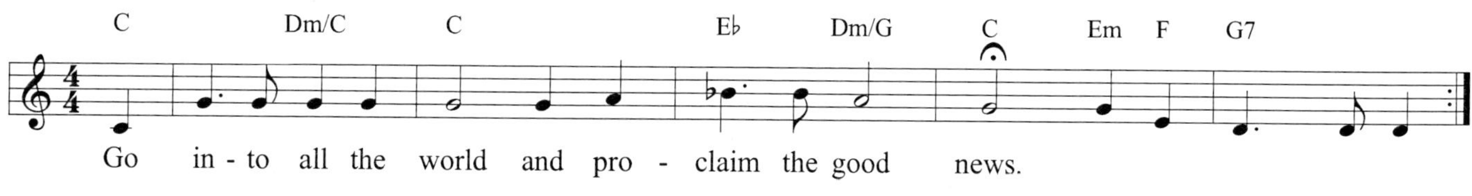

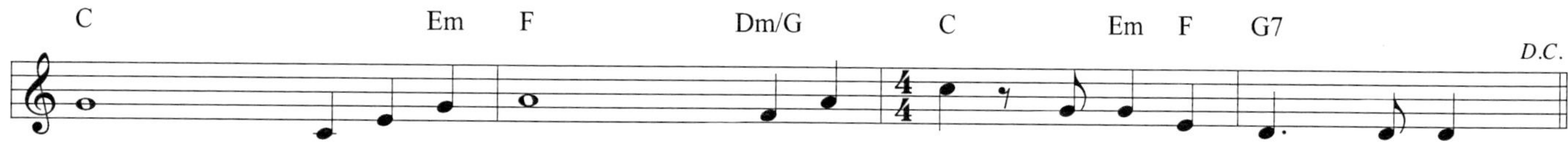

Praise the Lord, · **all** you nations!
Extol him, · **all** you peoples! R.

For great is his steadfast · **love** toward us,
and the faithfulness of the Lord en·-**dures** for-ever. R.

C Instrument

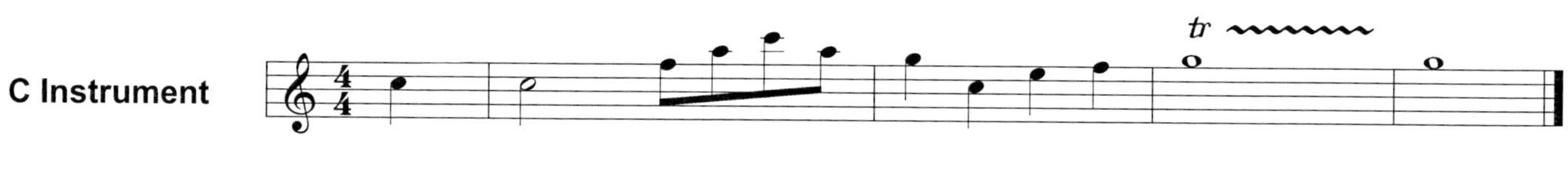

B♭ Instrument

Twenty-second Sunday in Ordinary Time – C

Psalm 68

Let the righteous be joyful; let them exult before · **God;**
let them be jubilant with · **joy.**
Sing to God, sing praises to his · **name;**
his name is the Lord, be exultant · **be**-fore_him. R.

Father of orphans and protector of · **widows**
is God in his holy habi·-**tation.**
God gives the desolate a home to · **live_in;**
he leads out the prisoners · **to_pros**-perity. R.

Rain in abundance, O God, you showered a·-**broad;**
you restored your heritage when it · **languished;**
your flock found a · **dwelling_in_it;**
in your goodness, O God, you provided · **for_the** needy. R.

Twenty-second Sunday in Ordinary Time – C

Psalm 68

Guitar

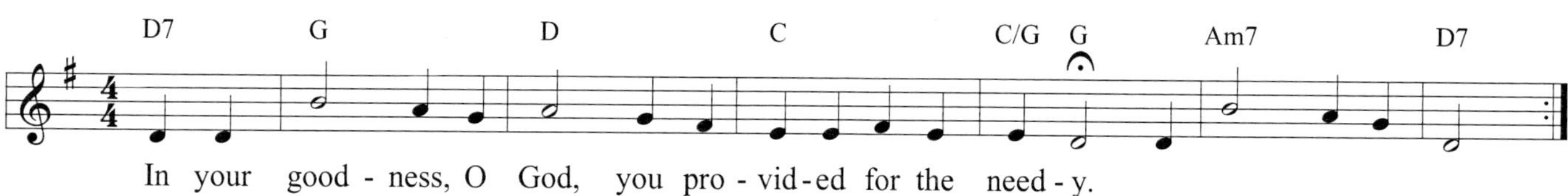

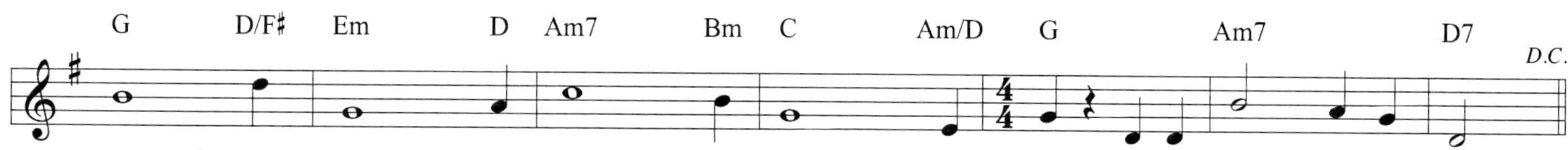

Let the righteous be joyful; let them exult before · **God;**
let them be jubilant with · **joy.**
Sing to God, sing praises to his · **name;**
his name is the Lord, be exultant · **be**-fore_him. R.

Father of orphans and protector of · **widows**
is God in his holy habi·-**tation.**
God gives the desolate a home to · **live_in;**
he leads out the prisoners · **to_pros**-perity. R.

Rain in abundance, O God, you showered a·-**broad;**
you restored your heritage when it · **languished;**
your flock found a · **dwelling_in_it;**
in your goodness, O God, you provided · **for_the** needy. R.

C Instrument

B♭ Instrument

Twenty-third Sunday in Ordinary Time – C

Psalm 90

You turn man back to · **dust**, and say,
"Turn back, you · **children** of Adam."
For a thousand years in your sight are like yesterday when · **it** is past,
or like a watch · **in** the night. R.

You sweep them away; they are · **like** a dream,
like grass that is re·-**newed_in** the morning;
in the morning it flourishes and · **is** re-newed;
in the evening it · **fades** and withers. R.

So teach us to · **count** our days
that we may gain · **a** wise heart.
Turn, O · **Lord**! How long?
Have compassion · **on** your servants! R.

Satisfy us in the morning with your · **stead**-fast love,
so that we may rejoice and be glad · **all** our days.
Let the favour of the Lord our · **God_be** up-on_us,
and prosper for us the · **work_of** our hands. R.

Twenty-third Sunday in Ordinary Time – C

Psalm 90

Guitar

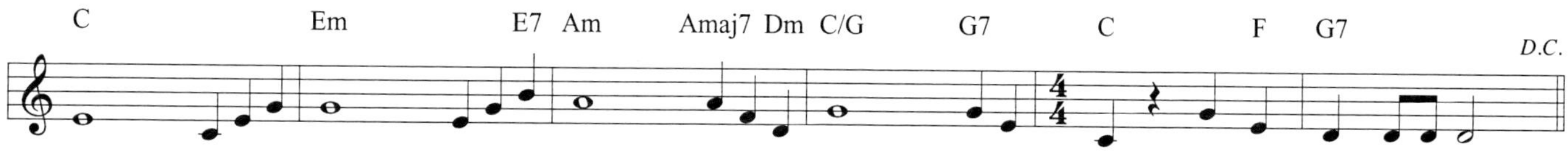

You turn man back to · **dust**, and say,
"Turn back, you · **children** of Adam."
For a thousand years in your sight are like yesterday when · **it** is past,
or like a watch · **in** the night. R.

You sweep them away; they are · **like** a dream,
like grass that is re·-**newed_in** the morning;
in the morning it flourishes and · **is** re-newed;
in the evening it · **fades** and withers. R.

So teach us to · **count** our days
that we may gain · **a** wise heart.
Turn, O · **Lord**! How long?
Have compassion · **on** your servants! R.

Satisfy us in the morning with your · **stead**-fast love,
so that we may rejoice and be glad · **all** our days.
Let the favour of the Lord our · **God_be** up-on_us,
and prosper for us the · **work_of** our hands. R.

C Instrument

B♭ Instrument

209

Twenty-fourth Sunday in Ordinary Time – C

Psalm 51

Have mercy on me, O God, according to your stead·-**fast** love;
according to your abundant mercy blot out my · **trans**-gressions.
Wash me thoroughly from my · **in**-iquity,
and cleanse me · **from** my sin. R.

Create in me a clean heart, · **O** God,
and put a new and right spirit · **with**-in_me.
Do not cast me away from · **your** presence,
and do not take your holy · **spirit** from me. R.

O Lord, open · **my** lips,
and my mouth will declare · **your** praise.
The sacrifice acceptable to God is a · **broken** spirit;
a broken and contrite heart, O God, you will · **not** des-pise. R.

Twenty-fourth Sunday in Ordinary Time – C

Psalm 51

Guitar

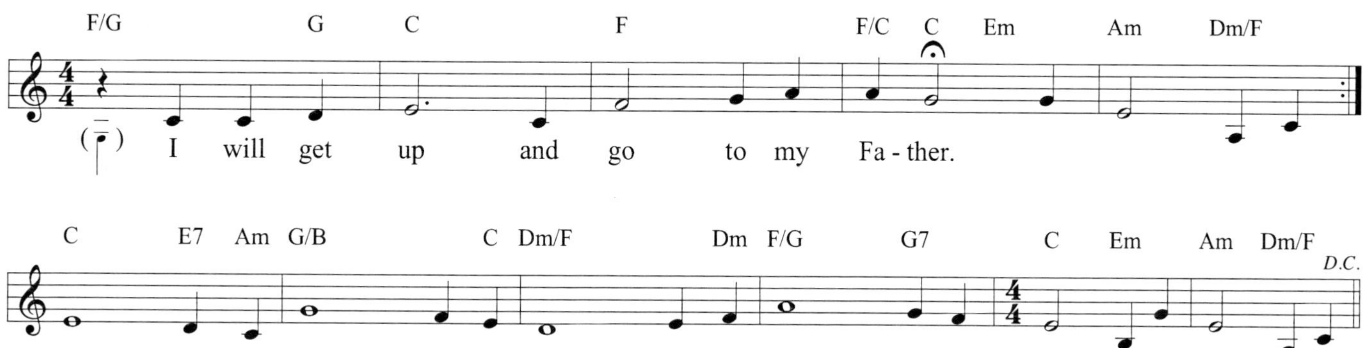

Have mercy on me, O God, according to your stead·-**fast** love;
according to your abundant mercy blot out my · **trans**-gressions.
Wash me thoroughly from my · **in**-iquity,
and cleanse me · **from** my sin. R.

Create in me a clean heart, · **O** God,
and put a new and right spirit · **with**-in_me.
Do not cast me away from · **your** presence,
and do not take your holy · **spirit** from me. R.

O Lord, open · **my** lips,
and my mouth will declare · **your** praise.
The sacrifice acceptable to God is a · **broken** spirit;
a broken and contrite heart, O God, you will · **not** des-pise. R.

C Instrument

B♭ Instrument

Twenty-fifth Sunday in Ordinary Time – C

Psalm 113

Praise, O servants of the · **Lord;**
praise the name of the · **Lord.**
Blessed be the name of the · **Lord**
from this time on and for·-**ever**-more. R.

The Lord is high above all · **nations,**
and his glory above the · **heavens.**
Who is like the Lord our God, who is seated on · **high,**
who looks far down on the heavens · **and_the** earth? R.

The Lord raises the poor from the · **dust,**
and lifts the needy from the · **ash_heap,**
to make them sit with · **princes,**
with the princes · **of_his** people. R.

Twenty-fifth Sunday in Ordinary Time – C

Psalm 113

Guitar

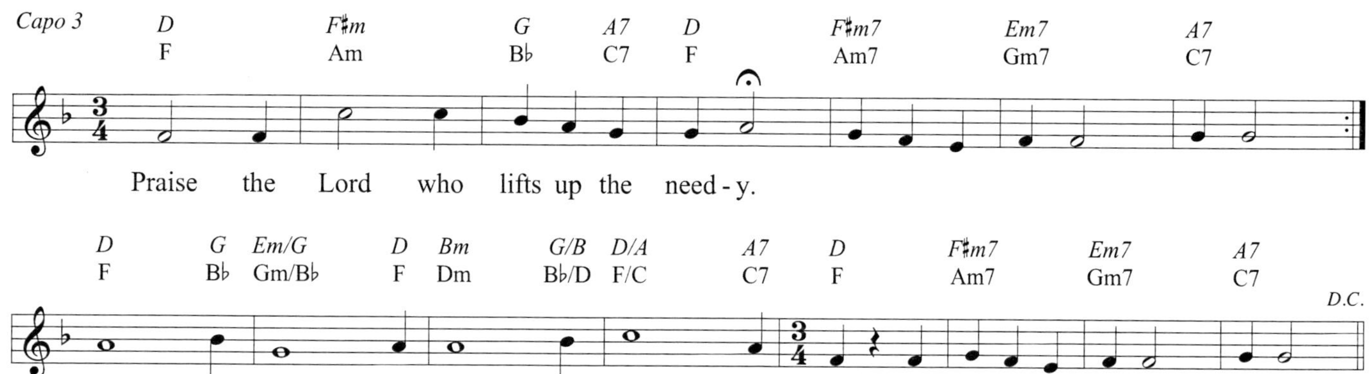

Praise, O servants of the · **Lord;**
praise the name of the · **Lord.**
Blessed be the name of the · **Lord**
from this time on and for·-**ever**-more. R.

The Lord is high above all · **nations,**
and his glory above the · **heavens.**
Who is like the Lord our God, who is seated on · **high,**
who looks far down on the heavens · **and_the** earth? R.

The Lord raises the poor from the · **dust,**
and lifts the needy from the · **ash_heap,**
to make them sit with · **princes,**
with the princes · **of_his** people. R.

C Instrument

B♭ Instrument

Twenty-sixth Sunday in Ordinary Time – C

Psalm 146

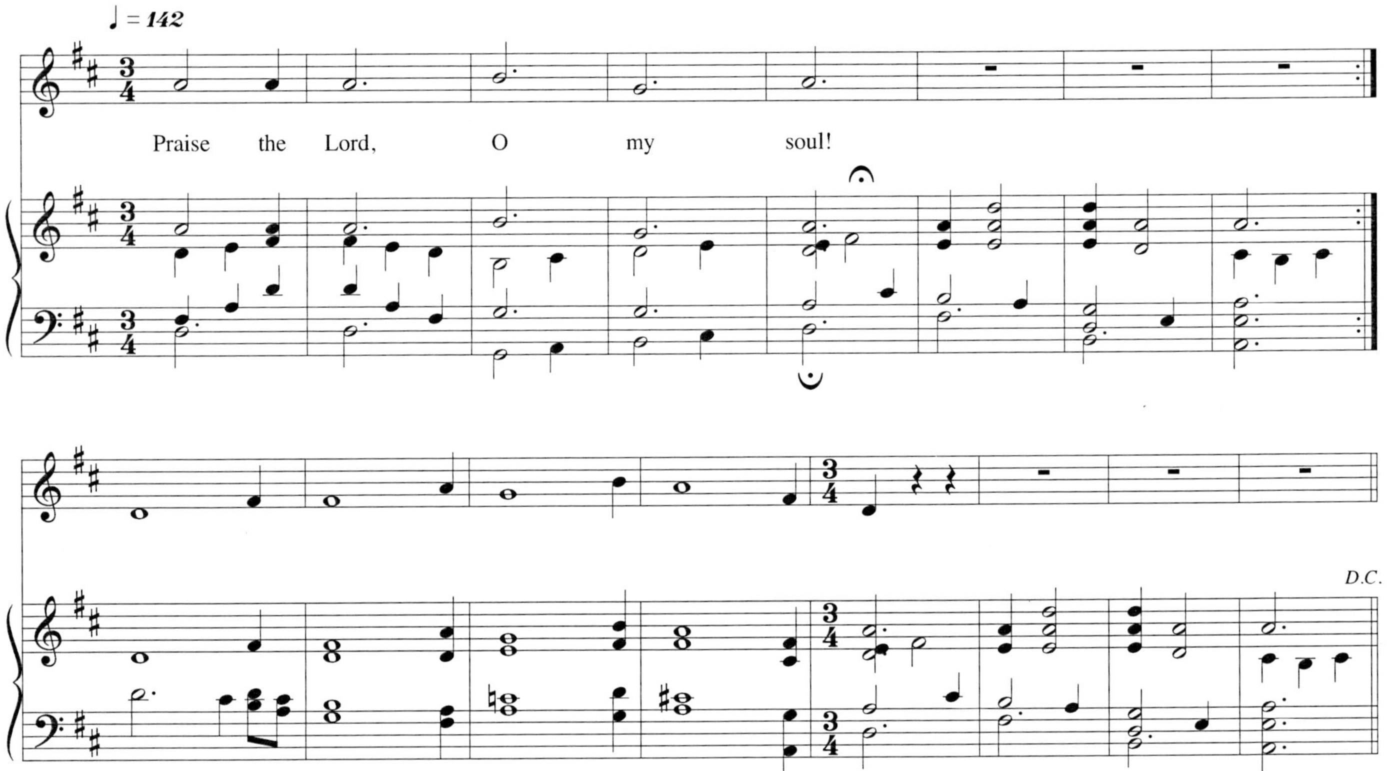

It is the Lord who keeps faith for·-**ever,**
who executes justice for the op·-**pressed;**
who gives food to the · **hungry.**
The Lord sets the · **prisoners** free. R.

The Lord opens the eyes of the · **blind**
and lifts up those who are bowed · **down;**
the Lord loves the · **righteous**
and watches over · **the** strangers. R.

The Lord upholds the orphan and the · **widow,**
but the way of the wicked he brings to · **ruin.**
The Lord will reign for·-**ever,**
your God, O Zion, for all · **gener**-ations. R.

Twenty-sixth Sunday in Ordinary Time – C
Psalm 146

Guitar

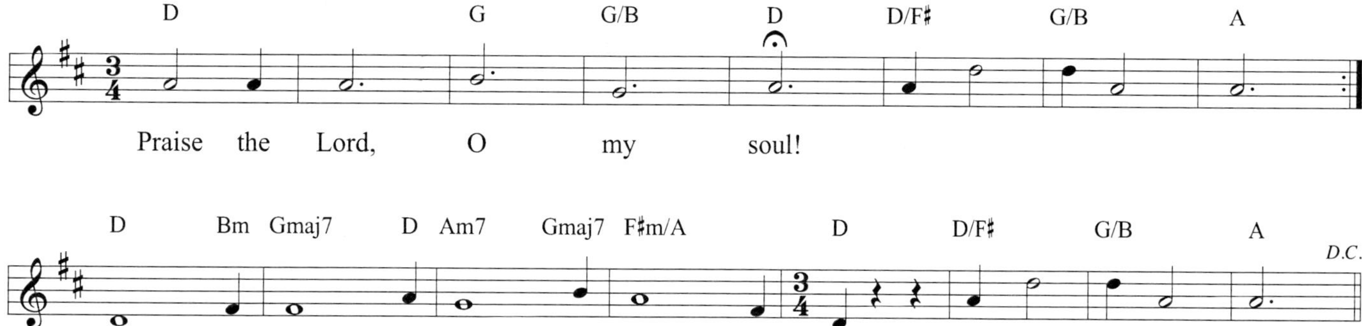

It is the Lord who keeps faith for·-**ever,**
who executes justice for the op·-**pressed;**
who gives food to the · **hungry.**
The Lord sets the · **prisoners** free. R.

The Lord opens the eyes of the · **blind**
and lifts up those who are bowed · **down;**
the Lord loves the · **righteous**
and watches over · **the** strangers. R.

The Lord upholds the orphan and the · **widow,**
but the way of the wicked he brings to · **ruin.**
The Lord will reign for·-**ever,**
your God, O Zion, for all · **gener**-ations. R.

C Instrument

B♭ Instrument

Twenty-seventh Sunday in Ordinary Time – C

Psalm 95

O come, let us sing to · **the** Lord.
Let us make a joyful noise to the rock of our · **sal**-vation!
Let us come into his presence with · **thanks**-giving;
let us make a joyful noise to him with songs · **of** praise! R.

O come, let us worship and · **bow** down,
let us kneel before the Lord, · **our** Maker!
For he is our God, and we are the people of · **his** pasture,
and the sheep of · **his** hand. R.

O that today you would listen to · **his** voice!
Do not harden your hearts, as at Meribah, as on the day at Massah in · **the** wilderness,
when your ancestors tested me, and put me to · **the** proof,
though they had seen · **my** work. R.

Twenty-seventh Sunday in Ordinary Time – C

Psalm 95

Guitar

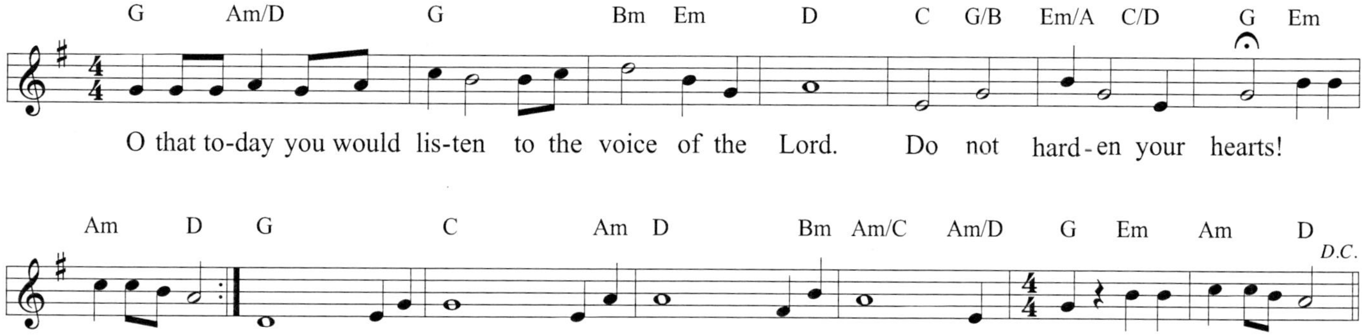

O come, let us sing to · **the** Lord.
Let us make a joyful noise to the rock of our · **sal**-vation!
Let us come into his presence with · **thanks**-giving;
let us make a joyful noise to him with songs · **of** praise! R.

O come, let us worship and · **bow** down,
let us kneel before the Lord, · **our** Maker!
For he is our God, and we are the people of · **his** pasture,
and the sheep of · **his** hand. R.

O that today you would listen to · **his** voice!
Do not harden your hearts, as at Meribah, as on the day at Massah in · **the** wilderness,
when your ancestors tested me, and put me to · **the** proof,
though they had seen · **my** work. R.

C Instrument

B♭ Instrument

217

Twenty-eighth Sunday in Ordinary Time – C

Psalm 98

O sing to the Lord · **a** new song,
for he has done · **marvel**-lous things.
His right hand and his · **ho**-ly arm
have · **brought** him victory. R.

The Lord has made · **known** his victory;
he has revealed his vindication in the · **sight_of** the nations.
He has remembered his · **stead**-fast love
and faithfulness to the · **house** of Israel. R.

All the ends of the · **earth** have seen
the victory · **of** our God.
Make a joyful noise to the Lord, · **all** the earth;
break forth into joyous · **song_and** sing praises. R.

Twenty-eighth Sunday in Ordinary Time – C

Psalm 98

Guitar

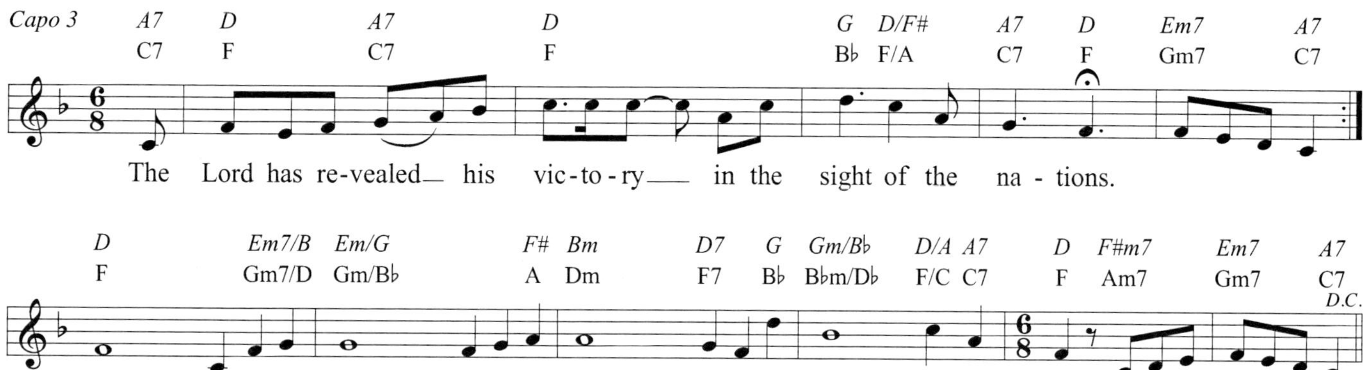

O sing to the Lord · **a** new song,
for he has done · **marvel**-lous things.
His right hand and his · **ho**-ly arm
have · **brought** him victory. R.

The Lord has made · **known** his victory;
he has revealed his vindication in the · **sight_of** the nations.
He has remembered his · **stead**-fast love
and faithfulness to the · **house** of Israel. R.

All the ends of the · **earth** have seen
the victory · **of** our God.
Make a joyful noise to the Lord, · **all** the earth;
break forth into joyous · **song_and** sing praises. R.

C Instrument

B♭ Instrument

219

Twenty-ninth Sunday in Ordinary Time – C

Psalm 121

I lift up my eyes to the · **hills**—
from where will my help · **come?**
My help comes from the · **Lord,**
who made heaven · **and** earth. R.

The Lord will not let your foot be · **moved;**
he who keeps you will not · **slumber.**
He who keeps · **Israel**
will neither slumber · **nor** sleep. R.

The Lord is your · **keeper;**
the Lord is your shade at your right · **hand.**
The sun shall not strike you by · **day,**
nor the moon · **by** night. R.

The Lord will keep you from all · **evil;**
he will keep your · **life.**
The Lord will keep your going out and your coming · **in**
from this time on and for·-**ever**-more. R.

Twenty-ninth Sunday in Ordinary Time – C

Psalm 121

Guitar

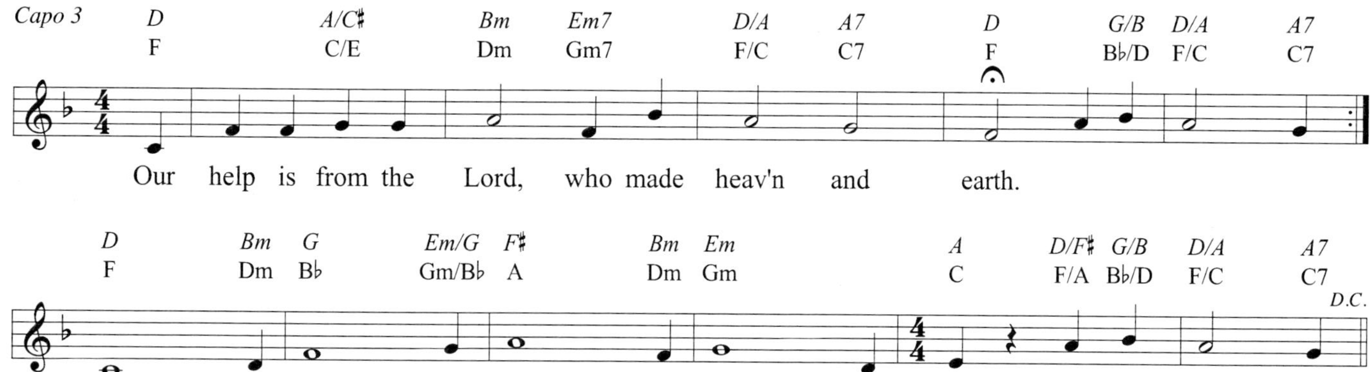

I lift up my eyes to the · **hills**—
from where will my help · **come?**
My help comes from the · **Lord,**
who made heaven · **and** earth. R.

The Lord will not let your foot be · **moved;**
he who keeps you will not · **slumber.**
He who keeps · **Israel**
will neither slumber · **nor** sleep. R.

The Lord is your · **keeper;**
the Lord is your shade at your right · **hand.**
The sun shall not strike you by · **day,**
nor the moon · **by** night. R.

The Lord will keep you from all · **evil;**
he will keep your · **life.**
The Lord will keep your going out and your coming · **in**
from this time on and for·-**ever**-more. R.

C Instrument

B♭ Instrument

Thirtieth Sunday in Ordinary Time – C

Psalm 34

I will bless the Lord at all · **times;**
his praise shall continually be in · **my** mouth.
My soul makes its boast in the · **Lord;**
let the humble hear and · **be** glad. R.

The face of the Lord is against · **evildoers,**
to cut off the remembrance of them · **from_the** earth.
When the righteous cry for help, the Lord · **hears,**
and rescues them from all · **their** troubles. R.

The Lord is near to the broken·**-hearted,**
and saves the crushed · **in** spirit.
The Lord redeems the life of his · **servants;**
none of those who take refuge in him will be · **con**-demned. R.

Thirtieth Sunday in Ordinary Time – C

Psalm 34

Guitar

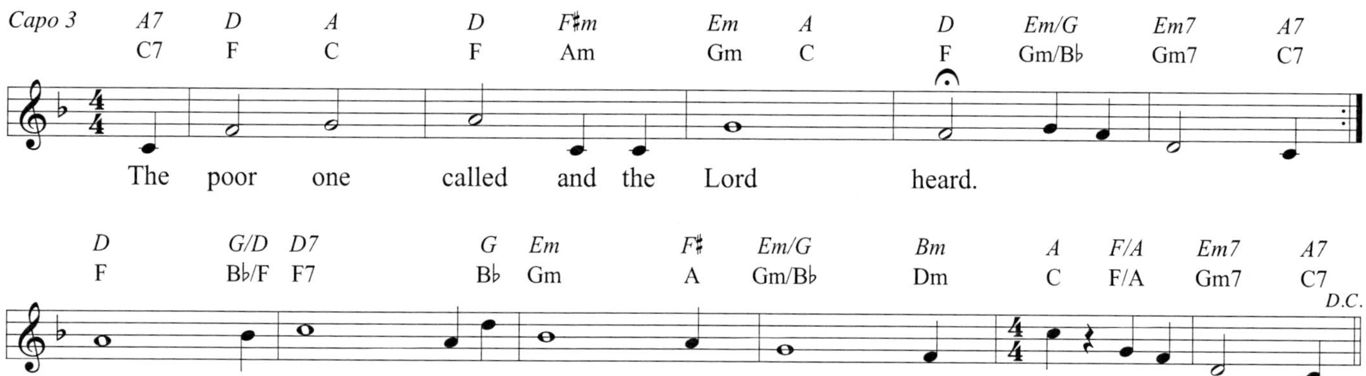

I will bless the Lord at all · **times;**
his praise shall continually be in · **my** mouth.
My soul makes its boast in the · **Lord;**
let the humble hear and · **be** glad. R.

The face of the Lord is against · **evildoers,**
to cut off the remembrance of them · **from_the** earth.
When the righteous cry for help, the Lord · **hears,**
and rescues them from all · **their** troubles. R.

The Lord is near to the broken·-**hearted,**
and saves the crushed · **in** spirit.
The Lord redeems the life of his · **servants;**
none of those who take refuge in him will be · **con**-demned. R.

C Instrument

Bb Instrument

223

Thirty-first Sunday in Ordinary Time – C

Psalm 145

I will extol you, my God and · **King,**
and bless your name forever and · **ever.**
Every day I will · **bless_you,**
and praise your name forever · **and** ever. R.

The Lord is gracious and · **merciful,**
slow to anger and abounding in steadfast · **love.**
The Lord is good to · **all,**
and his compassion is over all that he · **has** made. R.

All your works shall give thanks to you, O · **Lord,**
and all your faithful shall · **bless_you.**
They shall speak of the glory of your · **kingdom,**
and tell of · **your** power. R.

The Lord is faithful in all his · **words,**
and gracious in all his · **deeds.**
The Lord upholds all who are · **falling,**
and raises up all who are · **bowed** down. R.

Thirty-first Sunday in Ordinary Time – C

Psalm 145

Guitar

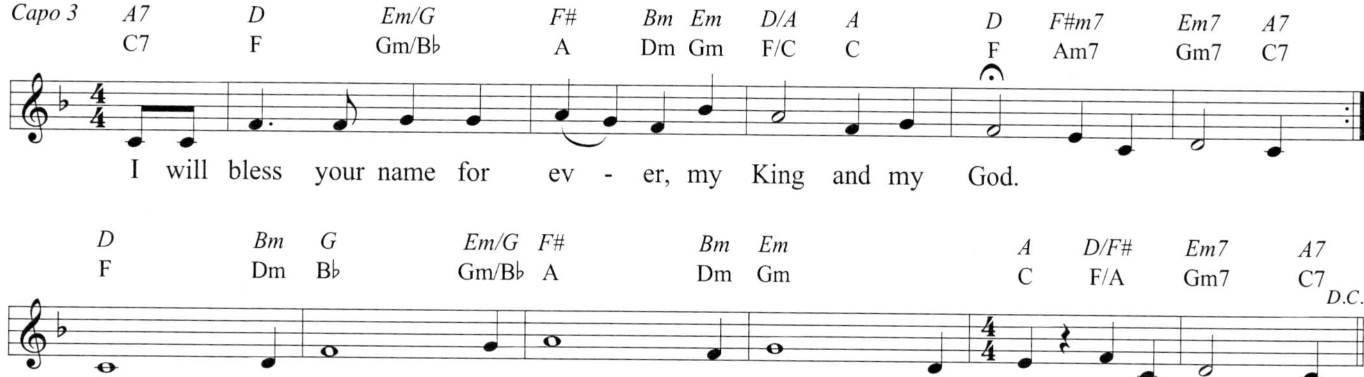

I will extol you, my God and · **King,**
and bless your name forever and · **ever.**
Every day I will · **bless_you,**
and praise your name forever · **and** ever. R.

The Lord is gracious and · **merciful,**
slow to anger and abounding in steadfast · **love.**
The Lord is good to · **all,**
and his compassion is over all that he · **has** made. R.

All your works shall give thanks to you, O · **Lord,**
and all your faithful shall · **bless_you.**
They shall speak of the glory of your · **kingdom,**
and tell of · **your** power. R.

The Lord is faithful in all his · **words,**
and gracious in all his · **deeds.**
The Lord upholds all who are · **falling,**
and raises up all who are · **bowed** down. R.

C Instrument

B♭ Instrument

Thirty-second Sunday in Ordinary Time – C

Psalm 17

Hear a just cause, O · **Lord;**
attend to my · **cry;**
give ear to my · **prayer**
from lips free of · **de**-ceit. R.

My steps have held fast to your · **paths;**
my feet have not · **slipped.**
I call upon you, for you will answer me, O · **God;**
incline your ear to me, hear · **my** words. R.

Guard me as the apple of the · **eye;**
hide me in the shadow of your · **wings.**
As for me, I shall behold your face in · **righteousness;**
when I awake I shall be satisfied, beholding · **your** likeness. R.

Thirty-second Sunday in Ordinary Time – C

Psalm 17

Guitar

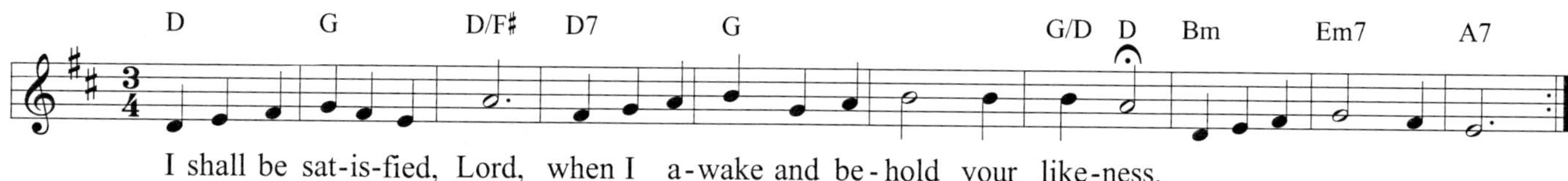

Hear a just cause, O · **Lord;**
attend to my · **cry;**
give ear to my · **prayer**
from lips free of · **de**-ceit. R.

My steps have held fast to your · **paths;**
my feet have not · **slipped.**
I call upon you, for you will answer me, O · **God;**
incline your ear to me, hear · **my** words. R.

Guard me as the apple of the · **eye;**
hide me in the shadow of your · **wings.**
As for me, I shall behold your face in · **righteousness;**
when I awake I shall be satisfied, beholding · **your** likeness. R.

C Instrument

B♭ Instrument

Thirty-third Sunday in Ordinary Time – C

Psalm 98

Sing praises to the Lord with the · **lyre,**
with the lyre and the sound · **of** melody.
With trumpets and the sound of the · **horn**
make a joyful noise before the King, · **the** Lord. R.

Let the sea roar, and all that · **fills_it;**
the world and those · **who** live_in_it.
Let the floods clap their · **hands;**
let the hills sing together for joy at the presence · **of_the** Lord. R.

For the Lord is · **coming,**
coming to judge · **the** earth.
He will judge the world with · **righteousness,**
and the peoples · **with** equity. R.

Thirty-third Sunday in Ordinary Time – C

Psalm 98

Guitar

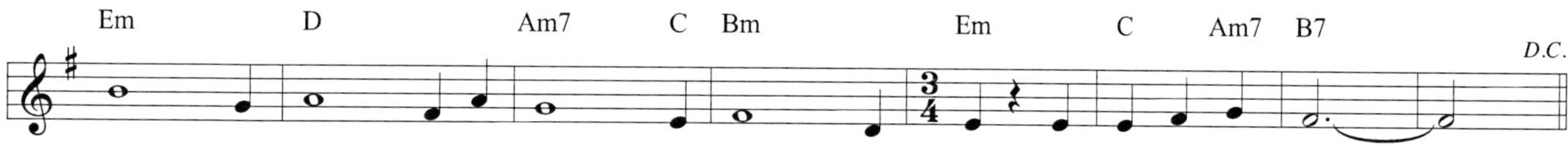

Sing praises to the Lord with the · **lyre,**
with the lyre and the sound · **of** melody.
With trumpets and the sound of the · **horn**
make a joyful noise before the King, · **the** Lord. R.

Let the sea roar, and all that · **fills_it;**
the world and those · **who** live_in_it.
Let the floods clap their · **hands;**
let the hills sing together for joy at the presence · **of_the** Lord. R.

For the Lord is · **coming,**
coming to judge · **the** earth.
He will judge the world with · **righteousness,**
and the peoples · **with** equity. R.

C Instrument

B♭ Instrument

Thirty-fourth Sunday in Ordinary Time (Christ the King) – C

Psalm 122

I was glad when they said · **to** me,
"Let us go to the house of · **the** Lord!"
Our feet · **are** standing
within your gates, O · **Je**-rusalem. R.

Jerusalem—built as · **a** city
that is bound firmly · **to**-gether.
To it the tribes · **go** up,
the tribes · **of_the** Lord. R.

As it was decreed · **for** Israel,
to give thanks to the name of · **the** Lord.
For there the thrones for judgment · **were_set** up,
the thrones of the · **house_of** David. R

Thirty-fourth Sunday in Ordinary Time (Christ the King) – C

Psalm 122

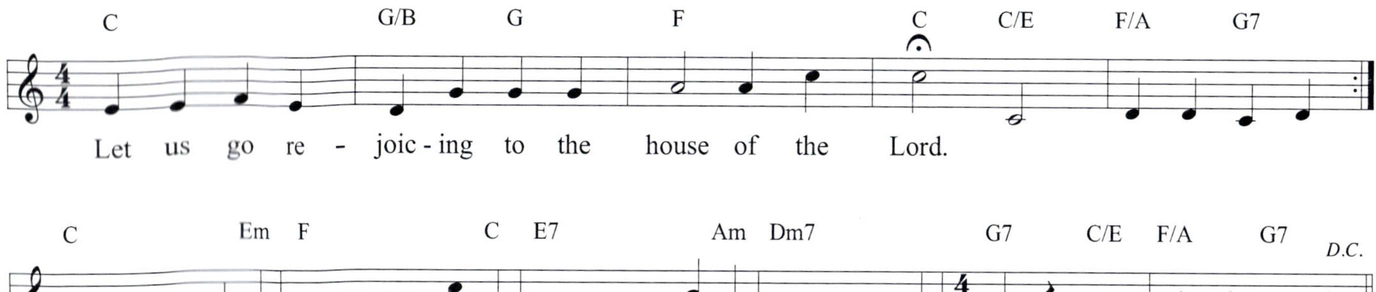

I was glad when they said · **to** me,
"Let us go to the house of · **the** Lord!"
Our feet · **are** standing
within your gates, O · **Je**-rusalem. R.

Jerusalem — built as · **a** city
that is bound firmly · **to**-gether.
To it the tribes · **go** up,
the tribes · **of_the** Lord. R.

As it was decreed · **for** Israel,
to give thanks to the name of · **the** Lord.
For there the thrones for judgment · **were_set** up,
the thrones of the · **house_of** David. R

February 2 – Presentation of the Lord – ABC

Psalm 24

Lift up your heads, · **O** gates!
and be lifted up, O · **ancient** doors!
that the King of glory · **may_come** in. R.

Who is the King · **of** glory?
The Lord, strong · **and** mighty,
the Lord, mighty · **in** battle. R.

Lift up your heads, · **O** gates!
and be lifted up, O · **ancient** doors!
that the King of glory · **may_come** in. R.

Who is this King · **of** glory?
The Lord · **of** hosts,
he is the King · **of** glory. R.

February 2 – Presentation of the Lord – ABC

Psalm 24

Guitar

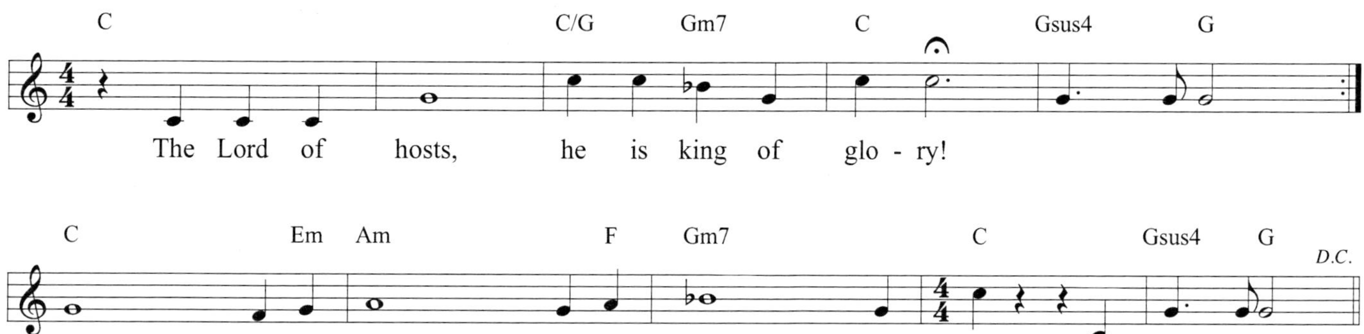

Lift up your heads, · **O** gates!
and be lifted up, O · **ancient** doors!
that the King of glory · **may_come** in. R.

Who is the King · **of** glory?
The Lord, strong · **and** mighty,
the Lord, mighty · **in** battle. R.

Lift up your heads, · **O** gates!
and be lifted up, O · **ancient** doors!
that the King of glory · **may_come** in. R.

Who is this King · **of** glory?
The Lord · **of** hosts,
he is the King · **of** glory. R.

C Instrument

B♭ Instrument

233

March 19 – St. Joseph, Husband of the Blessed Virgin Mary – ABC

Psalm 89

I will sing of your steadfast love, O Lord, for·-**ever;**
with my mouth I will proclaim your faithfulness to all gener·-**ations.**
I declare that your steadfast love is established for·-**ever;**
your faithfulness is as firm · **as_the** heavens. R.

You said, "I have made a covenant with my · **chosen_one,**
I have sworn to my servant · **David:**
I will establish your descendants for·-**ever,**
and build your throne for all · **gener**-ations." R.

He shall cry to me, "You are my · **Father,**
my God, and the Rock of my sal·-**vation!**"
Forever I will keep my steadfast · **love_for_him,**
and my covenant with him will · **stand** firm. R.

March 19 – St. Joseph, Husband of the Blessed Virgin Mary – ABC

Psalm 89

Guitar

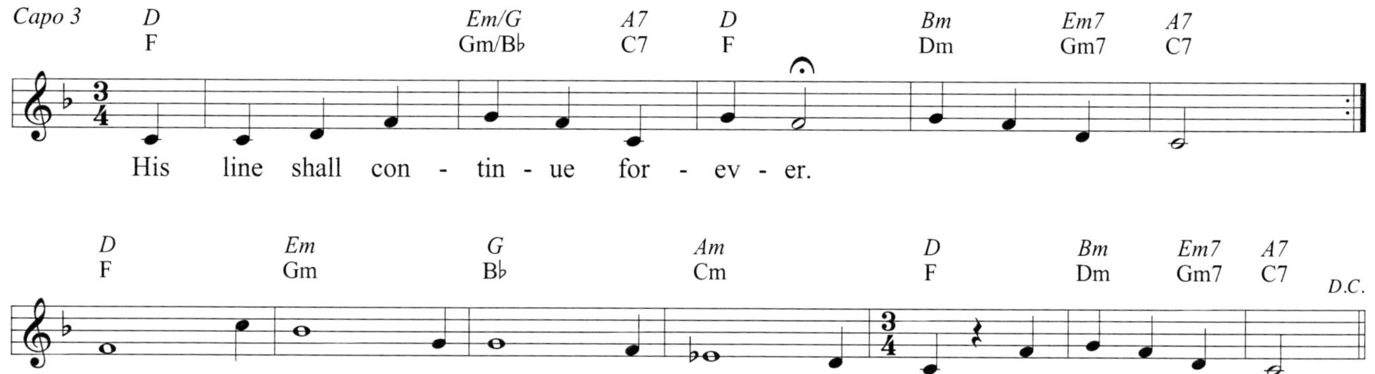

I will sing of your steadfast love, O Lord, for·-**ever;**
with my mouth I will proclaim your faithfulness to all gener·-**ations.**
I declare that your steadfast love is established for·-**ever;**
your faithfulness is as firm · **as_the** heavens. R.

You said, "I have made a covenant with my · **chosen_one,**
I have sworn to my servant · **David:**
I will establish your descendants for·-**ever,**
and build your throne for all · **gener**-ations." R.

He shall cry to me, "You are my · **Father,**
my God, and the Rock of my sal·-**vation!"**
Forever I will keep my steadfast · **love_for_him,**
and my covenant with him will · **stand** firm. R.

C Instrument

B♭ Instrument

235"""

March 25 – Annunciation of the Lord – ABC

Psalm 40

Sacrifice and offering you do not de·-**sire,**
but you have given me an · **o**-pen ear.
Burnt offering · **and** sin_offering
you have · **not** re-quired. R.

Then I said, "Here I · **am;**
in the scroll of the book it is · **written** of me.
I delight to do your will, O · **my** God;
your law is with·-**in** my heart." R.

I have told the glad news of de·-**liverance**
in the great · **con**-gre-gation;
see, I have not restrained · **my** lips,
as you · **know,** O Lord. R.

I have not hidden your saving help within my · **heart,**
I have spoken of your faithfulness and · **your** sal-vation;
I have not concealed your steadfast love and · **your** faithfulness
from the great · **con**-gre-gation. R.

Guitar

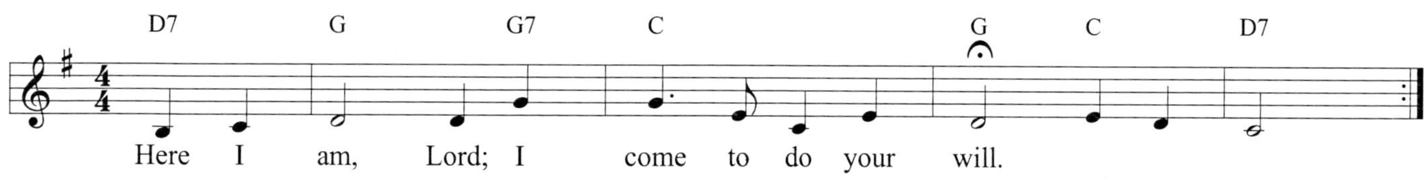

Sacrifice and offering you do not de·-**sire,**
but you have given me an · **o**-pen ear.
Burnt offering · **and** sin_offering
you have · **not** re-quired. R.

Then I said, "Here I · **am;**
in the scroll of the book it is · **written** of me.
I delight to do your will, O · **my** God;
your law is with·-**in** my heart." R.

I have told the glad news of de·-**liverance**
in the great · **con**-gre-gation;
see, I have not restrained · **my** lips,
as you · **know,** O Lord. R.

I have not hidden your saving help within my · **heart,**
I have spoken of your faithfulness and · **your** sal-vation;
I have not concealed your steadfast love and · **your** faithfulness
from the great · **con**-gre-gation. R.

C Instrument

B♭ Instrument

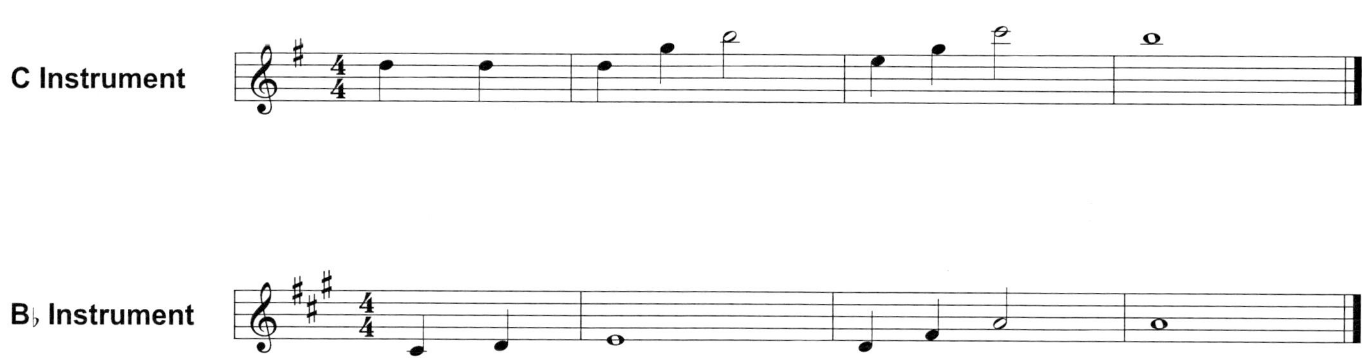

June 24 – Nativity of St. John the Baptist (Vigil) – ABC

Psalm 71

In you, O Lord, I · **take** refuge;
let me never be · **put** to shame.
In your righteousness de·-**liver_me** and rescue_me;
incline your ear to · **me** and save_me. R.

Be to me a rock · **of** refuge,
a strong · **fortress,** to save_me,
for you are my rock · **and** my fortress.
Rescue me, O my God, from the · **hand_of** the wicked. R.

For you, O Lord, are · **my** hope,
my trust, O Lord, · **from** my youth.
Upon you I have leaned · **from** my birth;
from my mother's womb you have · **been** my strength. R.

My mouth will tell of your right·-**eous** acts,
of your deeds of salvation · **all** day long.
O God, from my youth · **you** have taught_me,
and I still proclaim your · **won**-drous deeds. R.

June 24 – Nativity of St. John the Baptist (Vigil) – ABC

Psalm 71

Guitar

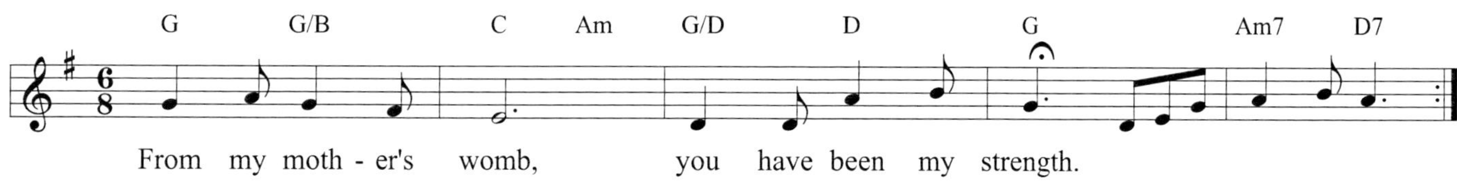

In you, O Lord, I · **take** refuge;
let me never be · **put** to shame.
In your righteousness de·-**liver_me** and rescue_me;
incline your ear to · **me** and save_me. R.

Be to me a rock · **of** refuge,
a strong · **fortress,** to save_me,
for you are my rock · **and** my fortress.
Rescue me, O my God, from the · **hand_of** the wicked. R.

For you, O Lord, are · **my** hope,
my trust, O Lord, · **from** my youth.
Upon you I have leaned · **from** my birth;
from my mother's womb you have · **been** my strength. R.

My mouth will tell of your right·-**eous** acts,
of your deeds of salvation · **all** day long.
O God, from my youth · **you** have taught_me,
and I still proclaim your · **won**-drous deeds. R.

C Instrument

B♭ Instrument

June 24 – Nativity of St. John the Baptist (Day) – ABC

Psalm 139

O Lord, you have searched me and · **known_me.**
You know when I sit down and when I · **rise** up;
you discern my thoughts from far a·-**way.**
You search out my path and my lying down, and are acquainted with all · **my** ways. R.

For it was you who formed my inward · **parts;**
you knit me together in my · **mother's** womb.
I · **praise_you,**
for I am fearfully and · **wonderfully** made. R.

Wonderful are your works; that I know very · **well.**
My frame was not hidden · **from** you,
when I was being made in · **secret,**
intricately woven in the depths of · **the** earth. R.

June 24 – Nativity of St. John the Baptist (Day) – ABC

Psalm 139

Guitar

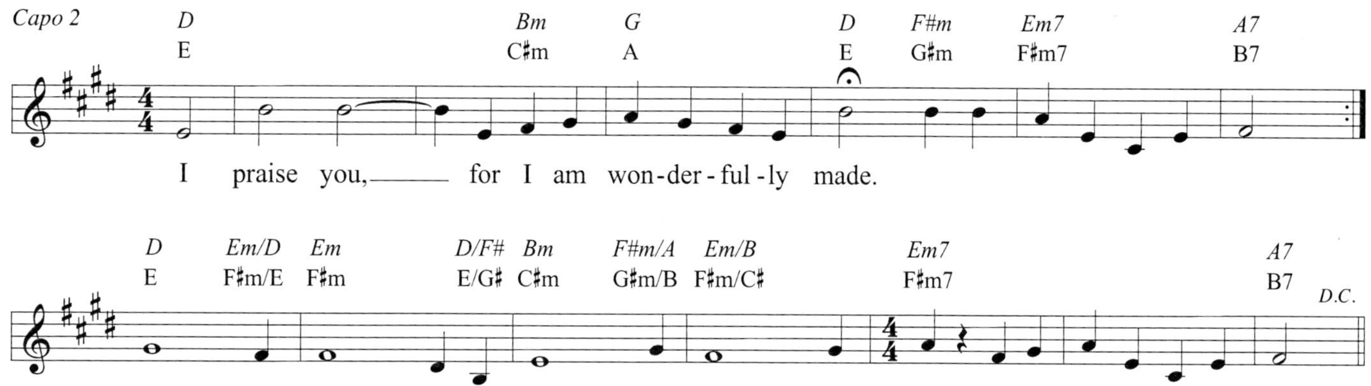

O Lord, you have searched me and · **known_me.**
You know when I sit down and when I · **rise** up;
you discern my thoughts from far a·-**way.**
You search out my path and my lying down, and are acquainted with all · **my** ways. R.

For it was you who formed my inward · **parts;**
you knit me together in my · **mother's** womb.
I · **praise_you,**
for I am fearfully and · **wonderfully** made. R.

Wonderful are your works; that I know very · **well.**
My frame was not hidden · **from** you,
when I was being made in · **secret,**
intricately woven in the depths of · **the** earth. R.

C Instrument

B♭ Instrument

241

June 29 – Sts. Peter and Paul, Apostles (Vigil) – ABC

Psalm 19

The heavens are telling the glory of God;
and the firmament proclaims his handiwork.
Day to day pours forth speech,
and night to night declares knowledge. R.

There is no speech, nor are there words;
their voice is not heard;
yet their voice goes out through all the earth,
and their words to the end of the world. R.

June 29 – Sts. Peter and Paul, Apostles (Vigil) – ABC

Psalm 19

Guitar

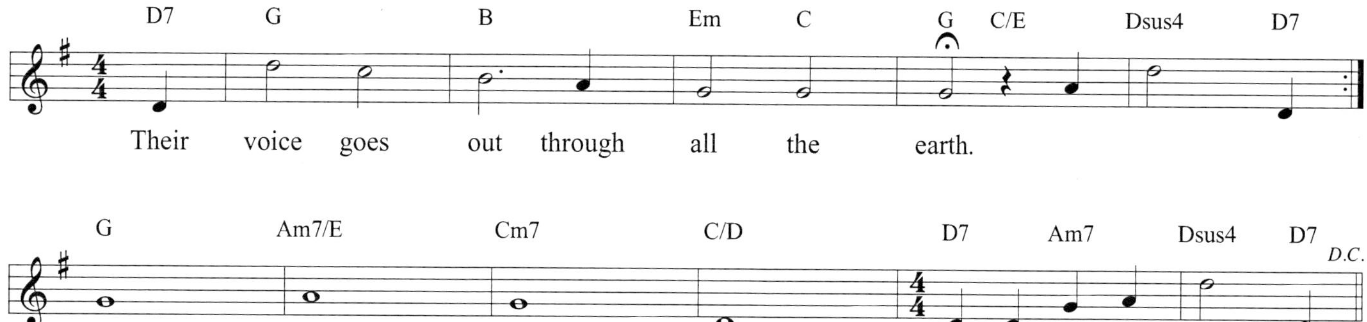

The heavens are telling the glory of God;
and the firmament proclaims his handiwork.
Day to day pours forth speech,
and night to night declares knowledge. R.

There is no speech, nor are there words;
their voice is not heard;
yet their voice goes out through all the earth,
and their words to the end of the world. R.

C Instrument

B♭ Instrument

June 29 – Sts. Peter and Paul, Apostles (Day) – ABC

Psalm 34

I will bless the Lord at all · **times;**
his praise shall continually be in · **my** mouth.
My soul makes its boast in the · **Lord;**
let the humble hear and · **be** glad. R.

O magnify the Lord with · **me,**
and let us exalt his name · **to**-gether.
I sought the Lord, and he · **answered_me,**
and delivered me from all · **my** fears. R.

Look to him, and be · **radiant;**
so your faces shall never · **be_a**-shamed.
The poor one called, and the Lord · **heard,**
and saved that person from ev·-**ery** trouble. R.

The Angel of the Lord en·-**camps**
around those who fear him, and · **de**-livers_them.
O taste and see that the Lord is · **good;**
blessed is the one who takes refuge · **in** him. R.

June 29 – Sts. Peter and Paul, Apostles (Day) – ABC

Psalm 34

Guitar

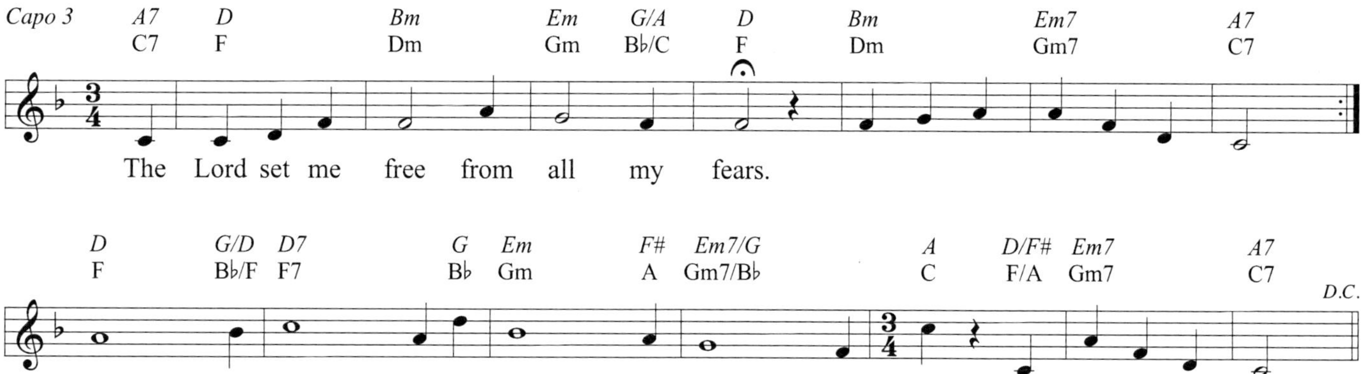

I will bless the Lord at all · **times;**
his praise shall continually be in · **my** mouth.
My soul makes its boast in the · **Lord;**
let the humble hear and · **be** glad. R.

O magnify the Lord with · **me,**
and let us exalt his name · **to**-gether.
I sought the Lord, and he · **answered_me,**
and delivered me from all · **my** fears. R.

Look to him, and be · **radiant;**
so your faces shall never · **be_a**-shamed.
The poor one called, and the Lord · **heard,**
and saved that person from ev·-**ery** trouble. R.

The Angel of the Lord en·-**camps**
around those who fear him, and · **de**-livers_them.
O taste and see that the Lord is · **good;**
blessed is the one who takes refuge · **in** him. R.

C Instrument

B♭ Instrument

245

August 6 – Transfiguration of the Lord – ABC

Psalm 97

The Lord is king! Let the earth re·-**joice;**
let the many coastlands · **be** glad!
Clouds and thick darkness are · **all** around him;
righteousness and justice are the foundation · **of** his throne. R.

The mountains melt like wax before the · **Lord,**
before the Lord of · **all_the** earth.
The heavens pro·-**claim** his righteousness;
and all the peoples be·-**hold** his glory. R.

1 - For you, O Lord, are most high over all the · **earth;**
4 - you are exalted far a·-**bove** all gods. R.

August 6 – Transfiguration of the Lord – ABC

Psalm 97

Guitar

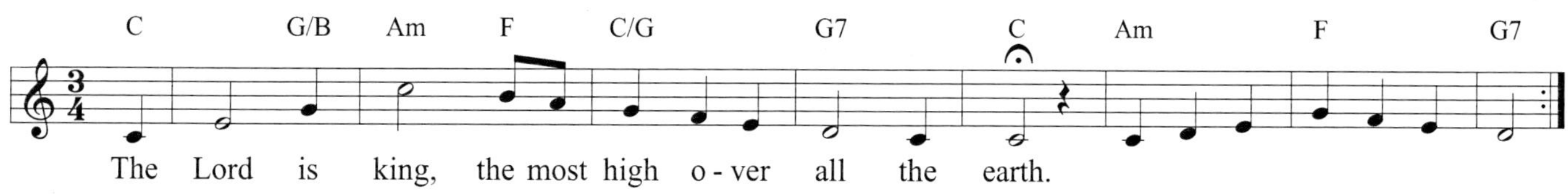

The Lord is king! Let the earth re-·-**joice;**
let the many coastlands · **be** glad!
Clouds and thick darkness are · **all** around him;
righteousness and justice are the foundation · **of** his throne. R.

The mountains melt like wax before the · **Lord,**
before the Lord of · **all_the** earth.
The heavens pro-·-**claim** his righteousness;
and all the peoples be-·-**hold** his glory. R.

1 - For you, O Lord, are most high over all the · **earth;**
4 - you are exalted far a-·-**bove** all gods. R.

C Instrument

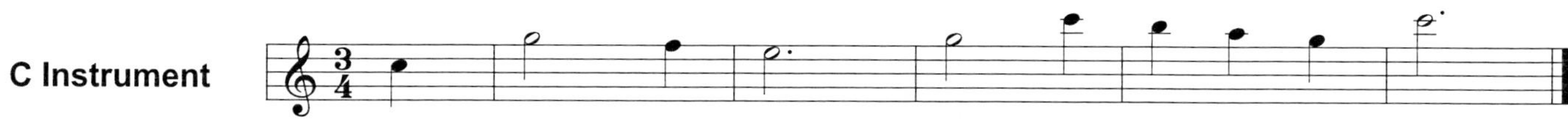

B♭ Instrument

August 15 – Assumption of the Blessed Virgin Mary (Vigil) – ABC

Psalm 132

We heard of the ark in · **Ephrathah;**
we found it in the fields · **of** Jaar.
"Let us go to his · **dwelling_place;**
let us worship · **at_his** footstool." R.

Let your priests be clothed with · **righteousness,**
and let your faithful shout · **for** joy.
For your servant David's · **sake**
do not turn away the face of · **your_a**-nointed_one. R.

For the Lord has chosen · **Zion;**
he has desired it for his ha·-**bi**·-tation.
"This is my resting place for·-**ever;**
here I will reside, for I have · **de**-sired_it." R.

August 15 – Assumption of the Blessed Virgin Mary (Vigil) – ABC

Psalm 132

Guitar

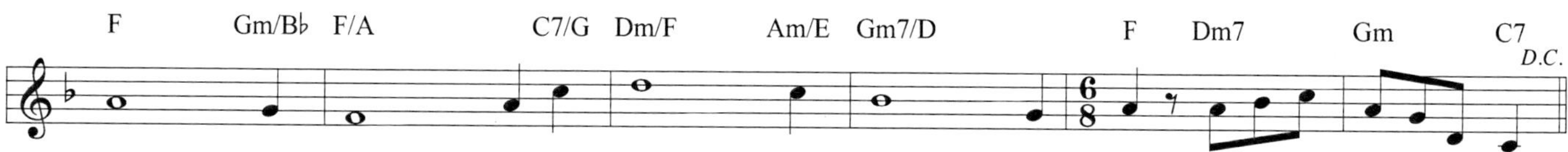

We heard of the ark in · **Ephrathah;**
we found it in the fields · **of** Jaar.
"Let us go to his · **dwelling_place;**
let us worship · **at_his** footstool." R.

Let your priests be clothed with · **righteousness,**
and let your faithful shout · **for** joy.
For your servant David's · **sake**
do not turn away the face of · **your_a**-nointed_one. R.

For the Lord has chosen · **Zion;**
he has desired it for his ha·-**bi**·-tation.
"This is my resting place for·-**ever;**
here I will reside, for I have · **de**-sired_it." R.

C Instrument

B♭ Instrument

August 15 – Assumption of the Blessed Virgin Mary (Day) – ABC

Psalm 45

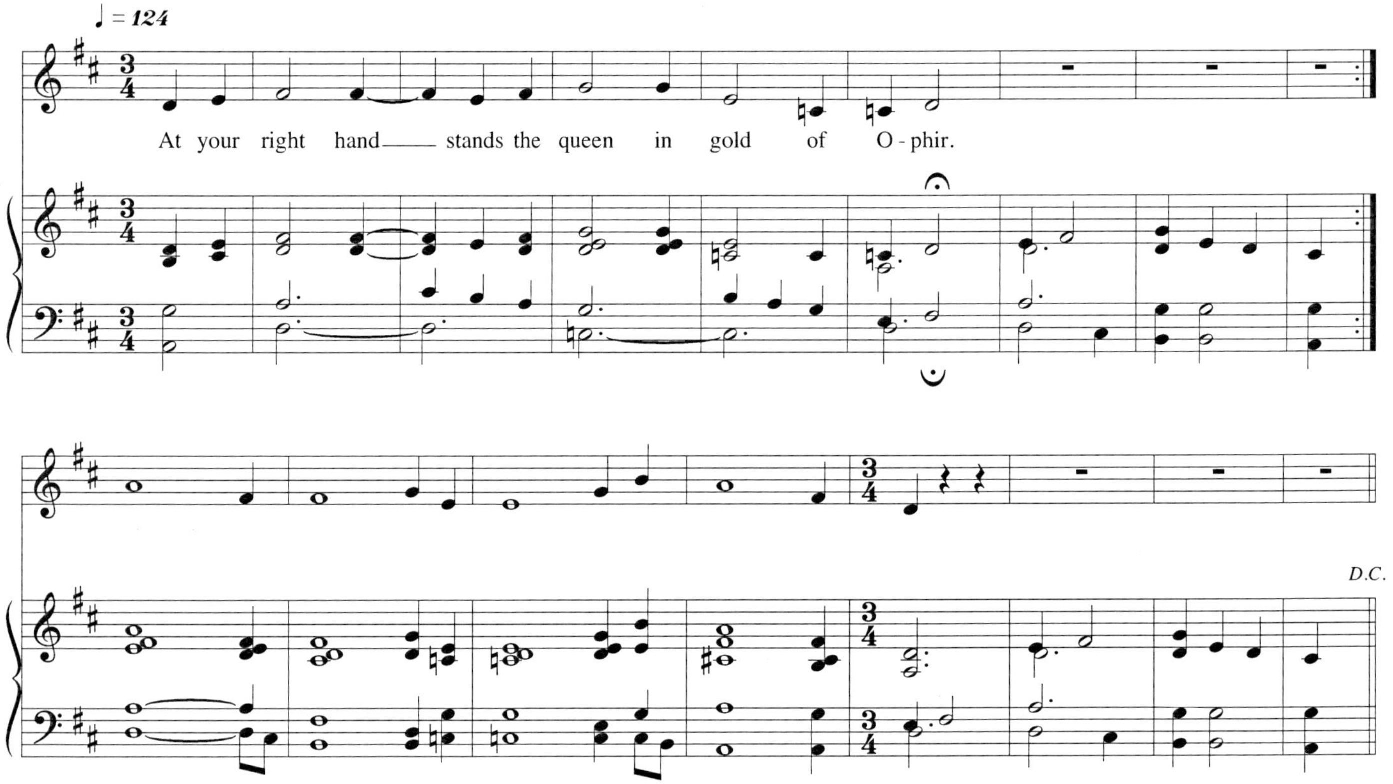

Daughters of kings are among your ladies of · **honour;**
at your right hand stands the queen in gold · **of** Ophir.
Hear, O daughter, consider and incline · **your** ear;
forget your people and your · **father's** house. R.

The king will desire your · **beauty.**
Since he is your lord, · **bow** to_him;
The princess is decked with golden robes; in many-coloured robes she is led to · **the** king;
behind her the virgins, her com·-**panions**, follow. R.

1 - With joy and gladness they are led a·-**long**
4 - as they enter the palace · **of_the** king. R.

August 15 – Assumption of the Blessed Virgin Mary (Day) – ABC

Psalm 45

Guitar

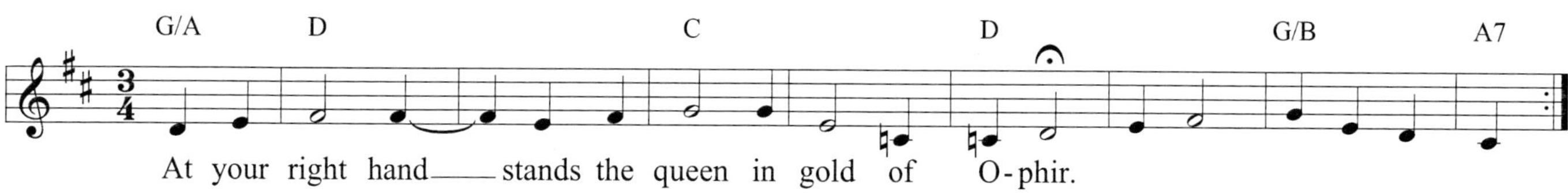

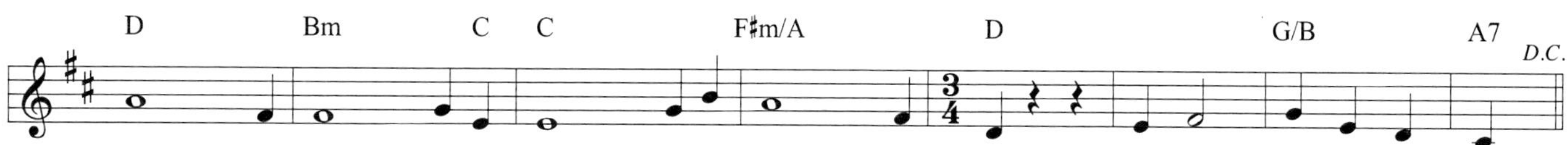

Daughters of kings are among your ladies of · **honour;**
at your right hand stands the queen in gold · **of** Ophir.
Hear, O daughter, consider and incline · **your** ear;
forget your people and your · **father's** house. R.

The king will desire your · **beauty.**
Since he is your · **lord,** bow_to_him;
The princess is decked with golden robes; in many-coloured robes she is led to · **the** king;
behind her the virgins, her com·-**panions**, follow. R.

1 - With joy and gladness they are led a·-**long**
4 - as they enter the palace · **of_the** king. R.

C Instrument

B♭ Instrument

September 14 – Exaltation of the Holy Cross – ABC

Psalm 78

Give ear, O my people, to my · **teaching;**
incline your ears to the words of my · **mouth.**
I will open my mouth in a · **parable;**
I will utter dark sayings · **from_of** old. R.

When God killed them, the people · **sought_for_him;**
they repented and sought him · **earnestly.**
They remembered that God was their · **rock,**
the Most High God · **their_re**-deemer. R.

But they flattered him with their · **mouths;**
they lied to him with their · **tongues.**
Their heart was not steadfast toward · **him;**
they were not true to · **his** covenant. R.

Yet he, being compassionate, forgave their in·-**iquity,**
and did not de·-**stroy_them;**
often he restrained his · **anger,**
and did not stir up all · **his** wrath. R.

September 14 – Exaltation of the Holy Cross – ABC

Psalm 78

Guitar

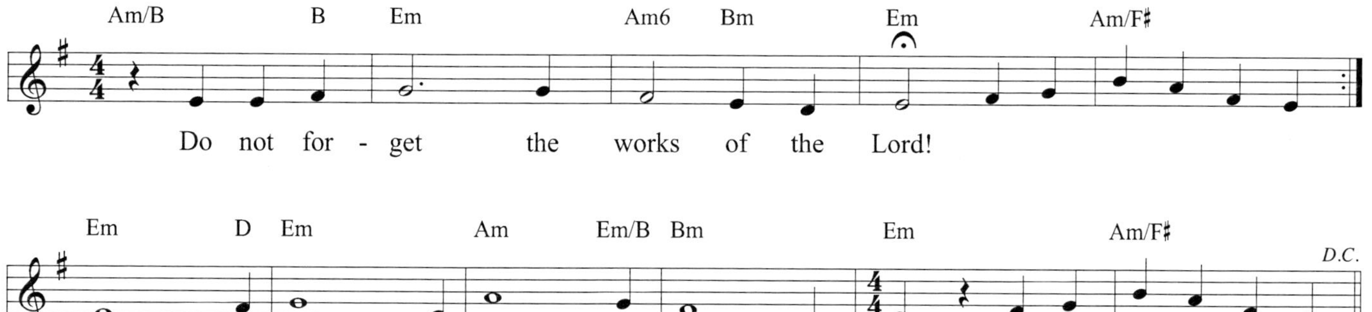

Give ear, O my people, to my · **teaching;**
incline your ears to the words of my · **mouth.**
I will open my mouth in a · **parable;**
I will utter dark sayings · **from_of** old. R.

When God killed them, the people · **sought_for_him;**
they repented and sought him · **earnestly.**
They remembered that God was their · **rock,**
the Most High God · **their_re**-deemer. R.

But they flattered him with their · **mouths;**
they lied to him with their · **tongues.**
Their heart was not steadfast toward · **him;**
they were not true to · **his** covenant. R.

Yet he, being compassionate, forgave their in·-**iquity,**
and did not de·-**stroy_them;**
often he restrained his · **anger,**
and did not stir up all · **his** wrath. R.

C Instrument

B♭ Instrument

253

November 1 – All Saints – ABC

Psalm 24

The earth is the Lord's and all that · **is** in_it,
the world, and those · **who** live_in_it;
for he has founded it · **on_the** seas,
and established it · **on_the** river. R.

Who shall ascend the hill · **of_the** Lord?
And who shall stand in his · **holy** place?
Someone who has clean hands and a · **pure** heart,
who does not lift up their soul to · **what_is** false. R.

That person will receive blessing · **from_the** Lord,
and vindication from the God of their · **sal**-vation.
Such is the company of those · **who** seek_him,
who seek the face of the God · **of** Jacob. R.

November 1 – All Saints – ABC

Psalm 24

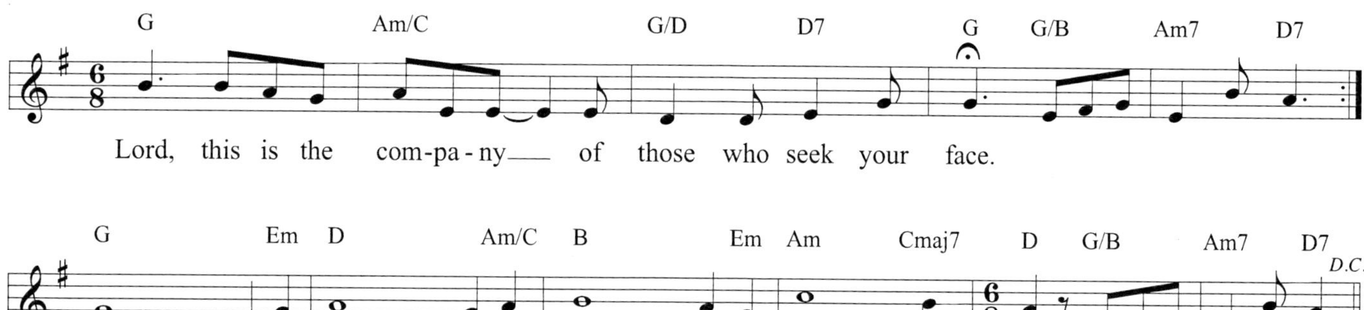

The earth is the Lord's and all that · **is in_it,**
the world, and those · **who** live_in_it;
for he has founded it · **on_the** seas,
and established it · **on_the** river. R.

Who shall ascend the hill · **of_the** Lord?
And who shall stand in his · **holy** place?
Someone who has clean hands and a · **pure** heart,
who does not lift up their soul to · **what_is** false. R.

That person will receive blessing · **from_the** Lord,
and vindication from the God of their · **sal**-vation.
Such is the company of those · **who** seek_him,
who seek the face of the God · **of** Jacob. R.

November 2 – Commemoration of All the Faithful Departed I – ABC

(All Souls)

Psalm 103

The Lord is merciful and · **gracious,**
slow to anger and abounding in stead·-**fast** love.
He does not deal with us according to our · **sins,**
nor repay us according to our · **in**-iquities. R.

As a father has compassion for his · **children,**
so the Lord has compassion for those · **who** fear_him.
For he knows how we were · **made;**
he remembers that we · **are** dust. R.

As for mortals, their days are like · **grass;**
they flourish like a flower · **of_the** field;
for the wind passes over it, and it is · **gone,**
and its place knows it · **no** more. R.

The steadfast love of the · **Lord**
is from everlasting to everlasting on those · **who** fear_him,
and his righteousness to children's · **children,**
to those who keep his covenant and remember to do his · **com**-mandments. R.

November 2 – Commemoration of All the Faithful Departed I – ABC

(All Souls)

Psalm 103

Guitar

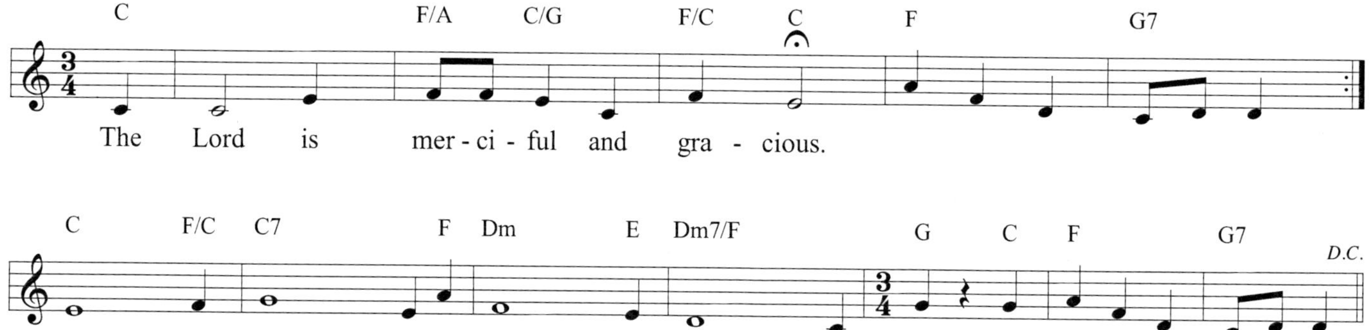

The Lord is merciful and · **gracious,**
slow to anger and abounding in stead·-**fast** love.
He does not deal with us according to our · **sins,**
nor repay us according to our · **in**-iquities. R.

As a father has compassion for his · **children,**
so the Lord has compassion for those · **who** fear_him.
For he knows how we were · **made;**
he remembers that we · **are** dust. R.

As for mortals, their days are like · **grass;**
they flourish like a flower · **of_the** field;
for the wind passes over it, and it is · **gone,**
and its place knows it · **no** more. R.

The steadfast love of the · **Lord**
is from everlasting to everlasting on those · **who** fear_him,
and his righteousness to children's · **children,**
to those who keep his covenant and remember to do his · **com**-mandments. R.

C Instrument

B♭ Instrument

November 2 – Commemoration of All the Faithful Departed II –ABC

(All Souls)

Psalm 23

The Lord is my shepherd, I shall · **not** want.
He makes me lie down in · **green** pastures;
he leads me be·-**side** still waters;
he re·-**stores** my soul. R.

He leads me in right paths for his · **name's** sake.
Even though I walk through the darkest valley, I fear · **no** evil;
for · **you** are with_me;
your rod and your · **staff**—they comfort_me. R.

You prepare a table · **be**-fore_me
in the presence · **of_my** enemies;
you anoint my · **head** with oil;
my · **cup** over-flows. R.

Surely goodness and mercy · **shall** follow_me
all the days of · **my** life,
and I shall dwell in the · **house_of** the Lord
my · **whole** life long. R.

November 2 – Commemoration of All the Faithful Departed II –ABC

(All Souls)
Psalm 23

Guitar

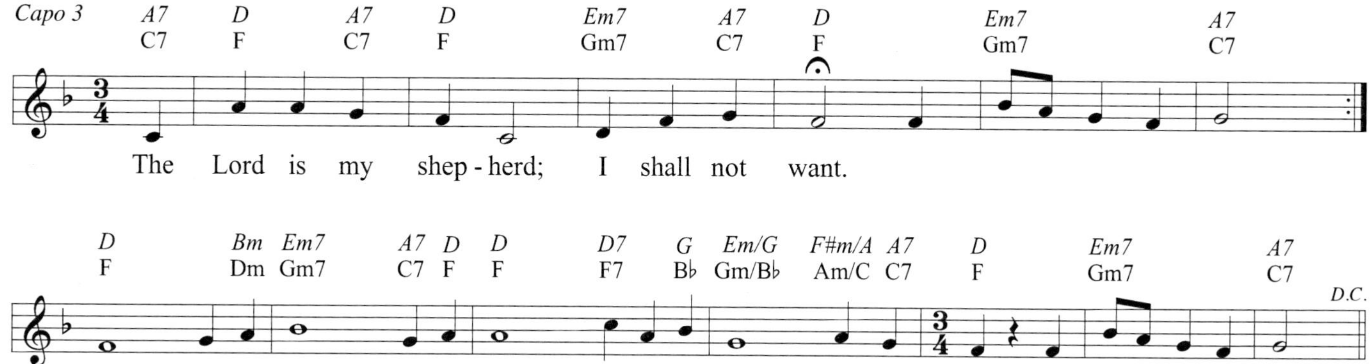

The Lord is my shepherd, I shall · **not** want.
He makes me lie down in · **green** pastures;
he leads me be·-**side** still waters;
he re·-**stores** my soul. R.

He leads me in right paths for his · **name's** sake.
Even though I walk through the darkest valley, I fear · **no** evil;
for · **you** are with_me;
your rod and your · **staff**—they comfort_me. R.

You prepare a table · **be**-fore_me
in the presence · **of_my** enemies;
you anoint my · **head** with oil;
my · **cup** over-flows. R.

Surely goodness and mercy · **shall** follow_me
all the days of · **my** life,
and I shall dwell in the · **house_of** the Lord
my · **whole** life long. R.

C Instrument

B♭ Instrument

November 2 – Commemoration of All the Faithful Departed III – ABC

(All Souls)

Psalm 116

Gracious is the Lord, and · **righteous;**
our God · **is** merciful.
The Lord protects the · **simple;**
when I was brought low, · **he** saved_me. R.

I kept my faith, even when I · **said,**
"I am greatly · **af**-flicted";
I said in my conster·-**nation,**
"Everyone is · **a** liar." R.

Precious in the sight of the · **Lord**
is the death of · **his** faithful_ones.
O Lord, I am your · **servant;**
you have loosed · **my** bonds. R.

November 2 – Commemoration of All the Faithful Departed III – ABC

(All Souls)

Psalm 116

Guitar

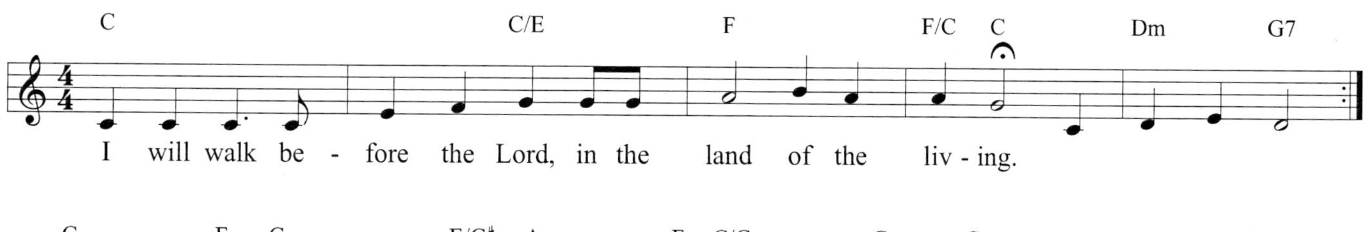

Gracious is the Lord, and · **righteous;**
our God · **is** merciful.
The Lord protects the · **simple;**
when I was brought low, · **he** saved_me. R.

I kept my faith, even when I · **said,**
"I am greatly · **af**-flicted";
I said in my conster·-**nation,**
"Everyone is · **a** liar." R.

Precious in the sight of the · **Lord**
is the death of · **his** faithful_ones.
O Lord, I am your · **servant;**
you have loosed · **my** bonds. R.

November 9 – Dedication of the Lateran Basilica – ABC

Psalm 46

God is our · **refuge** and strength,
a very present · **help** in trouble.
Therefore we will not fear, though the · **earth** should change,
though the mountains · **shake_in** the heart_of the sea. R.

There is a river whose streams make glad the · **city** of God,
the holy habitation · **of_the** Most High.
God is in the midst of the city; it shall · **not** be moved;
God will · **help_it** when_the morn-ing dawns. R.

The Lord of · **hosts** is with_us;
the God of Jacob · **is** our refuge.
Come, behold the · **works_of** the Lord;
see what awesome · **things_he** has brought_on the earth. R.

November 9 – Dedication of the Lateran Basilica – ABC

Psalm 46

Guitar

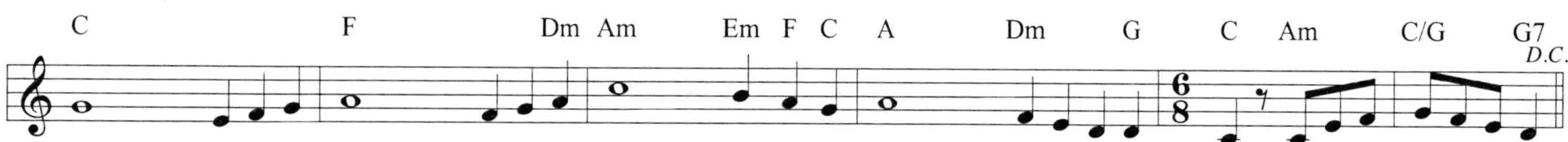

God is our · **refuge** and strength,
a very present · **help** in trouble.
Therefore we will not fear, though the · **earth** should change,
though the mountains · **shake_in** the heart_of the sea. R.

There is a river whose streams make glad the · **city** of God,
the holy habitation · **of_the** Most High.
God is in the midst of the city; it shall · **not** be moved;
God will · **help_it** when_the morn-ing dawns. R.

The Lord of · **hosts** is with_us;
the God of Jacob · **is** our refuge.
Come, behold the · **works_of** the Lord;
see what awesome · **things_he** has brought_on the earth. R.

C Instrument

B♭ Instrument

December 8 – Immaculate Conception of the Blessed Virgin Mary – ABC

Psalm 98

O sing to the Lord · **a** new song,
for he has done · **marvel**-lous things.
His right hand and his · **ho**-ly arm
have · **brought** him victory. R.

The Lord has made · **known** his victory;
he has revealed his vindication in the · **sight_of** the nations.
He has remembered his · **stead**-fast love
and faithfulness to the · **house** of Israel. R.

All the ends of the · **earth** have seen
the victory · **of** our God.
Make a joyful noise to the Lord, · **all** the earth;
break forth into joyous · **song_and** sing praises. R.

December 8 – Immaculate Conception of the Blessed Virgin Mary – ABC

Psalm 98

Guitar

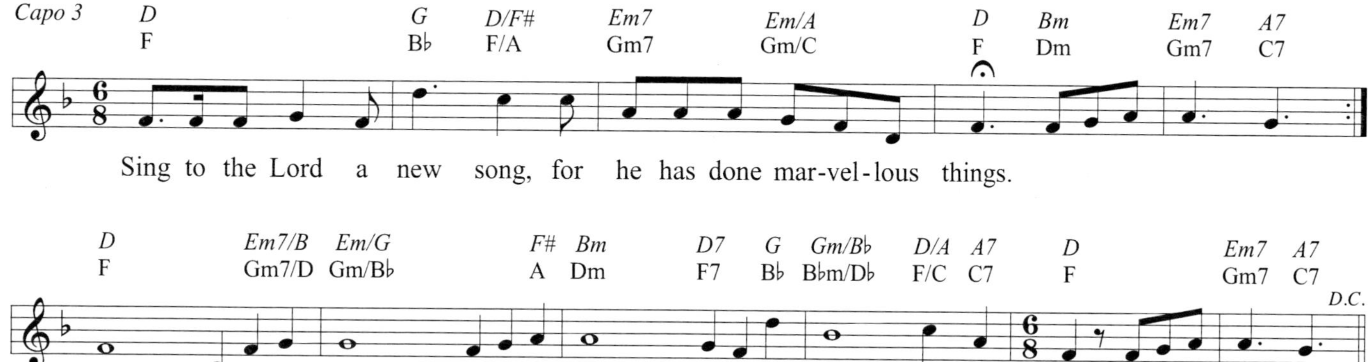

O sing to the Lord · **a** new song,
for he has done · **marvel**-lous things.
His right hand and his · **ho**-ly arm
have · **brought** him victory. R.

The Lord has made · **known** his victory;
he has revealed his vindication in the · **sight_of** the nations.
He has remembered his · **stead**-fast love
and faithfulness to the · **house** of Israel. R.

All the ends of the · **earth** have seen
the victory · **of** our God.
Make a joyful noise to the Lord, · **all** the earth;
break forth into joyous · **song_and** sing praises. R.

C Instrument

B♭ Instrument

Table of Responsorial Psalms and Canticles

001. 1-2, 3, 4+6	Year C - Sixth Sunday in Ordinary Time
004. 1, 3, 6, 8	Year B - Third Sunday of Easter
008. 3-4, 5-6, 7-8	Year C - Trinity Sunday
008. 3-4, 5-6, 7-8	Years ABC - Ext Vigil of Pentecost 1
015. 1b-3a, 3b-4a, 4b-5	Year B - Twenty-second Sunday in Ordinary Time
015. 1b-3a, 3b-4a, 4b-5	Year C - Sixteenth Sunday in Ordinary Time
016. 1-2+5, 7-8, 9-10, 11	Year A - Third Sunday of Easter
016. 1-2a+5, 7-8, 9-10, 11	Year C - Thirteenth Sunday in Ordinary Time
016. 5+8, 9-10, 11	Years ABC - Easter Vigil 2
016. 5+8, 9-10, 11	Year B - Thirty-third Sunday in Ordinary Time
017. 1, 5-6, 8+15	Year C - Thirty-second Sunday in Ordinary Time
018. 1-2, 3+6b, 46+50ab	Year A - Thirtieth Sunday in Ordinary Time
018. 1-2, 3+6b, 46+50ab	Year B - Thirty-first Sunday in Ordinary Time
019. 1-2, 3-4	Years ABC - Vigil of Peter and Paul
019. 7, 8, 9, 10	Years ABC - Common for Ordinary Time
019. 7, 8, 9, 10	Years ABC - Easter Vigil 6
019. 7, 8, 9, 10	Year C - Fifteenth Sunday in Ordinary Time 2
019. 7, 8, 9, 10	Year B - Third Sunday of Lent
019. 7, 8, 9, 14	Year C - Third Sunday in Ordinary Time
019. 7, 9, 11-12, 13	Year B - Twenty-sixth Sunday in Ordinary Time
022. 7-8, 16-17, 18-19, 22-23	Years ABC - Common for Holy Week
022. 7-8, 16-17, 18-19, 22-23	Year A - Passion Sunday
022. 7-8, 16-17, 18-19, 22-23	Year B - Passion Sunday
022. 7-8, 16-17, 18-19, 22-23	Year C - Passion Sunday
022. 25b-26, 27+29, 30-31	Year B - Fifth Sunday of Easter
023. 1-3a, 3b-4, 5, 6	Years ABC - All Souls II
023. 1-3a, 3b-4, 5, 6	Year C - Sacred Heart of Jesus
023. 1-3a, 3b-4, 5, 6	Year B - Sixteenth Sunday in Ordinary Time
023. 1-3a, 3b-4, 5, 6	Year A - Christ the King
023. 1-3a, 3b-4, 5, 6	Year A - Twenty-eighth Sunday in Ordinary Time
023. 1-3a, 3b-4, 5, 6	Year A - Fourth Sunday of Easter
023. 1-3a, 3b-4, 5, 6	Year A - Fourth Sunday of Lent
024. 1-2, 3-4ab, 5-6	Years ABC - All Saints
024. 1-2, 3-4ab, 5-6	Year A - Fourth Sunday of Advent
024. 7, 8, 9, 10	Years ABC - Presentation of the Lord
025. 4-5a, 6-7b, 8-9	Year B - Third Sunday in Ordinary Time
025. 4-5a, 6+7b, 8-9	Year B - First Sunday of Lent
025. 4-5a, 6+7b, 8-9	Year A - Twenty-sixth Sunday in Ordinary Time
025. 4-5a, 8-9, 10+14	Years ABC - Common for Advent
025. 4-5a, 8-9, 10+14	Year C - First Sunday of Advent
027. 1, 4, 7-8	Year A - Seventh Sunday of Easter
027. 1, 4, 13-14	Years ABC - Common for Ordinary Time
027. 1, 4, 13-14	Year A - Third Sunday in Ordinary Time
027. 1, 7-8, 9, 13-14	Year C - Second Sunday of Lent
029. 1-2, 3ac-4, 3b+9c-10	Years ABC - Baptism of the Lord
030. 1+3, 4-5, 10+11a+12b	Years ABC - Easter Vigil 4
030. 1+3, 4-5, 10+11a+12b	Year C - Tenth Sunday in Ordinary Time
030. 1+3, 4-5, 10+11a+12b	Year C - Third Sunday of Easter
030. 1+3, 4-5, 10+11a+12b	Year B - Thirteenth Sunday in Ordinary Time
031. 1-2a, 2b-3, 16+24	Year A - Ninth Sunday in Ordinary Time
031. 1+5, 11-12, 14-15, 16+24	Years ABC - The Lord's Passion
032. 1-2, 5, 7+10b	Year C - Eleventh Sunday in Ordinary Time
032. 1-2, 5, 10bc-11	Year B - Sixth Sunday in Ordinary Time
033. 1-2, 4-5, 18-19	Year A - Fifth Sunday of Easter
033. 1+12, 18-19, 20+22	Year C - Nineteenth Sunday in Ordinary Time
033. 4-5, 6-7, 12-13, 20+22	Years ABC - Easter Vigil 1.2

033. 4-5, 6+9, 18-19, 20+22	Year B - Trinity Sunday
033. 4-5, 18-19, 20+22	Year B - Twenty-ninth Sunday in Ordinary Time
033. 4-5, 18-19, 20+22	Year A - Second Sunday of Lent
034. 1-2, 3-4, 5-6	Year C - Fourth Sunday of Lent
034. 1-2, 3-4, 5-6, 7-8	Years ABC - Peter and Paul, Apostles
034. 1-2, 3-4, 5-6, 7-8	Years ABC - Common for Ordinary Time
034. 1-2, 3-4, 5-6, 7-8	Year B - Nineteenth Sunday in Ordinary Time
034. 1-2, 9-10, 11-12, 13-14	Years ABC - Common for Christmas
034. 1-2, 9-10, 11-12, 13-14	Year B - Twentieth Sunday in Ordinary Time
034. 1-2, 15-16, 17-18, 19-20 &c	Year B - Twenty-first Sunday in Ordinary Time
034. 1-2, 16-17, 18+22	Year C - Thirtieth Sunday in Ordinary Time
040. 1, 2, 3, 17	Year C - Twentieth Sunday in Ordinary Time
040. 1+3a, 6, 7-8, 9	Year B - Second Sunday in Ordinary Time
040. 1+3a, 6, 7-8, 9	Year A - Second Sunday in Ordinary Time
040. 6, 7-8, 9, 10	Years ABC - Annunciation of the Lord
041. 1-2, 3-4, 12-13	Year B - Seventh Sunday in Ordinary Time
042. 2, 4bcd; 43.3, 4,	Years ABC - Easter Vigil 7.1
045. 9-10, 11+12c+14, 15+17	Years ABC - Assumption of Mary
046. 1-2, 4-5, 7-8	Years ABC - Dedication of Lateran Basilica
047. 1-2, 5-6, 7-8	Years ABC - Common for Ascension
047. 1-2, 5-6, 7-8	Year A - Ascension of the Lord
047. 1-2, 5-6, 7-8	Year B - Ascension of the Lord
047. 1-2, 5-6, 7-8	Year C - Ascension of the Lord
050. 1+8, 12-13, 14-15	Year A - Tenth Sunday in Ordinary Time
051. 1-2, 3-4a, 10-11, 12+15	Year A - First Sunday of Lent
051. 1-2, 3-4a, 10-11, 12+15	Years ABC - Ash Wednesday
051. 1-2, 3-4a, 10-11, 12+15	Years ABC - Common for Lent
051. 1-2, 10-11, 12-13	Year B - Fifth Sunday of Lent
051. 1-2, 10-11, 15+17	Year C - Twenty-fourth Sunday in Ordinary Time
051. 10-11, 12-13, 16-17	Years ABC - Easter Vigil 7.2
054. 1-2, 3, 4+6	Year B - Twenty-fifth Sunday in Ordinary Time
062. 1-2, 5-6, 7-8	Year A - Eighth Sunday in Ordinary Time
063. 1, 2-3, 4-5, 6-7	Year A - Thirty-second Sunday in Ordinary Time
063. 1, 2-3, 4-5, 7-8	Years ABC - Common for Ordinary Time
063. 1, 2-3, 4-5, 7-8	Year C - Twelfth Sunday in Ordinary Time
063. 1, 2-3, 4-5, 7-8	Year A - Twenty-second Sunday in Ordinary Time
065. 9abcd, 9e-10, 11-12, 13	Year A - Fifteenth Sunday in Ordinary Time
066. 1-3a, 4-5, 6-7a, 16+20	Years ABC - Common for Easter
066. 1-3a, 4-5, 6-7a, 16+20	Year C - Fourteenth Sunday in Ordinary Time
066. 1-3a, 4-5, 6-7a, 16+20	Year A - Sixth Sunday of Easter
067. 1-2, 4-5, 6-7	Years ABC - Mary, Mother of God
067. 1-2, 4-5, 6-7	Year A - Twentieth Sunday in Ordinary Time
067. 1-2, 4-5a, 6-7	Year C - Sixth Sunday of Easter
068. 3-4, 5-6a, 9-10	Year C - Twenty-second Sunday in Ordinary Time
069. 7-9, 13+16, 32-33, 35ab-36	Year A - Twelfth Sunday in Ordinary Time
069. 13+16, 29-30, 32-33, 35&c	Year C - Fifteenth Sunday in Ordinary Time 1
071. 1-2, 3, 5-6, 15+17	Years ABC - Vigil of John the Baptist
071. 1-2, 3, 5-6, 15+17	Year C - Fourth Sunday in Ordinary Time
072. 1-2, 7-8, 10-11, 12-13	Years ABC - Epiphany of the Lord
072. 1-2, 7-8, 10-11, 12-13	Years ABC - Common for Christmas
072. 1-2, 7-8, 12-13	Year A - Second Sunday of Advent
078. 1-2, 34-35, 36-37, 38	Years ABC - Exaltation of the Cross
078. 3+4bc, 23-24, 25+54	Year B - Eighteenth Sunday in Ordinary Time
080. 1ab-2, 3-4, 14ab+18	Years ABC - Ext Vigil of Pentecost 2
080. 1ab+2, 14-15, 17-18	Year C - Fourth Sunday of Advent
080. 1ab+2, 14-15, 17-18	Year B - First Sunday of Advent
080. 8+11, 12-13, 14-15, 18-19	Year A - Twenty-seventh Sunday in Ordinary Time
081. 2-3, 4-5ab, 5c-7a, 9-10ab	Year B - Ninth Sunday in Ordinary Time
084. 1-2, 4-5, 8-9, 10	Year C - Holy Family
085. 8ab-9, 10-11, 12-13	Years ABC - Common for Advent
085. 8ab-9, 10-11, 12-13	Year B - Fifteenth Sunday in Ordinary Time

085. 8ab-9, 10-11, 12-13 — Year B - Second Sunday of Advent
085. 8ab-9, 10-11, 12-13 — Year A - Nineteenth Sunday in Ordinary Time
086. 5-6, 9-10, 15-16 — Year A - Sixteenth Sunday in Ordinary Time
089. 1-2, 3-4, 26+28 — Years ABC - Joseph, Husband of Mary
089. 1-2, 3-4, 26+28 — Year B - Fourth Sunday of Advent
089. 1-2, 15-16, 17-18 — Year A - Thirteenth Sunday in Ordinary Time
089. 3-4, 15-16, 26+28 — Years ABC - Vigil of Christmas
089. 20-21, 24+26, 27-28 — Years ABC - Mass of Chrism
090. 1-2, 3-4, 5-6, 14+16 — Years ABC - Ext Vigil of Pentecost 6
090. 3-4, 5-6, 12-13, 14+17 — Year C - Twenty-third Sunday in Ordinary Time
090. 3-4, 5-6, 12-13, 14+17 — Year C - Eighteenth Sunday in Ordinary Time
090. 12-13, 14-15, 16-17 — Year B - Twenty-eighth Sunday in Ordinary Time
091. 1-2, 10-11, 12-13, 14-15 — Years ABC - Common for Lent
091. 1-2, 10-11, 12-13, 14-15 — Year C - First Sunday of Lent
092. 1-2, 12-13, 14-15 — Year C - Eighth Sunday in Ordinary Time
092. 1-2, 12-13, 14-15 — Year B - Eleventh Sunday in Ordinary Time
093. 1ab, 1c-2, 5 — Year B - Christ the King
095. 1-2, 6-7ab, 7c-9 — Years ABC - Common for Ordinary Time
095. 1-2, 6-7ab, 7c-9 — Year C - Twenty-seventh Sunday in Ordinary Time
095. 1-2, 6-7ab, 7c-9 — Year B - Fourth Sunday in Ordinary Time
095. 1-2, 6-7ab, 7c-9 — Year A - Twenty-third Sunday in Ordinary Time
095. 1-2, 6-7ab, 7c-9 — Year A - Third Sunday of Lent
096. 1-2, 3-4, 11-12, 13 — Years ABC - Christmas during the night
096. 1-2, 3-4, 7-8, 9-10ac — Year C - Second Sunday in Ordinary Time
096. 1+3, 4-5, 7-8, 9+10ac — Year A - Twenty-ninth Sunday in Ordinary Time
097. 1-2, 3-4, 5-6, 11-12 — Years ABC - Ext Vigil of Pentecost 3
097. 1-2, 5-6, 9+12 — Years ABC - Transfiguration of the Lord
097. 1-2, 5-6, 11-12 — Years ABC - Christmas at dawn
097. 1-2, 6-7ac, 9+12 — Year C - Seventh Sunday of Easter
098. 1, 2-3ab, 3cd-4 — Years ABC - Immaculate Conception
098. 1, 2-3ab, 3cd-4 — Year C - Twenty-eighth Sunday in Ordinary Time
098. 1, 2-3ab, 3cd-4 — Year B - Sixth Sunday of Easter
098. 1, 2-3a, 3b-4, 5-6 — Years ABC - Christmas during the day
098. 1, 2-3a, 3b-4, 5-6 — Years ABC - Common for Christmas
098. 5-6, 7-8, 9 — Year C - Thirty-third Sunday in Ordinary Time
100. 1-2, 3, 4, 5 — Year A - Eleventh Sunday in Ordinary Time
100. 1-2, 3, 5 — Years ABC - Common for Ordinary Time
100. 1-2, 3, 5 — Year C - Fourth Sunday of Easter
103. 1-2, 3-4, 6-7, 8-9 — Year A - Sacred Heart of Jesus
103. 1-2, 3-4, 6-7, 8+11 — Year C - Third Sunday of Lent
103. 1-2, 3-4, 8+10, 12-13 — Years ABC - Common for Ordinary Time
103. 1-2, 3-4, 8+10, 12-13 — Year C - Seventh Sunday in Ordinary Time
103. 1-2, 3-4, 8+10, 12-13 — Year B - Eighth Sunday in Ordinary Time
103. 1-2, 3-4, 8+10, 12-13 — Year A - Seventh Sunday in Ordinary Time
103. 1-2, 3-4, 9-10, 11-12 — Year A - Twenty-fourth Sunday in Ordinary Time
103. 1-2, 11-12, 19-20 — Year B - Seventh Sunday of Easter
103. 8+10, 13-14, 15-16, 17 — Years ABC - All Souls I
104. 1b-2, 3-4, 24-25, 27+28 &c — Year C - Baptism of the Lord
104. 1-2a, 5-6, 10+12, 13-14, &c — Years ABC - Easter Vigil 1.1
104. 1-2a, 24+25c, 27-28, 29&c — Years ABC - Ext Vigil of Pentecost 7
104. 1-2a, 24+25c, 27-28, 29&c — Years ABC - Vigil of Pentecost
104. 1ab+24ac, 29b-30, 31+34 — Years ABC - Common for Pentecost
104. 1ab+24ac, 29b-30, 31+34 — Year A - Pentecost Sunday
104. 1ab+24ac, 29b-30, 31+34 — Year B - Pentecost Sunday
104. 1ab+24ac, 29b-30, 31+34 — Year C - Pentecost Sunday
105. 1-2, 3-4, 5-6, 8-9 — Year B - Holy Family
105. 1-2, 5-6, 7+8a+9a+10b — Years ABC - Ext Vigil of Pentecost 5
107. 23-24, 25-26, 28-29, 30-31 — Year B - Twelfth Sunday in Ordinary Time
110. 1, 2, 3, 4 — Year C - Body and Blood of Christ
112. 4-5, 6-7, 8a-9 — Year A - Fifth Sunday in Ordinary Time
113. 1-2, 4-6, 7-8 — Year C - Twenty-fifth Sunday in Ordinary Time

116. 1-2, 3-4, 5-6, 8-9 — Year B - Twenty-fourth Sunday in Ordinary Time
116. 5-6, 10-11, 15-16 — Years ABC - All Souls III
116. 10+15, 16-17, 18-19 — Year B - Second Sunday of Lent
116. 12-13, 15-16, 17-18 — Years ABC - Mass of the Lord's Supper
116. 12-13, 15-16, 17-18 — Year B - Body and Blood of Christ
117. 1, 2 — Year C - Twenty-first Sunday in Ordinary Time
117. 1, 2 — Year C - Ninth Sunday in Ordinary Time
118. 1-2, 16-17, 22-23 — Years ABC - Common for Easter
118. 1-2, 16-17, 22-23 — Years ABC - Easter Sunday
118. 1-2, 16-17, 22-23 — Years ABC - Easter Vigil - Solemn Alleluia
118. 1+8-9, 21-23, 26+28-29 — Year B - Fourth Sunday of Easter
118. 2-4, 13-15, 22-24 — Year A - Second Sunday of Easter
118. 2-4, 16-18, 22-24 — Year B - Second Sunday of Easter
118. 2-4, 22-24, 25-27a — Year C - Second Sunday of Easter
119. 1-2, 4-5, 17-18, 33-34 — Year A - Sixth Sunday in Ordinary Time
119. 57+72, 76-77, 127-128, &c — Year A - Seventeenth Sunday in Ordinary Time
121. 1-2, 3-4, 5-6, 7-8 — Year C - Twenty-ninth Sunday in Ordinary Time
122. 1-2, 3-4a, 4b-5 — Year C - Christ the King
122. 1-2, 3-4a, 4b-5, 6-7, 8-9 — Years ABC - Common Last Weeks of Ordinary Time
122. 1-2, 4-5, 6-7, 8-9 — Year A - First Sunday of Advent
123. 1-2a, 2b, 3-4 — Year B - Fourteenth Sunday in Ordinary Time
126. 1-2a, 2b-3, 4-5, 6 — Year C - Fifth Sunday of Lent
126. 1-2a, 2b-3, 4-5, 6 — Year C - Second Sunday of Advent
126. 1-2a, 2b-3, 4-5, 6 — Year B - Thirtieth Sunday in Ordinary Time
128. 1-2, 3, 4-5 — Year B - Twenty-seventh Sunday in Ordinary Time
128. 1-2, 3, 4-5 — Year A - Thirty-third Sunday in Ordinary Time
128. 1-2, 3, 4-5 — Years ABC - Holy Family
130. 1-2, 3-4, 5-6, 7b-8 — Years ABC - Common for Lent
130. 1-2, 3-4, 5-6, 7b-8 — Year B - Tenth Sunday in Ordinary Time
130. 1-2, 3-4, 5-6, 7b-8 — Year A - Fifth Sunday of Lent
131. 1, 2, 3 — Year A - Thirty-first Sunday in Ordinary Time
132. 6-7, 9-10, 13-14 — Years ABC - Vigil of the Assumption
137. 1-2, 3-4, 5-6 — Year B - Fourth Sunday of Lent
138. 1-2a, 2b-3, 4-5, 7c-8 — Year C - Fifth Sunday in Ordinary Time
138. 1-2a, 2b-3, 6-7ab, 7c-8 — Year C - Seventeenth Sunday in Ordinary Time
138. 1-2a, 2b-3, 6+8b — Year A - Twenty-first Sunday in Ordinary Time
139. 1-3, 4+6, 7-8, 10+17 — Years ABC - Ext Vigil of Pentecost 4
139. 1-3, 13-14a, 14b-15 — Years ABC - Birth of John the Baptist
145. 1-2, 8-9, 10-11, 13cd-14 — Years ABC - Common for Ordinary Time
145. 1-2, 8-9, 10-11, 13cd-14 — Year C - Thirty-first Sunday in Ordinary Time
145. 1-2, 8-9, 10-11, 13cd-14 — Year A - Fourteenth Sunday in Ordinary Time
145. 2-3, 8-9, 17-18 — Year A - Twenty-fifth Sunday in Ordinary Time
145. 8-9, 10-11, 12-13 — Year C - Fifth Sunday of Easter
145. 8-9, 15-16, 17-18 — Year A - Eighteenth Sunday in Ordinary Time
145. 10-11, 15-16, 17-18 — Year B - Seventeenth Sunday in Ordinary Time
146. 6c-7, 8-9a, 9b-10 — Years ABC - Common for Advent
146. 6c-7, 8-9a, 9b-10 — Year C - Twenty-sixth Sunday in Ordinary Time
146. 6c-7, 8-9a, 9b-10 — Year B - Thirty-second Sunday in Ordinary Time
146. 6c-7, 8-9a, 9b-10 — Year B - Twenty-third Sunday in Ordinary Time
146. 6c-7, 8-9a, 9b-10 — Year A - Fourth Sunday in Ordinary Time
146. 6c-7, 8-9a, 9b-10 — Year A - Third Sunday of Advent
147. 1-2, 3-4, 5-6 — Year B - Fifth Sunday in Ordinary Time
147. 12-13, 14-15, 19-20 — Years ABC - Second Sunday after Christmas
147. 12-13, 14-15, 19-20 — Year A - Body and Blood of Christ
Daniel 3. 52, 53, 54, 55, 56 — Year A - Trinity Sunday
Exodus 15.1-2, 3-5, 6-7, 17-18 — Years ABC - Easter Vigil 3
Isaiah 12. 2-3, 4bcd, 5-6 — Years ABC - Easter Vigil 5
Isaiah 12. 2-3, 4bcd, 5-6 — Year B - Sacred Heart of Jesus
Isaiah 12. 2-3, 4bcd, 5-6 — Year B - Baptism of the Lord
Isaiah 12. 3, 4bcd, 5-6 — Year C - Third Sunday of Advent
Luke 1. 47-48, 49-50, 53-54 — Year B - Third Sunday of Advent

Table of Psalm Refrains

Refrain	Psalm	Occasion
A light will shine on us this day: The Lord is born for us.	097. 1-2, 5-6, 11-12	Years ABC - Christmas at dawn
All the ends of the earth have seen the victory of our God.	098. 1, 2-3a, 3b-4, 5-6	Years ABC - Christmas during the day
	098. 1, 2-3a, 3b-4, 5-6	Years ABC - Common for Christmas
Alleluia! Alleluia! Alleluia!	118. 1-2, 16-17, 22-23	Years ABC - Easter Vigil - Alleluia
As a deer longs for flowing streams, my soul longs for you, O God.	042. 2, 4bcd; 43.3, 4,	Years ABC - Easter Vigil 7.1
Ascribe to the Lord glory and strength.	096. 1+3, 4-5, 7-8, 9+10ac	Year A - Twenty-ninth Sunday in OT
At your right hand stands the queen in gold of Ophir.	045. 9-10, 11+12c+14, 15+17	Years ABC - Assumption
Be with me, Lord, when I am in trouble.	091. 1-2, 10-11, 12-13, 14-15	Year C - First Sunday of Lent
	091. 1-2, 10-11, 12-13, 14-15	Years ABC - Common for Lent
Before the Angels I sing your praise, O Lord.	138. 1-2a, 2b-3, 4-5, 7c-8	Year C - Fifth Sunday in OT
Blessed are the poor in spirit; the kingdom of heaven is theirs!	146. 6c-7, 8-9a, 9b-10	Year A - Fourth Sunday in OT
Blessed are those who live in your house, O Lord.	084. 1-2, 4-5, 8-9, 10	Year C - Holy Family
Blessed are those who walk in the law of the Lord!	119. 1-2, 4-5, 17-18, 33-34	Year A - Sixth Sunday in OT
Blessed is everyone who fears the Lord.	128. 1-2, 3, 4-5	Year A - Thirty-third Sunday in OT
Blessed is everyone who fears the Lord, who walks in his ways.	128. 1-2, 3, 4-5	Years ABC - Holy Family
Blessed the one who fears the Lord.	034. 1-2, 9-10, 11-12, 13-14	Years ABC - Common for Christmas
Blessed the one who trusts in the Lord.	001. 1-2, 3, 4+6	Year C - Sixth Sunday in OT
Blessed the people the Lord has chosen as his heritage.	033. 1+12, 18-19, 20+22	Year C - Nineteenth Sunday in OT
	033. 4-5, 6+9, 18-19, 20+22	Year B - Trinity Sunday
Create in me a clean heart, O God.	051. 1-2, 10-11, 12-13	Year B - Fifth Sunday of Lent
	051. 10-11, 12-13, 16-17	Years ABC - Easter Vigil 7.2
Declare the marvellous works of the Lord among all the peoples.	096. 1-2, 3-4, 7-8, 9-10ac	Year C - Second Sunday in OT
Do not forget the works of the Lord!	078. 1-2, 34-35, 36-37, 38	Years ABC - Exaltation of the Holy Cross
Father, into your hands I commend my spirit.	031. 1+5, 11-12, 14-15, 16+24	Years ABC - The Lord's Passion
Fill us with your love, O Lord, that we may rejoice and be glad.	090. 12-13, 14-15, 16-17	Year B - Twenty-eighth Sunday in OT
Forever I will sing of your steadfast love, O Lord.	089. 1-2, 3-4, 26+28	Year B - Fourth Sunday of Advent
	089. 1-2, 15-16, 17-18	Year A - Thirteenth Sunday in OT
	089. 3-4, 15-16, 26+28	Years ABC - Vigil of Christmas
	089. 20-21, 24+26, 27-28	Years ABC - Mass of Chrism
For God alone my soul waits in silence.	062. 1-2, 5-6, 7-8	Year A - Eighth Sunday in OT
From my mother's womb, you have been my strength.	071. 1-2, 3, 5-6, 15+17	Years ABC - John the Baptist (Vigil)
Give thanks to the Lord for he is good; his steadfast love endures forever.	118. 2-4, 13-15, 22-24	Year A - Second Sunday of Easter
	118. 2-4, 16-18, 22-24	Year B - Second Sunday of Easter
	118. 2-4, 22-24, 25-27a	Year C - Second Sunday of Easter
Give thanks to the Lord; his steadfast love endures forever.	107. 23-24, 25-26, 28-29, 30-31	Year B - Twelfth Sunday in OT
Give us your spirit, O Lord, and we shall live.	090. 1-2, 3-4, 5-6, 14+16	Years ABC - Ext Vigil of Pentecost 6
Glory and praise for ever!	Daniel 3. 52, 53, 54, 55, 56	Year A - Trinity Sunday

Antiphon	Psalm	Liturgical Day
Go into all the world and proclaim the good news.	117. 1, 2	Year C - Ninth Sunday in OT
	117. 1, 2	Year C - Twenty-first Sunday in OT
God has gone up with a shout, the Lord with the sound of a trumpet.	047. 1-2, 5-6, 7-8	Year A - Ascension of the Lord
	047. 1-2, 5-6, 7-8	Year B - Ascension of the Lord
	047. 1-2, 5-6, 7-8	Year C - Ascension of the Lord
	047. 1-2, 5-6, 7-8	Years ABC - Common for Ascension
Have mercy, O Lord, for we have sinned.	051. 1-2, 3-4a, 10-11, 12+15	Year A - First Sunday of Lent
	051. 1-2, 3-4a, 10-11, 12+15	Years ABC - Ash Wednesday
	051. 1-2, 3-4a, 10-11, 12+15	Years ABC - Common for Lent
Heal me, O Lord, for I have sinned against you.	041. 1-2, 3-4, 12-13	Year B - Seventh Sunday in OT
Here I am, Lord; I come to do your will.	040. 1+3a, 6, 7-8, 9	Year A - Second Sunday in OT
	040. 1+3a, 6, 7-8, 9	Year B - Second Sunday in OT
	040. 6, 7-8, 9, 10	Years ABC - Annunciation of the Lord
His line shall continue forever.	089. 1-2, 3-4, 26+28	Years ABC - Joseph, Husband of Mary
I believe that I shall see the good things of the Lord in the land of the living.	027. 1, 4, 7-8	Year A - Seventh Sunday of Easter
I love you, O Lord, my strength.	018. 1-2, 3+6b, 46+50ab	Year A - Thirtieth Sunday in OT
	018. 1-2, 3+6b, 46+50ab	Year B - Thirty-first Sunday in OT
	139. 1-3, 13-14a, 14b-15	Years ABC - Birth of John the Baptist
I praise you, for I am wonderfully made.	017. 1, 5-6, 8+15	Year C - Thirty-second Sunday in OT
I shall be satisfied, Lord, when I awake and behold your likeness.	023. 1-3a, 3b-4, 5, 6	Year A - Twenty-eighth Sunday in OT
I shall dwell in the house of the Lord my whole life long.	145. 1-2, 8-9, 10-11, 13cd-14	Year A - Fourteenth Sunday in OT
I will bless your name for ever, my King and my God.	145. 1-2, 8-9, 10-11, 13cd-14	Year C - Thirty-first Sunday in OT
	145. 1-2, 8-9, 10-11, 13cd-14	Years ABC - Common for OT
	145. 8-9, 10-11, 12-13	Year C - Fifth Sunday of Easter
I will extol you, Lord, for you have raised me up.	030. 1+3, 4-5, 10+11a+12b	Year B - Thirteenth Sunday in OT
	030. 1+3, 4-5, 10+11a+12b	Year C - Tenth Sunday in OT
	030. 1+3, 4-5, 10+11a+12b	Year C - Third Sunday of Easter
	030. 1+3, 4-5, 10+11a+12b	Years ABC - Easter Vigil 4
I will get up and go to my Father.	051. 1-2, 10-11, 15+17	Year C - Twenty-fourth Sunday in OT
I will lift up the cup of salvation, and call on the name of the Lord.	116. 12-13, 15-16, 17-18	Year B - Body and Blood of Christ
I will walk before the Lord, in the land of the living.	116. 1-2, 3-4, 5-6, 8-9	Year B - Twenty-fourth Sunday in OT
	116. 5-6, 10-11, 15-16	Years ABC - All Souls III
	116. 10+15, 16-17, 18-19	Year B - Second Sunday of Lent
In his days may righteousness flourish, and peace abound forever.	072. 1-2, 7-8, 12-13	Year A - Second Sunday of Advent
In you, Lord, I have found my peace.	131. 1, 2, 3	Year A - Thirty-first Sunday in OT
In your goodness, O God, you provided for the needy.	068. 3-4, 5-6a, 9-10	Year C - Twenty-second Sunday in OT
Let my tongue cling to my mouth if I do not remember you!	137. 1-2, 3-4, 5-6	Year B - Fourth Sunday of Lent
Let the light of your face shine on us, O Lord.	004. 1, 3, 6, 8	Year B - Third Sunday of Easter
Let the peoples praise you, O God, let all the peoples praise you.	067. 1-2, 4-5, 6-7	Year A - Twentieth Sunday in OT
	067. 1-2, 4-5a, 6-7	Year C - Sixth Sunday of Easter

Antiphon	Reference	Occasion
Let us go rejoicing to the house of the Lord.	122. 1-2, 3-4a, 4b-5	Year C - Christ the King
	122. 1-2, 3-4a, 4b-5, 6-7, 8-9	Years ABC - Common Last Weeks of OT
	122. 1-2, 4-5, 6-7, 8-9	Year A - First Sunday of Advent
Let us sing to the Lord; he has covered himself in glory.	Exodus 15.1-2, 3-5, 6-7, 17-18	Years ABC - Easter Vigil 3
Let your love be upon us, Lord, even as we hope in you.	033. 1-2, 4-5, 18-19	Year A - Fifth Sunday of Easter
	033. 4-5, 18-19, 20+22	Year A - Second Sunday of Lent
	033. 4-5, 18-19, 20+22	Year B - Twenty-ninth Sunday in OT
Light rises in the darkness for the upright.	112. 4-5, 6-7, 8a-9	Year A - Fifth Sunday in OT
Lord, be a rock of refuge for me.	031. 1-2a, 2b-3, 16+24	Year A - Ninth Sunday in OT
Lord, be mindful of your mercy.	025. 4-5a, 6+7b, 8-9	Year A - Twenty-sixth Sunday in OT
Lord, come and save us.	146. 6c-7, 8-9a, 9b-10	Year A - Third Sunday of Advent
	146. 6c-7, 8-9a, 9b-10	Years ABC - Common for Advent
Lord, every nation on earth will adore you.	072. 1-2, 7-8, 10-11, 12-13	Years ABC - Common for Christmas
	072. 1-2, 7-8, 10-11, 12-13	Years ABC - Epiphany of the Lord
Lord, forgive the guilt of my sin.	032. 1-2, 5, 7+10b	Year C - Eleventh Sunday in OT
Lord, from you comes my praise in the great congregation.	022. 25b-26, 27+29, 30-31	Year B - Fifth Sunday of Easter
Lord, how I love your law!	119. 57+72, 76-77, 127-128, &c	Year A - Seventeenth Sunday in OT
Lord, in your steadfast love, answer me.	069. 7-9, 13+16, 32-33, 35ab-36	Year A - Twelfth Sunday in OT
Lord, it is good to give thanks to you.	092. 1-2, 12-13, 14-15	Year B - Eleventh Sunday in OT
	092. 1-2, 12-13, 14-15	Year C - Eighth Sunday in OT
Lord, make haste to help me!	040. 1, 2, 3, 17	Year C - Twentieth Sunday in OT
Lord, make me know your ways.	025. 4-5a, 6-7b, 8-9	Year B - Third Sunday in OT
Lord, send forth your Spirit, and renew the face of the earth.	104. 1-2a, 5-6, 10+12, 13-14, &c	Years ABC - Easter Vigil 1.1
	104. 1-2a, 24+25b, 27-28, 29&c	Years ABC - Ext Vigil of Pentecost 7
	104. 1-2a, 24+25c, 27-28, 29&c	Years ABC - Vigil of Pentecost
	104. 1ab+24ac, 29b-30, 31+34	Year A - Pentecost Sunday
	104. 1ab+24ac, 29b-30, 31+34	Year B - Pentecost Sunday
	104. 1ab+24ac, 29b-30, 31+34	Year C - Pentecost Sunday
	104. 1ab+24ac, 29b-30, 31+34	Years ABC - Common for Pentecost
Lord, this is the company of those who seek your face.	024. 1-2, 3-4ab, 5-6	Years ABC - All Saints
Lord, you are good and forgiving.	086. 5-6, 9-10, 15-16	Year A - Sixteenth Sunday in OT
Lord, you have been our dwelling place in all generations.	090. 3-4, 5-6, 12-13, 14+17	Year C - Eighteenth Sunday in OT
	090. 3-4, 5-6, 12-13, 14+17	Year C - Twenty-third Sunday in OT
Lord, you have the words of eternal life.	019. 7, 8, 9, 10	Year B - Third Sunday of Lent
	019. 7, 8, 9, 10	Years ABC - Common for OT
	019. 7, 8, 9, 10	Years ABC - Easter Vigil 6
Lord, you will show me the path of life.	016. 1-2+5, 7-8, 9-10, 11	Year A - Third Sunday of Easter
Make a joyful noise to God, all the earth!	066. 1-3a, 4-5, 6-7a, 16+20	Year A - Sixth Sunday of Easter
	066. 1-3a, 4-5, 6-7a, 16+20	Year C - Fourteenth Sunday in OT
	066. 1-3a, 4-5, 6-7a, 16+20	Years ABC - Common for Easter

May God be gracious to us and bless us.	067. 1-2, 4-5, 6-7	Years ABC - Mary, Mother of God
May the Lord bless us all the days of our lives.	128. 1-2, 3, 4-5	Year B - Twenty-seventh Sunday in OT
May the Lord come in; he is king of glory.	024. 1-2, 3-4ab, 5-6	Year A - Fourth Sunday of Advent
My God, my God, why have you forsaken me?	022. 7-8, 16-17, 18-19, 22-23	Year A - Passion Sunday
	022. 7-8, 16-17, 18-19, 22-23	Year B - Passion Sunday
	022. 7-8, 16-17, 18-19, 22-23	Year C - Passion Sunday
	022. 7-8, 16-17, 18-19, 22-23	Years ABC - Common for Holy Week
My mouth will tell, O Lord, of your deeds of salvation.	071. 1-2, 3, 5-6, 15+17	Year C - Fourth Sunday in OT
My soul shall exult in my God.	Luke 1. 47-48, 49-50, 53-54	Year B - Third Sunday of Advent
My soul thirsts for you, O Lord my God.	063. 1, 2-3, 4-5, 7-8	Year A - Twenty-second Sunday in OT
	063. 1, 2-3, 4-5, 6-7	Year A - Thirty-second Sunday in OT
	063. 1, 2-3, 4-5, 7-8	Year C - Twelfth Sunday in OT
	063. 1, 2-3, 4-5, 7-8	Years ABC - Common for OT
O bless the Lord, my soul!	104. 1b-2, 3-4, 24-25, 27+28 &c	Year C - Baptism of the Lord
O Lord, our God, how majestic is your name in all the earth!	008. 3-4, 5-6, 7-8	Year C - Trinity Sunday
O Lord, our God, you have given us the breath of life!	008. 3-4, 5-6, 7-8	Years ABC - Ext Vigil of Pentecost 1
O Lord, who may abide in your tent?	015. 1b-3a, 3b-4a, 4b-5	Year B - Twenty-second Sunday in OT
	015. 1b-3a, 3b-4a, 4b-5	Year C - Sixteenth Sunday in OT
O that today you would listen to the voice of the Lord. Do not harden your hearts!	095. 1-2, 6-7ab, 7c-9	Year A - Third Sunday of Lent
	095. 1-2, 6-7ab, 7c-9	Year A - Twenty-third Sunday in OT
	095. 1-2, 6-7ab, 7c-9	Year B - Fourth Sunday in OT
	095. 1-2, 6-7ab, 7c-9	Year C - Twenty-seventh Sunday in OT
	095. 1-2, 6-7ab, 7c-9	Years ABC - Common for OT
On the day I called, O Lord, you answered me.	138. 1-2a, 2b-3, 6-7ab, 7c-8	Year C - Seventeenth Sunday in OT
Our eyes look to the Lord, until he has mercy upon us.	123. 1-2a, 2b, 3-4	Year B - Fourteenth Sunday in OT
Our help is from the Lord, who made heaven and earth.	121. 1-2, 3-4, 5-6, 7-8	Year C - Twenty-ninth Sunday in OT
Praise the Lord, Jerusalem.	147. 12-13, 14-15, 19-20	Year A - Body and Blood of Christ
Praise the Lord, O my soul!	146. 6c-7, 8-9a, 9b-10	Year B - Twenty-third Sunday in OT
	146. 6c-7, 8-9a, 9b-10	Year B - Thirty-second Sunday in OT
	146. 6c-7, 8-9a, 9b-10	Year C - Twenty-sixth Sunday in OT
Praise the Lord who lifts up the needy.	113. 1-2, 4-6, 7-8	Year C - Twenty-fifth Sunday in OT
Proclaim the wonders of the Lord.	139. 1-3, 4+6, 7-8, 10+17	Years ABC - Ext Vigil of Pentecost 4
Protect me, O God, for in you I take refuge.	016. 5+8, 9-10, 11	Year B - Thirty-third Sunday in OT
	016. 5+8, 9-10, 11	Years ABC - Easter Vigil 2
Restore us, O God; let your face shine, that we may be saved.	080. 1ab-2, 3-4, 14ab+18	Years ABC - Ext Vigil of Pentecost 2
	080. 1ab+2, 14-15, 17-18	Year B - First Sunday of Advent
	080. 1-ab+2, 14-15, 17-18	Year C - Fourth Sunday of Advent
Rise up, O Lord, and go to your resting place; you and the ark of your might.	132. 6-7, 9-10, 13-14	Years ABC - Assumption (Vigil)
Seek God in your need, and let your hearts revive.	069. 13+16, 29-30, 32-33, 35&c	Year C - Fifteenth Sunday in OT 1
Shout aloud and sing for joy: great in your midst is the Holy One of Israel.	Isaiah 12.3, 4bcd, 5-6	Year C - Third Sunday of Advent

Show us your steadfast love, O Lord, and grant us your salvation.	085. 8ab-9, 10-11, 12-13	Year A - Nineteenth Sunday in OT
	085. 8ab-9, 10-11, 12-13	Year B - Second Sunday of Advent
	085. 8ab-9, 10-11, 12-13	Year B - Fifteenth Sunday in OT
	085. 8ab-9, 10-11, 12-13	Years ABC - Common for Advent
Sing aloud to God our strength.	081. 2-3, 4-5ab, 5c-7a, 9-10ab	Year B - Ninth Sunday in OT
Sing praises to the Lord who heals the brokenhearted.	147. 1-2, 3-4, 5-6	Year B - Fifth Sunday in OT
Sing to the Lord a new song, for he has done marvellous things.	098. 1, 2-3ab, 3cd-4	Years ABC - Immaculate Conception
Taste and see that the Lord is good.	034. 1-2, 3-4, 5-6, 7-8	Year B - Nineteenth Sunday in OT
	034. 1-2, 9-10, 11-12, 13-14	Year B - Twentieth Sunday in OT
	034.1-2, 15-16, 17-18, 19-20 &c	Year B - Twenty-first Sunday in OT
	034. 1-2, 3-4, 5-6	Year C - Fourth Sunday of Lent
	034. 1-2, 3-4, 5-6, 7-8	Years ABC - Common for OT
The cup of blessing that we bless is a sharing in the Blood of Christ.	116. 12-13, 15-16, 17-18	Years ABC - Mass of the Lord's Supper
The earth is full of the steadfast love of the Lord.	033. 4-5, 6-7, 12-13, 20+22	Years ABC - Easter Vigil 1.2
The Lord gave them the bread of heaven.	078. 3+4bc, 23-24, 25+54	Year B - Eighteenth Sunday in OT
The Lord has done great things for us; we are filled with joy.	126. 1-2a, 2b-3, 4-5, 6	Year B - Thirtieth Sunday in OT
	126. 1-2a, 2b-3, 4-5, 6	Year C - Fifth Sunday of Lent
	126. 1-2a, 2b-3, 4-5, 6	Year C - Second Sunday of Advent
The Lord has established his throne in the heavens.	103. 1-2, 11-12, 19-20	Year B - Seventh Sunday of Easter
The Lord has revealed his victory in the sight of the nations.	098. 1, 2-3ab, 3cd+4	Year B - Sixth Sunday of Easter
	098. 1, 2-3ab, 3cd-4	Year C - Twenty-eighth Sunday in OT
The Lord is coming to judge the peoples with equity.	098. 5-6, 7-8, 9	Year C - Thirty-third Sunday in OT
The Lord is king; he is robed in majesty.	093. 1ab, 1c-2, 5	Year B - Christ the King
The Lord is king! Let the peoples tremble!	097. 1-2, 3-4, 5-6, 11-12	Years ABC - Ext Vigil of Pentecost 3
The Lord is king, the most high over all the earth.	097. 1-2, 6-7ac, 9+12	Year C - Seventh Sunday of Easter
	097. 1-2, 5-6, 9+12	Years ABC - Transfiguration of the Lord
The Lord is merciful and gracious.	103. 1-2, 3-4, 6-7, 8+11	Year C - Third Sunday of Lent
	103. 1-2, 3-4, 8+10, 12-13	Year A - Seventh Sunday in OT
	103. 1-2, 3-4, 8+10, 12-13	Year B - Eighth Sunday in OT
	103. 1-2, 3-4, 8+10, 12-13	Year C - Seventh Sunday in OT
	103. 1-2, 3-4, 8+10, 12-13	Years ABC - Common for OT
	103. 8+10, 13-14, 15-16, 17	Years ABC - All Souls I
The Lord is merciful and gracious; slow to anger, and abounding in steadfast love.	103. 1-2, 3-4, 9-10, 11-12	Year A - Twenty-fourth Sunday in OT
The Lord is my light and my salvation.	027. 1, 4, 13-14	Year A - Third Sunday in OT
	027. 1, 7-8, 9, 13-14	Year C - Second Sunday of Lent
	027. 1, 4, 13-14	Years ABC - Common for OT
The Lord is my shepherd; I shall not want.	023. 1-3a, 3b-4, 5, 6	Year A - Fourth Sunday of Lent
	023. 1-3a, 3b-4, 5, 6	Year A - Fourth Sunday of Easter
	023. 1-3a, 3b-4, 5, 6	Year A - Christ the King
	023. 1-3a, 3b-4, 5, 6	Year B - Sixteenth Sunday in OT
	023. 1-3a, 3b-4, 5, 6	Year C - Sacred Heart of Jesus
	023. 1-3a, 3b-4, 5, 6	Years ABC - All Souls II

The Lord is near to all who call on him.	145. 2-3, 8-9, 17-18	Year A - Twenty-fifth Sunday in OT
The Lord is our God, mindful of his covenant forever.	105. 1-2, 3-4, 5-6, 8-9	Year B - Holy Family
The Lord of hosts: he is king of glory!	024. 7, 8, 9, 10	Years ABC - Presentation of the Lord
The Lord remembers his covenant forever.	105. 1-2, 5-6, 7+8a+9a+10b	Years ABC - Ext Vigil of Pentecost 5
The Lord set me free from all my fears.	034. 1-2, 3-4, 5-6, 7-8	Years ABC - Peter and Paul, Apostles
The Lord upholds my life.	054. 1-2, 3, 4+6	Year B - Twenty-fifth Sunday in OT
The Lord will bless his people with peace.	029. 1-2, 3ac-4, 3b+9c-10	Years ABC - Baptism of the Lord
The poor one called and the Lord heard.	034. 1-2, 16-17, 18+22	Year C - Thirtieth Sunday in OT
The precepts of the Lord are right, and give joy to the heart.	019. 7, 9, 11-12, 13	Year B - Twenty-sixth Sunday in OT
	019. 7, 8, 9, 10	Year C - Fifteenth Sunday in OT 2
The seed that fell on good soil produced a hundredfold.	065. 9abcd, 9e-10, 11-12, 13	Year A - Fifteenth Sunday in OT
The steadfast love of the Lord is everlasting on those who fear him.	103. 1-2, 3-4, 6-7, 8-9	Year A - Sacred Heart of Jesus
The stone that the builders rejected has become the cornerstone.	118. 1+8-9, 21-23, 26+28-29	Year B - Fourth Sunday of Easter
The streams make glad the city of God, the habitation of the Most High.	046. 1-2, 4-5, 7-8	Years ABC - Lateran Basilica
The vineyard of the Lord is the house of Israel.	080. 8+11, 12-13, 14-15, 18-19	Year A - Twenty-seventh Sunday in OT
The Word became flesh and lived among us.	147. 12-13, 14-15, 19-20	Years ABC - Second Sunday after Xmas
Their voice goes out through all the earth.	019. 1-2, 3-4	Years ABC - Peter and Paul (Vigil)
This is the day the Lord has made; let us rejoice and be glad.	118. 1-2, 16-17, 22-23	Years ABC - Easter Sunday
	118. 1-2, 16-17, 22-23	Years ABC - Common for Easter
To the upright I will show the salvation of God.	050. 1+8, 12-13, 14-15	Year A - Tenth Sunday in OT
To you, O Lord, I lift my soul.	025. 4-5a, 8-9, 10+14	Year C - First Sunday of Advent
	025. 4-5a, 8-9, 10+14	Years ABC - Common for Advent
Today is born our Saviour, Christ the Lord.	096. 1-2, 3-4, 11-12, 13	Years ABC - Christmas during the night
We are his people: the sheep of his pasture.	100. 1-2, 3, 5	Year C - Fourth Sunday of Easter
	100. 1-2, 3, 5	Years ABC - Common for OT
	100. 1-2, 3, 4, 5	Year A - Eleventh Sunday in OT
With joy you will draw water from the wells of salvation.	Isaiah 12. 2-3, 4bcd, 5-6	Year B - Baptism of the Lord
	Isaiah 12. 2-3, 4bcd, 5-6	Year B - Sacred Heart of Jesus
	Isaiah 12. 2-3, 4bcd, 5-6	Years ABC - Easter Vigil 5
With the Lord there is steadfast love and great power to redeem.	130. 1-2, 3-4, 5-6, 7b-8	Year A - Fifth Sunday of Lent
	130. 1-2, 3-4, 5-6, 7b-8	Year B - Tenth Sunday in OT
	130. 1-2, 3-4, 5-6, 7b-8	Years ABC - Common for Lent
You are a priest forever, according to the order of Melchizedek.	110. 1, 2, 3, 4	Year C - Body and Blood of Christ
You are my chosen portion, O Lord.	016. 1-2a+5, 7-8, 9-10, 11	Year C - Thirteenth Sunday in OT
You are my refuge, Lord; with deliverance you surround me.	032.1-2, 5, 10bc-11	Year B - Sixth Sunday in OT
You open your hand to feed us, Lord, and satisfy our needs.	145. 8-9, 15-16, 17-18	Year A - Eighteenth Sunday in OT
You open your hand to feed us, Lord; you satisfy all our needs.	145. 10-11, 15-16, 17-18	Year B - Seventeenth Sunday in OT
Your paths, Lord, are love and faithfulness for those who keep your covenant.	025. 4-5a, 6+7b, 8-9	Year B - First Sunday of Lent
Your steadfast love, O Lord, endures forever. Do not forsake the work of your hands.	138. 1-2a, 2b-3, 6+8b	Year A - Twenty-first Sunday in OT
Your words, Lord, are spirit and life.	019. 7, 8, 9, 14	Year C - Third Sunday in OT

Achevé d'imprimer en Novembre 2009
sur les presses numériques de
umen | digital, à Montréal